Praise for *Ladies Who Punch*

"It's already stirring up so much drama I'm considering asking it to be a New York housewife next season . . . This book is hot."

—Andy Cohen

"Juicy and revealing."

—*Orlando Sentinel*

"A bombshell."

—*Inside Edition*

"This book is very juicy."

—*Page Six TV*

"Talk about a tell-all! It's full of juicy inside information." —*US Weekly*

"A lot of juicy stuff in here."

—CNN *New Day*

"The hottest book on the market."

—*E! News Daily Pop*

"This book's blowing peoples' minds."

—*ET*

"It's one of the best page-turners I've ever read." —Jillian Barberie

"A veritable Spill-the-Tea Party. With interviews from nearly everyone involved in the twenty-two-year-old series, including a gloriously candid Rosie O'Donnell, it is dishy in the way entertainment reporting frankly never is anymore. Come for the stories of cattiness, All-About-Eve machinations, and behind-the-scenes blowups, but stay for the sharp distillation of why this talk show completely changed television as we know it. *The View* is responsible for the very conflagration of news and opinion that today defines media and gives us all three to five rage strokes per week."

—*The Daily Beast*

"And you thought the *The View* could get crazy on-screen (Joy Behar and Meghan McCain, we're looking at you). This pull-back-the-curtain story of almost two decades of the groundbreaking talk show delivers. This is everything a behind-the-scenes book should be—dishy, surprising, and written with the unprecedented help of those who lived it."   —*Booklist*

"Terrifically fun to read. Setoodeh has been reporting on the show for years, and he knows everyone. The book is studded with juicy little scoops, including firing stories, backstage drama (wait for the story about Walters, Jenny McCarthy, and the tampon), and details about Star Jones's freebie-laden wedding."   —*Slate*

"By comparison, Trump's White House is far more functional."
—*Toronto Star*

"With a random array of hosts and plenty of drama to go around, Setoodeh manages to peel back the composed facade of what viewers see on their screens in order to focus on raw feelings and teetering emotions of those closely involved with *The View. Ladies Who Punch* is an exciting read that proves there's always a little soap opera even if a show presents itself as hard news."   —Associated Press

"Jenny McCarthy reached out to Ramin to tell him the book is 'fair and honest.' But when you write a book like this, not everyone's going to love it, but with all the juicy info, he's got a bestseller on his hands for sure."
—*DailyMailTV*

Ladies Who Punch

The Explosive Inside Story of *The View*

Ramin Setoodeh

THOMAS DUNNE BOOKS
NEW YORK

First published in the United States by Thomas Dunne Books, an imprint of St. Martin's Publishing Group

LADIES WHO PUNCH. Copyright © 2019 by Ramin Setoodeh. Epilogue. Copyright © 2020 by Ramin Setoodeh. All rights reserved. Printed in the United States of America. For information, address St. Martin's Publishing Group, 120 Broadway, New York, NY 10271.

Designed by Devan Norman

www.thomasdunnebooks.com

The Library of Congress Cataloging-in-Publication Data is available upon request.

ISBN 978-1-250-11209-5 (hardcover)
ISBN 978-1-250-25198-5 (trade paperback)
ISBN 978-1-250-11210-1 (ebook)

Our books may be purchased in bulk for promotional, educational, or business use. Please contact your local bookseller or the Macmillan Corporate and Premium Sales Department at 1-800-221-7945, extension 5442, or by email at MacmillanSpecialMarkets@macmillan.com.

First Thomas Dunne Books Paperback Edition: February 2020

10 9 8 7 6 5 4 3 2 1

To my mom, who taught me to always listen to
a woman with a strong point of view

From Lisa Ling to Debbie Matenopoulos, every person who has left that show has been fired—except for me! And it's like the Trump administration. They will just continually lie and present a false front. They would go on TV and pretend to be friends when bad things were happening. You have to talk about it.

—Rosie O'Donnell

Contents

Part Two: Rosie's View

Part Three: Whoopi's View

Ladies
Who
Punch

Prologue

Out, Damned Cohost!

Barbara Walters was creating a scene. Not that she minded it. As the most powerful woman in the news business, her mere presence at Spago in Beverly Hills infused the room with an aura of royalty. The chef came over to welcome her. Other patrons leaned over their plates to get a better look. Any meal with Barbara was always an intimidating exercise, which started with her dropping the names of some people she'd recently run into: Hillary Clinton, Michael Bloomberg, Jennifer Lopez, and more. On this evening in the winter of 2007, her dining companion—Brian Frons, the president of ABC Daytime—tried his best to keep up.

The View, the daytime talk show that Barbara had created in 1997 with a panel of mild-mannered women, had peaked in Season 10. The show was averaging an impressive 3.5 million viewers, up 17 percent from the previous year. Normally, nothing made Barbara happier than strong ratings, like the high school valedictorian that gloated over every percentage point on a math quiz. Yet, despite a surge in viewership, Barbara felt miserable.

In just a few months, *The View* had suffered through a series of embarrassing controversies, drawing the anger of Donald Trump (mocked for his hair and, even worse, his finances), Kelly Ripa (accused of homophobic behavior after she told a guest, Clay Aiken, not to cover her mouth with his hand), and the entire Asian American community (subjected to a racist impersonation). One culprit was behind all these fires: Rosie O'Donnell.

Barbara knew what had to be done. In the past, she'd quietly orchestrated the firings of other cohosts on *The View* as they outlasted their welcome: Debbie Matenopoulos in 1999, Lisa Ling in 2002, and Star Jones in 2006. Even though Barbara had recruited Rosie herself, she admitted that she'd made a terrible mistake, telling Trump that much in a private conversation.

Barbara's decision to push out Rosie wasn't simply a power play. It was an act of self-preservation. Rosie had disrupted the normal mechanisms of a talk show. She fought constantly with the show's director, Mark Gentile, and berated the senior staff. She hated the executive producer, Bill Geddie, so much that he took a temporary leave of absence to get away from her. On top of that, Rosie was running around telling the staff that Barbara, at seventy-seven, was much too old to be on TV.

For most of her career, Barbara had been known as a serious news anchor. Now, all that had changed. Her empire had expanded in a lopsided direction, unheard of for a news icon. She looked more like the matriarch of an out-of-control family—a septuagenarian Kris Jenner before the world knew who that was. Camera crews from *TMZ* regularly camped out on the sidewalk of Barbara's Upper East Side apartment, trying to ask her about the latest drama unfolding on *The View*. She didn't like it one bit.

"I know you've been very calm this year, and I really appreciate that," Barbara told Frons after they'd exchanged pleasantries.

"I want the best for you and the show." He sighed, momentarily relieved.

Barbara was nothing if not direct. "I do want you to know," she calmly announced, "if you re-sign Rosie to this show, Bill and I are going to quit."

Barbara Walters, the griller-in-chief of world leaders and presidents, had a soft spot for a heroine that gulped cosmopolitans. Barbara loved *Sex and the City*, the HBO series about four girlfriends trying to have it all in New York City. Sometimes, for a fleeting moment, she'd imagine herself in Carrie Bradshaw's Manolo Blahniks. "I watch old reruns," she told me one afternoon, sitting in her dressing room at *The View*, decorated with framed pictures of her daughter, Jackie, and her beloved Havanese dog, Cha-Cha. "I still think Sarah Jessica Parker is adorable, and I want her to meet Mr. Big and live happily ever after." *The View*, which debuted one year before *Sex and the City*, even played like the unscripted version—minus the one-night stands, but with just as much yakking, fussing, and chatter about defining a woman's worth on the journey to having it all.

In television history, *The View*'s influence is significant in a way that doesn't usually get said out loud. When Barbara started the show, with a group of pals (Meredith Vieira, Star Jones, Joy Behar, and Debbie Matenopoulos), news and opinion were clearly separated. In the pre-Twitter age, reporters such as Barbara weren't allowed to tell the public what they thought, let alone speculate about a president's marriage or relationship to his mistress or children (which *The View* made into a national pastime). The show offered a venue where opinion wasn't just as important as news, it *was* the news in some cases, such as when Rosie O'Donnell made noise with her September 11 conspiracy theories or Whoopi Goldberg refused to believe her friend Bill Cosby was a rapist. "We didn't create a new format," Barbara said. "We created a new atmosphere." In 2011, Anderson Cooper unveiled an afternoon talk show while keeping his anchor job at CNN—nobody questioned him because Barbara had already done it.

Speaking of CNN, its political coverage had come to look a lot like *The View*, with Trump supporters playing the role of Elisabeth Hasselbeck. It's hard to watch television now without running up against a row of bickering pundits. *The View* got there first, as the Martha Washington of panel shows, and it made the idea of a single talk show host (Jerry Springer, Sally Jessy Raphael, Ricki Lake, etc.) seem quaint. In our supersize culture, why settle for one voice when you can have five—even if that means straining to hear them scream over one another?

Barbara handpicked all the original cohosts of *The View,* called them "the ladies," and treated them like her TV daughters. As each of the ingénues rose to fame, their own personal lives and dramas became mini-sagas that unfolded in real time. To be a cohost of *The View* meant excavating your deepest secrets—a foreshadowing of our *TMZ* (and TMI) culture. In a way, *The View* was TV's first mainstream reality show after *The Real World.* Yes, three years later, *Survivor* took credit for that, but *The View* opened a window into the personal relationships among strong women, a predecessor to Bravo's *Real Housewives* or MTV's *The Hills.* "It was like a reality show and a soap opera," said Debbie Matenopoulos, the youngest cohost, who got the job when she was twenty-two. "There's something about how raw and real it would be."

The View certainly paved the way for the CBS knockoff series *The Talk,* which emphasized less politics and more celebrity; the Fox show *The Real,* targeted to younger women of color; the ABC cooking show *The Chew;* the failed Tyra Banks offering *FABLife;* and Fox News's *Outnumbered,* the Republican edition. "We are copied almost line by line by other programs," Barbara said. "It's sort of flattering." *The View* wasn't TV's first panel show (*Politically Incorrect* and *Crossfire* ran before it), but it brought the genre to daytime.

The View made it socially acceptable for men to yammer about their feelings, too. Dick Clark cribbed the conceit for 2001's *The Other Half,* costarring Mario Lopez and Danny Bonaduce. Joan Rivers spearheaded her own *View* pilot with several loud gay men, called *Straight Talk*—her cohosts were the then unknown Andy Cohen and Billy Eichner. Come to think of it, even Rivers's *Fashion Police,* which had a panel of experts dissing celebrity frocks on the red carpet, traced its origins back to you know where. "I think they would absolutely slit their wrists if I managed to draw a line between *Fashion Police* and *The View,*" said Melissa Rivers, who cohosted the E! series with her mom.

The mood across the country in 1997, *The View*'s birth year, was dramatically different from what it is now. Ellen DeGeneres had just kicked down the door as TV's first openly gay sitcom star, although it was clear she wouldn't be successful. Hillary Clinton was a full-time first lady, hiding her ambitions to run for a seat in the Senate. As the baby boomer generation raised their own kids, college-educated women weren't as likely to give up their careers. Yet for those who did, Barbara carved out a room of one's own. *The View* was like the walking, talking antithesis to *The Feminine Mystique,* the groundbreaking 1963 book by Betty Friedan, which explored the causes of unhappiness among housewives. According to Joy Behar, a reason that *The View* succeeded was that it was an unapologetically feminist show: "We basically embody a feminist. We are self-employed. We have control over our personal lives. We try to do as much with our lives as we can."

While the show tried to celebrate its empowered stars, that didn't always happen. Sometimes *The View* was overshadowed by "catfights," as the media loved to speculate about how the ladies really felt about one another. When it comes to women in Hollywood, the press has always had a double standard. Then again, the ladies of *The View* never masked their true feelings. "They all had a lot of relational aggression," shrugged Tina Fey, who cowrote the *Saturday Night Live* sketches of *The View*, starring Cheri Oteri as Barbara.

The View got hip early on that treating happenings on Capitol Hill like a soap opera could be riveting TV. It was ahead of its time in thinking that politicians were celebrities. Back in 1992, Bill Clinton's appearance as a saxophone-playing governor on *The Arsenio Hall Show* was considered an exception to the norms of late-night TV. But *The View* made daytime hospitable to senators, from Elizabeth Warren to John McCain; vice presidents, such as Dick Cheney and Joe Biden; and President Barack Obama, who stopped by the show twice in 2012 to rally women voters for his reelection bid. "I like hanging out with women, what can I tell you?" said Obama, the first sitting president in history to appear on daytime TV.

Michelle Obama counted herself a loyal viewer. So did Nancy Reagan, who would call up if she felt the show's signature Hot Topics debates sounded too critical of her late husband's legacy. Nicolle Wallace, a cohost who had worked as George W. Bush's communications director, watched *The View* from the White House—"It's this iconic show," she said—as a barometer of national moods. "If a political topic was on their radar, I used it as ammunition with the president or the White House staff," she recalled. She'd tell them, "This is such a big deal. They are talking about it on the damn *View*."

The show inadvertently offered a bridge between Hillary Clinton and Trump before they knew they'd become political adversaries. Both attended the much-hyped Star Jones wedding in 2004, where they sat at the same table. Trump was a regular guest on *The View*. Clinton's presence loomed larger. Over the years, she was like a phantom sixth cohost, an easy conversation starter for Barbara's ladies. Hillary was a prism through which the cohosts viewed themselves, from the Monica Lewinsky scandal through Clinton's years as a US senator and secretary of state. In the lead-up to her first presidential run, Clinton used *The View* as a warm-up for how she'd fare with tough questions.

So in December 2006, days before Christmas, Clinton made an appearance on *The View*, with anecdotes about opening presents with Bill and Chelsea. But she was eclipsed by a figure who would later haunt her. Rosie opened the show that day with a historic roast of Trump, which led to an infamous and bitter feud. Clinton watched the routine from her dressing room, not knowing that ten years later she'd be facing off against Trump for her dream job, and that Rosie's name would be dragged into one of their presidential debates. "I was laughing so hard backstage, I didn't think I'd get out," Clinton said, when she settled on the couch, channeling a friendly pal.

"Every day we're in trouble on this show," Joy offered, correctly predicting the firestorm ahead.

"Isn't that interesting?" Clinton asked. "I wonder why that happens?"

"I don't know," Joy said. "We're just women."

Part One

Barbara's View

I

Everybody's a Critic

For a long time, nobody had any clue why Barbara Walters—who symbolized the gold standard of the TV news business—would dip her feet in the murky waters of daytime. This was the genre that gave rise to paternity tests, plastic surgery, and "too fat to wear." In 1983, a serious broadcaster named Sally Jessy Raphael started a talk show with the goal of tackling lofty societal issues. But a few years in, she caved and went the tabloid route. All her competitors were doing the same. Geraldo Rivera staged so many fights he ended up with a broken nose during an episode called "Teen Hatemongers." Maury Povich made a cottage industry out of unfaithful boyfriends. Jenny Jones was on a constant search for guests who didn't know their real daddies. Jerry Springer presided over a circus of angry misfits who threw chairs and fists. The nuclear arms race for smut TV was the complete opposite of Barbara's brand, as an erudite ambassador of world news—with access to everybody from Barbra Streisand to Mu'ammar Gaddafi.

Most daytime talk had evolved from Phil Donahue, who in 1967 launched his eponymous show that changed the culture. Donahue had no fear of boundaries or taboos—he tackled homosexuality decades before *Will & Grace,* once invited a Nazi to speak to an audience of Jews, and challenged a young Donald Trump about his real estate dealings. "We can't continue to give you guys these big tax breaks," Donahue scolded. Just as important, he taped his show in front of a live audience, taking their questions and concerns into living rooms across the country.

His no-holds-barred approach cleared the way for Oprah Winfrey, who duplicated the template. Winfrey started on local TV news as a reporter who studied Walters on NBC's *Today,* imitating her interviewing techniques and style. When Winfrey landed her own nationally syndicated talk show in 1986, she gravitated toward education and information, emulating a best friend you can trust with your deepest secrets. By the midnineties, Oprah ruled the cult of stay-at-home moms with "remember your spirit" segments and book club recommendations. The inspirational programming made Winfrey the mightiest woman on TV, with up to 20 million daily viewers.

But in 1996, she finally got some competition. Rosie O'Donnell, a comedic actress from movies (*Sleepless in Seattle, A League of Their Own,* and *The Flintstones*), wanted to take a shot at her own talk show. She modeled her venture on a staple from her childhood: 1961's *Mike Douglas Show,* on which the squeaky-clean host chatted playfully with rising celebrities such as Aretha Franklin and Mel Brooks. Douglas was an early adopter of celebrity gab, an afternoon counterpart to *The Tonight Show*, which had started seven years before. In Rosie's reboot, the format stayed the same, but she revved up the pace with Broadway musical numbers, audience giveaways, and lengthy discussions about her crush—back when she was closeted—on Tom Cruise. As two of TV's biggest moguls, O and Ro built up their kingdoms, shaping pop culture and raking in fortunes.

Unlike soap operas, most talk shows are cobbled together quickly and inexpensively. There's no need for actors or too many writers toiling on scripts. The biggest expense is usually the host's salary, assuming he or she is a marquee name. Many of the giants in the industry started out small, such as Regis Philbin, who climbed into his seat on *Live with Regis and*

Kathie Lee in 1988 after years as a local morning emcee in New York and LA. The measure of a successful host is genuine connection, imitating a BFF with jokes, self-help tips, and makeovers. It's not so easy, though. The daytime audience is impatient and fickle, with an appetite for sauce. Since Oprah's rise, an army of A- and B-list personalities have tried to mimic her—Katie Couric, Anderson Cooper, and Megyn Kelly (anchors); Queen Latifah and Harry Connick Jr. (singers); Roseanne Barr, Tony Danza, Megan Mullally, and Fran Drescher (sitcom actors); Kris Jenner and Bethenny Frankel (reality stars)—only to fall flat on their coiffed heads.

But if you make it, the job is lucrative. Advertisers embrace successful daytime talk shows because they reach stay-at-home moms, who typically control their family budgets and watch the programs live, even the ads. As a result, Ellen DeGeneres, Dr. Phil, and Kelly Ripa earn multimillion-dollar salaries, in the same range as movie stars such as Jennifer Lawrence and Brad Pitt. Above them, there's that short-tempered brunette with a gavel, Judith Sheindlin, who cashes a check for $47 million a year. Her courtroom series, *Judge Judy,* which started in 1996, isn't really a talk show, but it plays like *Jerry Springer* meets *Matlock,* with wounded plaintiffs battling over unpaid dues and broken promises. "I would have been so happy if we had done three years, and I had enough money to buy a condo two blocks off the beach of Miami," Sheindlin told me. "That was my dream."

Sheindlin's perch in daytime is so towering and profitable that she scoffed when she heard that Trump had been considering her for a vacancy to the US Supreme Court. "It must have been one of those moments when he wasn't thinking," Sheindlin said. "I have too good of a day job."

⁂

By the midnineties, Barbara Walters was at the head of her class at ABC, carrying a hefty workload as the number one star of TV news. She served as the coanchor of *20/20,* then a place for meaty investigations, cranked out Oscars specials, aired her *10 Most Fascinating People* (which began in 1993 with Hillary Clinton at the top), and constantly outhustled her peers for exclusives. In 1995, she scored the first interview with a paralyzed Christopher Reeve, making headlines around the world. A year later, after the O. J. Simpson verdict, prosecutor Christopher Darden sat down with Barbara before anyone else.

Barbara grew up in New York and Florida, where she lived in a pistachio-colored house. Her father, Lou, ran a string of nightclubs, packed with showgirls and hit singers, which gave her early brushes with famous people—he was constantly socializing with the likes of Milton Berle, Johnnie Ray, and Frank Sinatra. "It made me the way I am," Barbara told me one day. "I'm not in awe of any celebrity." Her mother, Dena, stayed at home with Barbara's older sister, Jacqueline, who was mentally disabled. "My childhood was totally influenced by my sister," Barbara said. "It gave me a childhood that was sad and kind of lonely because there were things I couldn't do, like have friends over."

Barbara had a few false starts to her career. She wanted to be an actress, but she was too scared of rejection. "You can't be an actress if you're afraid of being turned down," she recalled. After a stint as a publicist (during which she learned how to manipulate the press, a skill that came in handy later), Barbara joined the staff of *Today* in 1961 as a writer. Because of her gender, this was groundbreaking for the time. "There were six male writers and one female," Barbara said. "And you didn't get to be the female writer unless she got married or died."

Through sheer determination, Barbara migrated in front of the camera, reporting segments about fashion or a night out with a Playboy Bunny. "I was not the natural choice when I began," Barbara said. "I was not beautiful. I had a speech impediment. That didn't help." She said the standards were different back then. "Most of the women in television now are very lovely, but they are also talented. In my time, they were maybe not as talented." Her secret to success was perseverance. "What I had was this creative curiosity and ability to ask questions," she said.

Her agent slipped a clause in her contract that if the current host left, she'd assume the title. Nobody thought he'd go anywhere, but when Frank McGee suddenly died of bone cancer in 1974, Barbara took over as the first female cohost, opposite Jim Hartz. "Since then, a woman is the cohost on the *Today* show," Barbara said. "That's my legacy." (In fact, now there are two women: Savannah Guthrie and Hoda Kotb.) Barbara drew in viewers with her tenacity as she interrogated powerful men such as Richard Nixon and Henry Kissinger with her prickly questions. Because of Walters's success, TV executives started to let more women cover hard news, enter war zones, and tackle politics.

In 1976, she shattered another glass ceiling, when she left NBC for ABC to be the first woman coanchor of a nightly newscast. Her new employer shelled out a record $1 million a year to nab their new star—a deal that, forty years later, created a culture where Megyn Kelly could demand $25 million from Fox News, before ultimately fleeing to NBC. The hysteria over Barbara's move to ABC was followed by questions of whether she could cut it. The press ran sexist stories about how she owned a pink typewriter. Her coanchor, Harry Reasoner, hated her, and the tension was awkward. "We were terrible together," Barbara said. "From the beginning, viewers were angry with me for doing this to poor Harry."

She survived by leaving the news desk and reinventing herself through her trademark specials. Barbara would convene three newsmakers—a celebrity, a world leader, and a miscellaneous person in the news—for an hour of prime time. She wanted to capture her subjects in intimate settings, so she devised the novel conceit of visiting their habitats. Barbara popularized the idea of bringing cameras into celebrity homes, long before audiences were used to MTV's *Cribs* or the Kardashians. She became just as famous as the people she interviewed, as she rode a wave of success for the next two decades.

But in her own home, Barbara's personal life was fraught. In the fifties, her father gambled away her family's fortune on a series of bad investments, putting pressure on Barbara to support her parents and her sister with her money. This was an especially odd arrangement for a woman of her generation, who would normally rely on a husband's paycheck for security. It meant that Barbara had to stay employed—in spite of Lou Walters's concerns about her longevity on TV. "He was afraid I was going to get fired," Barbara said about her father. His doubts instilled two traits in her that followed her for the rest of her career: a boundless desire for success and a lurking, irrational fear that her savings could vanish overnight. "I had to support them for so long," Barbara said of her family. "I knew I had to work, and I just worked harder."

Barbara consistently chose her job over her marriages (she had three, with the last one ending in 1992) and raised her adopted daughter, Jackie (who she named after her sister), as a single mother. "I don't think there was a person I should have been with," Barbara said. "I don't look back and think, 'How did he get away?'"

In 1984, she met the man who would become her most important companion—her hairdresser, Bryant Renfroe, who always stood by her, just a few feet away from the cameras. He came into Walters's life after he'd left his salon in Florida to perform miracles at ABC on Joan Lunden and Kathie Lee Johnson (who later married Frank Gifford). Fate led him to Barbara's apartment one afternoon, after her stylist had to bail. "When I finished, she looked at me and said, 'I can't go out like this.'"

Renfroe ripped up the instructions from the previous stylist and started over. "I always thought her hair looked awful," Renfroe confessed. "It was choppy, uneven, messy, unconstructed." He created Barbara's modern-day look, a bob haircut that was emulated by millions of career-climbing women (just ask Hillary Clinton). "It's called giving you cheekbones and jawlines," Renfroe said.

From then on, Barbara was inseparable from her gay best friend. Renfroe traveled with Walters to all her big interviews and meetings, such as a lunch with Princess Diana at Buckingham Palace. (Barbara always personally introduced him.) Renfroe not only tended to her hair, he provided her with constant moral support. "There were times where the producers gave me headphones because it was important that I heard," Renfroe said. After she'd wrap an interview with anyone from Cher to Barack Obama, Barbara would scan the room to make sure she hadn't missed anything, usually calling out one person by name (*"Bryant!"*) for last-minute feedback. Barbara's idea of hell was forgetting an obvious question and waking up in the middle of the night in a cold sweat about what she should have asked. She relied on Renfroe to be her safety net.

No matter how successful she became, Barbara always pondered new ways to expand her empire. So in her late sixties, when most TV journalists are winding down—if not already deep in retirement—Barbara had a fresh idea. In the spirit of Gatsby, she gazed out at the green light from Oprah's and Rosie's docks and envisioned a rival creation, a competing act.

The View was born out of a conversation between a mom and her daughter, which seems right because of the maternal relationships—between Barbara and her cohosts—that would fuel the show.

In the summer of 1996, while wrapping one of her celebrity specials, Barbara took aside her producer Bill Geddie to tell him about a conversation she'd had with Jackie, then in her late twenties. "It's so interesting," she told Geddie. "She comes at the world from a completely different point of view." Barbara wondered if they could create a show around that premise, with women of different generations debating the headlines of the day.

Her inspiration for the format of *The View* came from two places. The first was ABC's *This Week*, a Sunday news program in which anchor David Brinkley held a roundtable with pundits arguing about politics. The other, *Girl Talk*, which aired from 1963 to 1969, lived up to its name with its host, Virginia Graham, booking trailblazers such as Cindy Adams,

Olivia de Havilland, and Joan Rivers for cozy chats—Barbara herself had been a guest repeatedly. "I thought if you could combine those two together, you'd have a successful show," Barbara said.

And then there was a show from Barbara's own history, a missed opportunity that still gnawed at her. In the seventies, she hosted a local NBC program called *Not for Women Only* (the title alone hinted at the bias women in the TV industry faced). Barbara, who juggled the gig in addition to *Today*, would assemble a weekly panel of experts—among them soap opera writers, inventors, politicians' wives—to talk about important issues in the culture, at a time when the women's movement was on the rise, personified by strong heroines on such shows as *The Mary Tyler Moore Show* and *One Day at a Time*. Barbara's side project, which she binge-taped in an afternoon, was essentially a predecessor to *The View*, with rotating cohosts. "I sometimes think I should have hung on to that show, syndicated it, and I would have been a very rich person," recalled Barbara, momentarily forgetting her own considerable worth. "I didn't. But it taught me a lesson for *The View*."

Barbara didn't just want to headline her talk show, she also wanted a piece of ownership through her company, Barwall Productions. If it worked, it would be a big step forward, moving Barbara from TV star to entrepreneur. She picked Geddie as an ally because she trusted him. He'd spent a decade with her as the steady hand that oversaw her specials. Geddie, an imposing six-foot-four Republican from Texas in his early forties, could look like a bodyguard next to his five-foot-five boss; he acted as her protector. In his spare time, he'd written a screenplay for the little-seen 1996 thriller *Unforgettable,* starring Ray Liotta as a man wrongfully accused of murdering his wife.

It taught him how he didn't want to spend the rest of his career. "I was not allowed on the set and it was rewritten many times," Geddie said about his foray into Hollywood. "So I go to a test screening with a bunch of New Yorkers. It was very exciting for me and my wife. The first third of the movie is exactly what I wrote. Then it changes and people start laughing—it's not a comedy. By the end, it was a horrific experience, and we both sat up like ghosts, thinking, 'Oh my God, this is the worst movie ever made!' We walked through a crowd of smoking teenagers in front of the theater. And I remember one young girl took a big inhale and said, 'Who writes shit like that?'"

Geddie plotted to move up the ladder in TV. After he received a tip that ABC was canceling one of its daytime offerings, he told Barbara that this was their chance. They wrote up a proposal for what they could slot into that hour. In that first draft, they needed a name for their show, so they used a placeholder, *Everybody's a Critic*. It hinted at the tone for what the man behind the curtain hoped to achieve. "I wanted it to be a bitchy show," Geddie said. "Barbara did not want it to be bitchy. I got my wish, by the way."

The ABC Daytime team, run by executive Patricia Fili-Krushel (who'd go on to head NBC News for a time), was in a bind. Nothing they had programmed at 11:00 a.m. eastern time had worked—their latest casualty was *Caryl & Marilyn: Real Friends,* a talk show starring two Kathie Lee wannabes who'd appeared in a failed NBC sitcom, *The Mommies.* Because the hour had been so beaten up, roughly 40 percent of the affiliates had taken it back for local programming. As opposed to prime time, when everybody in the country sees the same shows, daytime TV operates under a different system—one in which regional managers can pick and choose what to air in their towns.

Think of it like the electoral college, but for entertainment. "In daytime, a show must earn the right to stay on, as you clear the country piece by piece," said Stuart Krasnow, a veteran talk-show producer at Telepictures Productions who worked on *Caryl & Marilyn* and later *The View.* Other series aren't held to that standard, which makes the hurdles for daytime TV greater. "You have a couple hundred different bosses in all these stations that are not going to be happy if the numbers aren't good," Krasnow said. "They expect drastic changes. Or get out of the way."

At the time, Barbara wasn't even aware of these intricacies. She was just trying to get her idea approved. She met with Fili-Krushel, who was skeptical at first: "She comes in with the pitch, and I loved the idea, but it was a half-hour show at that point. I said to her, 'We need an hour. If we can develop the back half, let's pilot it.'"

Fili-Krushel had another note. She said that the show's featured stories needed to be juicier items ripped from the headlines of the *New York Daily News*.

"No, *The New York Times*," Barbara insisted. "I want to talk about Syria."

"I said, 'That's not going to work in daytime,'" Fili-Krushel remembered. "So we took Barbara to a daytime focus group. Barbara is nothing if not really smart about television. And she says to me, 'I got it. *USA Today* and the *Daily News*. This is our audience.'"

Barbara had initially shopped her idea to Roone Arledge, the broadcasting titan who oversaw ABC News. Arledge had saved Barbara after he first arrived, in 1977, by giving her a second chance with the specials after her botched shotgun wedding to Reasoner (who left for CBS). Arledge had also created *This Week,* the political talk show that Barbara was copying.

Arledge, who previously ran sports at ABC and pioneered *Monday Night Football,* managed his news division like an Olympics team. Anchors weren't just expected to fight competitors from other networks for scoops—they often faced off against one another. For Barbara, this was no problem.

Competitiveness ran in her veins. She was one of the few TV reporters who dialed publicists and lawyers herself, instead of relying on producers to ask them to deliver their clients. But this anything-goes hierarchy at ABC created tension in the newsroom and sparked rumors (which were true) that Barbara and Diane Sawyer were always trampling over each other for a story. "There were no rules," Sawyer told me. "Roone thought that competition even in the family would be good." Sawyer met with him in 1990, a year after arriving at ABC, to protest: "I really felt that it would be impossible for me to be put in a situation where I would be calling and Barbara would be calling, too. That's not what families do."

Arledge had the clout to take Barbara's enterprise under his wing. But instead, in a decision that would shape the future of *The View* and create a two-decade tug-of-war, he punted Barbara's baby to the daytime division. He did worse than that. He strongly advised her against pursuing such a foolish lark. "Roone did not want me to do the show," Barbara said. "He felt it was too frivolous. He thought it would lessen my reputation."

As confident as she was on camera, Barbara hated making decisions about her career. Even the smallest fork in the road turned her into a puddle of uncertainty, a result of having to fight so hard for every opportunity. At NBC, she'd tormented herself for months about leaving for ABC. Once the ink had dried—and faded—on her contract, she spent years at ABC wondering whether she'd made the wrong decision. "Editors love to work with me because I know what I want," Barbara said. "But not in real life."

Arledge's disapproval spooked his star. She felt backed into a corner and started second-guessing herself. She worried that her talk show would interfere with her stature—how could she fly to the Middle East in a moment's notice if she expected to greet all those stay-at-home moms in the morning? She loved rolling the dice with trick questions during an interview, but she didn't like personal risks.

"I'm not really sure I want to do this," she told Geddie.

He pushed back. "It's really important to me," Geddie pleaded. "I can't keep doing the Barbara Walters shows for the rest of my life."

She trusted him, and she agreed to dive in. He provided this consolation: "If it's embarrassing, it's going to be two years of embarrassing. Not twenty years of embarrassment."

Before they took off, the show needed a new name. Calling it *Everybody's a Critic* suggested something less approachable. Outside of *Siskel & Ebert,* which featured two middle-aged white men reviewing movies, most TV shows didn't thrive on so much opinion. It would be another five years before *American Idol* debuted and opened the floodgates on a parade of self-appointed experts doling out their nasty critiques on everything from fashion (*Project Runway*) to food (*Top Chef*) to ballroom moves (*Dancing with the Stars*).

Geddie kept coming back to the idea of different views at the table. Late in the process he thought up a new name.

"I've got the greatest title," he told Barbara. "It's going to be called *The View from Here*."

She liked it, but ABC ran a trademark search and came back with an obstacle. A show in Canada already went by that name, so Geddie went with the abridged version.

"They ran another search, and there was nothing called *The View*," said Geddie. "I always thought it was a terrible title. It just didn't make any sense." He laughed. "But now I think, 'What a great title!'"

2

Audition

A fter Barbara Walters had secured the daytime division's stamp of approval for *The View,* she was missing just one key ingredient— her outspoken sidekicks. She cast a wide net for the women who'd soon simply be known as "the ladies," the coconspirators in her shenanigans. As Barbara came to announce every day in the show's opening credits, she wanted *The View* to be multigenerational. That didn't matter much to Geddie, but Barbara insisted on it based on the wide gap that separated her and Jackie. She arrived at the number of cohosts, four, through TV math. Three would be too few, and with five, not everybody might be able to speak before the next commercial break.

Barbara, who couldn't resist being a journalist even in social settings, probing dinner guests for intimate secrets, left no stone unturned in her search for the perfect *View* cohosts. She had Geddie research every female TV personality between the ages of twenty and fifty. They couldn't aim too high, for a Joan Rivers or Brooke Shields, because they didn't have a budget for real salaries.

Barbara knew that she couldn't devote all her time to *The View.* With her other commitments at ABC News, Barbara planned on appearing on her talk show two to three days a week. The other reason to keep some distance: her lawyer told her not to position herself as the lead on *The View*, in the likely scenario that the show imploded. That meant someone else would need to steer the daily Hot Topics debates. "I did not make myself the moderator, which I regret," Barbara said. "Yes, it's much more fun being the moderator."

Meredith Vieira, an ex–*60 Minutes* correspondent, crept on the short list for that role, based on a recommendation from the show's supervising producer, Jessica Stedman Guff. Meredith, forty-three at the time, knew Barbara from bumping into her in the elevators at ABC, and she needed a job, since her newsmagazine show, *Turning Point*, was on the verge of cancellation. But Meredith wasn't sure if this was the right step for her career. Before social media, serious women in journalism couldn't dish on a talk show about their opinions. "Once she crossed the line, she was afraid she was going to be a joke," Geddie said.

"I remember being very hesitant about even going to audition," Meredith told me over breakfast near her home on the Upper West Side. "I wasn't somebody who watched daytime." Not that she was a snob about it: "I was working, and it had never been an area of television that interested me." She knew her options as a reporter were limited because she didn't want to travel so that she could be at home with her three kids. "What's the worst that can happen?" she thought.

Barbara wasn't convinced that Meredith was the right fit either—they wanted funny. So Stedman Guff, who knew Meredith through their children in school, took her out for a bite with Geddie, at the upscale Italian restaurant Café Fiorello. After the lunch, Geddie turned to Stedman Guff and told her that she was right. He liked that Meredith had a wicked sense of humor beneath her cool exterior. "Believe me, she wanted the job," Stedman Guff said.

Star Jones was another woman on the wish list. The thirty-five-year-old African-American lawyer was a rising star on TV from her legal commentary on *Inside Edition* and other shows. As a former prosecutor based out of Brooklyn, Star saw her profile rise through her coverage of the O. J. Simpson trial. She had attempted her own talk show for NBC, but the pilot didn't impress executives, who decided she couldn't carry a program on her own.

"I thought to myself, 'I am at a crossroads,'" Star recalled. "What do I do? And the phone rang." It was a producer that she had worked with in the past, asking if she'd be interested in a panel show. Barbara's name sold her. "Tell me more and send me the information," she responded. Star agreed to fly to New York from Los Angeles, where she lived in a spacious Hollywood Hills house with a swimming pool, for a chemistry test.

As the search barreled on, Barbara attended a charity event for Milton Berle, whom she'd known from his performances years ago at her dad's nightclub. There, she witnessed a hilarious set from a bawdy red-haired comedian who reminded her of Carol Burnett. Joy Behar, fifty-four, riffed about feminism and the sex life of author Salman Rushdie. It made Barbara laugh—on the inside.

From the stage, Joy had no idea she was leaving such a strong impression. She'd griped to her boyfriend Steve about the "Turner Classic Movies crowd" of Regis Philbin and Maureen O'Hara. "I did a joke about men who marry, how easy it is for them to get a young woman," Joy said. When she wrapped, Steve told her that everybody in the room was in stitches except for Walters. "So what?" Joy told him. "I'm not going to work for her." A few months later, ABC asked her to try out for *The View*.

The most surprising contender came through the door by accident. Debbie Matenopoulos, twenty-two, a senior at New York University, had been working part-time at MTV as a production assistant. One night, at a party downtown, a casting director told her that ABC was looking for new talent. She should give it a shot.

For a pre-interview with Geddie, Debbie arrived dressed to kill— if only she'd been trying out for *The Real World*. She'd donned a baby T-shirt with John Travolta's mug from *Welcome Back, Kotter*, a black miniskirt, and knee-high boots. Her hair was dyed Kool-Aid pink for a segment that she'd just taped for MTV's *House of Style,* as a free extra. She carried a blue bowling bag for a purse. "It was actually a Kate Spade bowling bag purse," Debbie recalled.

Geddie immediately liked her offbeat style, and Barbara stopped by to offer a quick hello. "I met Barbara with my pink hair," Debbie said. He wanted a reel of her best clips; she didn't have one. She ran back to MTV and asked her friends to splice together the few minutes that comprised the totality of her on-air experience. "If you were cute and in the office and willing, they put you on television—that's how MTV was back then." She was laughing the whole time. "I thought, 'This is as far as I'm going to get.' I'm really out of my league here. But I'd have a cocktail story for years."

On a morning in April 1997, ABC secretly held an audition for *The View* at the Essex House, the stuffy midtown hotel on Central Park South. The network had rented two adjoining suites. One was used as a waiting pen for the roughly fifty aspiring cohosts who had been selected by Geddie as viable candidates. The other room had been configured with a mock table and chairs. The bedroom was set up with a TV for Geddie and other top honchos to watch how this scrimmage would play out.

As soon as Debbie entered the waiting area, she felt sick to her stomach. She would habitually throw up when she got nervous—a drawback for a potential TV star. "I was the only person in the room that didn't have some sort of notoriety," Debbie said. She sized up her competition, which included actress and motivational speaker Mother Love, NBC anchor Mary Alice Williams, and supermodels Veronica Webb, Emme, and Catherine McCord.

While these weren't exactly big celebrities, they were famous enough faces to spook a college student with only a vague interest in broadcasting.

"My heart was beating really fast," Debbie said. "I was intimidated." She convinced herself that she'd never get the job and decided to flee. But just as she made her way for the exit, she was spotted.

"Oh, Debbie, I'm so glad you came," Barbara cooed, having already committed her name to memory.

Barbara clutched Debbie by the shoulder and slowly moved her back to the center of the room. Barbara then parceled out instructions to the group without loosening her grip, as if she'd just caught a scared puppy. "I'm frozen," Debbie said. "That's the reason I stayed, because I was opening the door to leave and she was there."

To audition, four women at a time were summoned to the table, with mock topics printed out on note cards. Then they had to make small talk, to see how they'd interact individually and as a group, with new applicants rotating in and old ones out. Barbara wanted the vibe to resemble coffee with girlfriends, but it wasn't as effortless as it looked. A rhythm had to be mastered, so that the cohosts weren't shouting over one another. "A topic is like a hot potato," said Star, who stood out that day in a red cashmere power suit. "You pass it and it moves." Those that tried to suck up all the oxygen with soliloquies would get the ax.

Meredith introduced the first group—Barbara, Star, and Debbie—and read the topics from the note cards. "It seemed like a safe role for me," Meredith said. To get started, the women discussed a story about the Heaven's Gate cult in San Diego where thirty-nine of its members had committed suicide to gain entrance into heaven. After Barbara condemned the incident as a senseless tragedy, Meredith pushed back: *How do you know? You haven't been to heaven.* Barbara blushed, but she liked the back-and-forth. The ladies were onto something.

Another topic from the note cards asked for each of the cohosts to pick the most important people of the twentieth century. In addition to Albert Einstein and Bill Gates, Debbie had an unconventional name on her list—Madonna. The room suddenly erupted in shrieks, as Star addressed her in outrage: *You must be crazy.*

Debbie's choice cemented her fate in TV history. "Later on, they told me that's why I got the job," Debbie said. "And I swear to God, that's how I felt at the time." She chose Madonna for "what she had done for AIDS, gay rights, women's rights, and empowerment." Back then, before reality TV legitimized fame, the reach of even the biggest celebrities had its limits. It would be hard to imagine sitting across from Barbara and justifying that Madonna had accomplished as much as a US president. But it worked. Geddie wagered it would make for must-see TV.

Once the first session had ended, Barbara got up. She took a spot in the bedroom with Geddie and watched the next group on the TV screen: Joy, her replacement, cozied up to Star, Debbie, and Meredith. The chemistry still crackled without Barbara, and she and Geddie were overjoyed.

"We're geniuses," they said, chuckling to each other. "This is going to be a great show."

"Then we pulled Joy out and put in another comedian, and it didn't work," Geddie recalled. "We pulled Debbie out and put in another young person, and it didn't work. We pulled Meredith out and put in another journalist type, and it didn't work. We tried four completely different fresh people. It never worked again. It was never engaging for the rest of the day."

One of the early front-runners decided she had to get a look for herself. After Star's turn was up, she didn't pack up. Instead, she snuck into the executive suite, taking a seat right next to them. "All of a sudden, the mattress sags and I look over and Star is sitting on the bed," said Stedman Guff, who had to escort her out.

"You can't sit here while we're auditioning," Stedman Guff told her.

Star, who was never one to surrender in an argument, listed her career accomplishments. "I'm in this business," she protested. "I've been a producer. I'm a lawyer."

"I don't care what you are, honey," Stedman Guff said. "You're getting out."

That tiff offered an early glimpse into Star's personality. After word got out that Geddie was considering Star for the show, he was bombarded with horror stories. "She was considered difficult, a problem person," Geddie said. He wasn't put off by the warnings because he'd worked with challenging talent before. "I always said the same thing: everybody is difficult, and everybody could be terrible." Geddie paused. "I hadn't met Rosie yet."

There was no need for lengthy deliberations. "The first group was the group we hired," Barbara said. Joining her as the new cohosts of *The View* would be Meredith, Star, Debbie, and Joy. Over the years, Barbara loved to speculate about the fairy dust that brought the women to her audition in that exact order. However, it wasn't entirely coincidental that the foursome they opened with was the group they picked. "We started with them," said Geddie, "because we liked them best—a comedian in her fifties, a journalist mom in her forties, a professional lawyer in her thirties, and someone in her twenties."

Walters personally called all of her new cohosts to tell them the good news. "I thought, 'I'll give this a chance,'" Meredith said. "I never thought twenty years later I'd be talking about this. It was an interim thing for me until I figured out what I wanted to do."

Joy's job wasn't full-time like that of the other cohosts. She'd be filling in as the alternate on the mornings when Barbara wasn't there. "It was nice to have a couple days off," said Joy, who was contemplating a sitcom but didn't want to move to LA from New York. "My agent at the time told me not to do it. The money wasn't enough. But I wanted to do it because it was in New York and right near my house."

At least she had an agent. Debbie was in the wilderness, without any representation. Or electricity. She'd been ducking notices from Con Edison about her unpaid bills. One night, returning home from class, she clicked the red button on her answering machine to find a familiar voice. "Oh, Debbie, it's Barbara," the room purred. "I just want you to know that you've got the job. I couldn't do this without you."

Debbie rewound the tape and listened to it again, in case a friend was

playing a prank on her. It sounded real. She only believed it after her room-
mate confirmed that it wasn't a joke.

"You got the job!"

They ran downstairs to buy a bottle of champagne to celebrate. When
they got back, the unpaid electricity bill had caught up with them. "In one
day, my lights go out and I get the job of a lifetime," Debbie said. "Here
we are drinking champagne in the dark."

One last important hire was left. The show needed a director. Barbara met
with a handful of prospects, but her favorite was a lanky guy who owned
his own production company devoted to low-budget music videos and series on MTV, Comedy Central, and Lifetime. Mark Gentile convinced
Barbara that he'd be a steadfast workaholic for *The View*.

"It was a time for me where I had quite a few shows on the air, and I
was making a lot of good money," Gentile said. "But I wanted to move to
a higher place in my career. I wanted to find a single show that I would
focus all my energies on and would make successful."

He chatted with Barbara for fifteen minutes. At the end of their conversation, he closed with a hard sell. "I'll tell you what," he vowed. "I'll
work with you for six months. If you don't love everything I do, I'll give
you all your money back. Every dime. I don't want it."

The next day, he got a call from the network with the job offer. True
to his word, Gentile refused to cash a single paycheck for many months,
until he'd received the A-plus from his boss.

The look and feel of *The View* needed to be worked out. To curb her
nerves about the show ruining her reputation, Barbara pushed to make
The View unlike other daytime talk shows. She nixed the idea of a live
studio audience, preferring to do the debates in a small room, reminiscent of her own quiet studio at *20/20*. Cameras were set up, but that

bare-bones version tested miserably. She caved and agreed to what she described as "a small audience."

The network shot one pilot with Barbara and another without her. The early feedback suggested that the intrepid journalist might not be as beloved in a different environment. "The show with Joy tested better than the one with Barbara," Fili-Krushel revealed. "I said to Bill, 'We have to edit this report!'" Geddie told her that Barbara, as the executive producer, would want to know the truth. "Not a good idea," Fili-Krushel recalled.

When Barbara saw the results, she was genuinely hurt: "Why do they like the show better with Joy than with me?" That led Barbara and Joy to have a rocky first year, as Barbara continually worried that Joy was out to sabotage her. Barbara even jokingly compared her new colleague to *All About Eve*. The daytime executives were unnerved that the thick-skinned Barbara would be so insecure. They tried to assure her that Joy rated better simply because she was funny, which the audience liked.

In another complication, Arledge phoned Fili-Krushel to try to kill the project: "Pat, I understand you don't like Barbara's pilot."

"I go, 'Roone, where did you hear that from? I love Barbara's pilot,'" Fili-Krushel recalled. It quickly dawned on her what he was trying to do. "So I called Bob Iger"—now the CEO of the Walt Disney Co., who then was the chairman of ABC—"and I said, 'We can't afford not to put programming on air.'" He was on her side. "Don't worry," he told her. "I'll handle Roone." (Iger had his doubts, too. "We can't get one host to work. How are we going to get five?" he asked after watching the test episodes.)

The odds were stacked against *The View* because research indicated that the audience at home wasn't highly educated women—but primarily made up of low-income moms. According to a survey by Frank N. Magid Associates, 40 percent of daytime viewers lived in households with an income of less than $20,000 a year, and 85 percent of them hadn't graduated from a four-year college. Black women watched the most daytime TV, followed by Latina and Asian women. White women came in last. The conventional wisdom was that this demographic didn't want to catch up on news stories in the middle of the day. They were seeking an escape with beauty tips, makeovers, celebrity sightings, and fights on *Jerry Springer*—or so everyone thought.

The new home for *The View* was a sign of just how long ABC thought the show would last. The network didn't furnish Barbara with a shiny studio near *Regis and Kathie Lee* or *Good Morning America*. Instead, *The View* took over the digs from the recently canceled soap opera *The City* on West Sixty-Sixth Street, just a block from the Hudson River.

The building was a schlep for celebrities coming from Rockefeller Center (where Rosie held court) or Times Square. The producers' offices were in the basement. The dressing rooms didn't even come with individual toilets, but rather a communal bathroom for all the ladies to share. "Oh my God!" said Star, when asked about the arrangement. "Until this moment, I didn't even realize it was one bathroom. We were a family. You share a bathroom with your sisters."

The loftlike stage where the soap opera had taped needed to be reimagined for a talk show. Gentile, who was commanding the makeover, was trying to wrap his brain around how to squeeze all four (and later five) ladies behind a single table. He found the solution one weekend at a Pottery Barn in Connecticut, where he spotted a piece that would make TV history: "It was just a wooden table with a leaf. It was low-rent." He'd have the cohosts sit on one side, and *The View*'s logo at the end, shined from a spotlight that he set up next to the camera. "Just don't walk in front of it," he said. "That's the show." Although the table changed over the years, the basic concept never did, a testament to Gentile's engineering.

For a theme song, Gentile tapped Edd Kalehoff, who had penned the anthems to *Monday Night Football* and *World News Tonight*. His jingle for *The View* was just as catchy, with an upbeat melody that brought to mind a circus act, for a troupe of women about to attempt the flying trapeze. At jam sessions, the lead guitarist proudly rocked out with his tattoos and nose rings. "I used to always say, 'Man, if Barbara ever saw the guy doing the music, she'd shit a brick,'" Gentile mused.

Like presidential candidates preparing for a debate, the ladies of *The View* spent the two weeks prior to launch practicing in real time, even faking the commercials. The show would open with the so-called Hot Topics, a name that Barbara coined, before going to a celebrity interview and closing on a musical act or a self-help segment, such as improving your finances or sex life.

Even when she wasn't supposed to be there, Barbara crashed some of the rehearsals—leaving her cohosts aghast that they hadn't worn any makeup. It was one thing to attend a scrimmage just among themselves. But it was another to be with TV royalty. "It would throw us all off our game, because everyone was still so scared of Barbara," Debbie said.

As ABC started to promote the show, the executives looked at the cohosts as the backup singers for a band. Barbara's name was prominently displayed on early posters, but not theirs—the other cohosts were so anonymous, they were simply identified by their professions (lawyer, comedian, journalist, etc.). Yet there was no need to despair. Barbara pulled them aside with an upbeat career forecast: "If this show is successful, none of you ladies will be able to walk down the street without people stopping you."

They all laughed it off at the time. "That's exactly what happened," said Debbie. "It gives me chills even saying it. Within six months, it was insane."

3

Barbara Does Daytime

I t was like a college seminar in which the students don't know whether they would get along with their new professor—Barbara Walters. On August 11, 1997, on the first episode of *The View*, Meredith Vieira admitted she had trouble sleeping the night before. Debbie Matenopoulos broke out into hives on her neck. Star Jones piped up about the importance of using the word *allegedly* whenever possible.

In its original incarnation, *The View* looked different. The Hot Topics debates, soon mimicked by most cable-TV producers ("Now everything is a Hot Topic," Barbara lamented), lasted for only a single segment, as Meredith shuffled through print copies of the morning newspapers, pulling out the best headlines. The celebrity interviews were such an integral part of the show that the stage was reconfigured and the other cohosts disappeared to make room for an intimate one-on-one. "Originally, I was supposed to be the key interviewer because Barbara was taking a backseat," Meredith said.

The atmosphere felt like *20/20* meets *Live with Regis and Kathie Lee*. In fact, Barbara borrowed a touch of Regis Philbin's flair, after guest cohosting on his show for a string of days. On *The View*'s pilot, she had asked

Philbin to pitch in as the pretend celebrity. "It had never been done on TV before by a great team of girls like that," remembered Philbin, who dropped in over the years from his flashier studio. "They were terrific together, and they had respect for each other."

That was true early on. Since Barbara didn't want her extracurricular activity to distract from her news jobs, *The View* wasn't conceived as a hotbed for controversy. "It wasn't as political then," said Barbara, who as a journalist couldn't reveal whom she'd voted for or where she stood on issues such as abortion. Just take the premiere: Tom Selleck was the first guest, promoting his role—which he claimed to have modeled after Barbara—as a reporter in the gay romantic comedy *In & Out*.

"You are such a nice guy for coming here on the first show," Meredith greeted him. "And so smart, to know that this is going to be such a hit."

"I did it because Barbara asked," Selleck responded stiffly.

In the next segment, the ladies ("my pals," Barbara called them) re-emerged for the Question of the Day: "If your house was burning, what is the one thing you would grab on your way out?" Selleck picked his shotgun, a response that wasn't as polarizing in the pre-Columbine era, while Star nailed the biggest laughs with her answer, "My fur coat," as she flashed a brown frock straight out of Cruella de Vil's closet. After that, an earnest author offered tips on how to talk to your man. Then Joy Behar snuck out at the very end, to mutter a quick hello, as the substitute. "They've been keeping me in the broom closet all this time, but now I'm here," she joked on air. It was an awkward and forgettable hour of TV.

When the cameras stopped, the youngest cohost made a run for it. "I walked off the stage and I almost threw up," Debbie told me. "My nerves were so bad. I was sick to my stomach the whole time, like almost hyperventilating, because I was so scared. I'd never done live TV before."

If that weren't hard enough, the Hot Topics debates required keeping up with Barbara. "I didn't understand why there was nothing substantive in daytime," Geddie said. "We really wanted to break the mold."

The premiere opened on a political note, as Meredith detailed a story involving a supposed spat in the Kennedy family. Then she turned her attention to even saucier terrain. "It feels like the summer of infidelity," Meredith cheekily observed, citing such high-profile scandals as Paula Jones's civil suit against Bill Clinton, Bill Cosby's having to testify in an extortion trial in which he revealed he'd had an affair, and Frank Gifford's being caught cheating on Kathie Lee with a flight attendant. The studio crowd was asked by Barbara to cheer if they cared about a politician's private life (half did), while the cohosts piled on. "That's Hillary's problem," Star said, fourteen minutes into *The View*, about the president's rumored cheating, the first mention of a name that would soon become a Hot Topics staple.

On Tuesday ("They kept us on another day," Meredith said, exhaling), the ladies argued about who should portray Hillary in a biopic about the White House couple. The president had suggested Meryl Streep, but Debbie brought up another idea: "I think Cybill Shepherd should play Hillary."

"The Republicans would rather have . . . Roseanne," Barbara said, chuckling.

On Wednesday, *The View* set its sights on a man who would eventually become the show's biggest villain. Donald Trump was in the news as a result of his nasty separation from his second wife, Marla Maples. "You know what? They name a kid after a jewelry store," Joy said, referring to the three-year-old Tiffany. "Give me a break!" The conversation shifted to the new fashion trend, adopted by Calvin Klein, of women showing their bra straps in public. "This bothers me," Star protested.

On Friday, Trump managed to make more headlines, with a sexist comment about the Miss America beauty pageant allowing its contestants to wear a two-piece bikini in the swimsuit competition. "Thank you, Donald," Meredith shot back. "I can judge an ass when he's fully dressed."

~

The View got off to an inauspicious start by design. Barbara and Bill Geddie debuted the show in mid-August, during a quiet period on TV when
most women were on vacation with their families, to get out ahead of the
splashy fall premieres. "We sort of snuck it on," Barbara said, "because we
figured it would give us time to get into shape. So when people finally
tuned in, we would be there."

The show wasn't bolstered by an aggressive advertising campaign. Nor
did it have a team of caffeinated publicists working overtime to secure
press. At a small party for reporters, Barbara craftily observed that a rain-
bow in the sky was a good omen, and Debbie (described by *The New York
Times* the next day as "a bit like Deborah Norville by way of Cameron
Diaz") bawled on cue while telling the story of how she got hired.

As a mazel tov, all the cohosts had received a bouquet of flowers from
Disney's then CEO Michael Eisner. Yet there were no illusions. *The View*'s
future rested solely on Barbara's shoulder pads—fortunately, they were formidable. Her wardrobe mirrored that of a stateswoman, with colorful
pantsuits and shimmering brooches, while her unpierced ears restricted
her to costume earrings. (She used to complain that her lobes sagged.) Barbara recorded a soon-to-be-iconic introduction in the opening credits,
explaining the conceit ("I've always wanted to do a show with women of
different generations, backgrounds, and views . . ."), and she took her job
as the executive producer seriously.

Barbara showed up at her *View* office early each morning, traveling
mostly by foot, if the weather permitted, with a posse that included her
hairdresser, Bryant Renfroe; makeup artist, Lori Klein; and housekeeper,
Icodel Tomlinson, who had been with Barbara for thirty-five years. Renfroe would take a car to Barbara's apartment, arriving at 8:00 a.m. She'd
dump her belongings in the vehicle, trudge through Central Park with
her team, and meet the driver on the other side. "I miss those walks,"
Renfroe said. "We'd talk about everything. My life. Her life. Not so much
the cohosts."

Barbara would get back into the car for the last blocks, as they inched forward in traffic to West End Avenue. Didn't she get recognized? Barbara liked to quip that she could disappear in public if she wasn't wearing any makeup or didn't utter a word, because her distinct Boston accent gave away her identity.

Once she was in the building, she'd thumb through a folder with the juiciest stories of the day, which had been compiled by an overnight producer. She didn't choose them by herself. She wanted all the ladies to agree on what they'd talk about, inviting them to take part. At 9:00 a.m., Geddie oversaw the Hot Topics meeting in the communal makeup room, with the other cohosts—often minus Meredith, who called in on speakerphone because she was dropping off her kids at school in Westchester. If the scene resembled a sleepover, it was because the ladies wore their wet hair in towels, with their faces still unmade. These discussions were so exclusive that not even the publicists of the guests were allowed to eavesdrop. Admission was reserved for high-tier *View* staff, the cohosts, and Renfroe.

After Meredith arrived, she worked with a writer so that all her lines sounded like words she'd actually say. "I used to drive Barbara crazy because I would take time," Meredith said. "It was literally up to the wire. I was always just making it to set."

In preparing for *The View,* Barbara had several ironclad broadcasting rules, which she passionately imparted to her staff. She loved to lecture on the value of research—watching a TV show or a movie before an interview, so that her cohosts would ask informed questions. "Even when we were doing a cooking segment, I read the cookbook," Barbara said years later in her dressing room, while nibbling on an egg sandwich. "I like to do homework."

Barbara didn't allow for any preshow arguments about the Hot Topics before they went on TV so that their debates wouldn't sound canned. She worried about targeting Middle America, and not just the elite coasts, with the stories they selected. "Do they care in Wyoming?" was a favorite refrain. "I have an expression that I use," Barbara explained. "And I say, 'It's

great for New York, but I live in Wyoming.'" But she was comically un-
aware that she had wielded this retort so often, it had lost meaning.

"Nobody cares about the Kardashians in Wyoming," Barbara would
pipe up, in the later seasons.

"Yes, they do," her producers would push back. "Barbara, they have
newspapers in Wyoming."

On TV, Barbara wasted no time and tried to familiarize viewers with
her new protégées. At first, her aggressive reporting style sounded strange
for the leisurely pace of daytime. Even at her most relaxed, Barbara
seemed like a QVC host trying to convince housewives to buy the latest
accessories—her cohosts. Barbara kept pushing Debbie to do impressions
of her immigrant mother, a hairstylist from Greece. Barbara branded Star
"a combination of Cinderella and Perry Mason" (or, better yet, "a star in
every sense of the word!") and sent Joy to get a fancy haircut at Bergdorf
Goodman with the cameras trailing along. And Barbara tried to hand the
reins—as much as possible—to Meredith.

"I'm supposed to be the normal one in this group, which isn't hard,"
Meredith teased that first week. Her soothing cadence offered viewers a
point of entry. Joy played the comedic foil with zingers, and Debbie did
her best to keep up, although her favorite stories centered on college loans
and her gross car. "I was a little too young," Debbie said. "I had no idea
about the majority of things happening in the world." Star quickly grew
into the MVP. For the target demographic of stay-at-home moms, she
sounded the most relatable, eagerly dishing about her dream husband,
career ambitions, and fashion obsessions (she owned three hundred pairs
of shoes). "Live television never makes me nervous," Star said. "Do you
know why? That's the litigator training. When you do a closing statement,
you only get one shot."

In the tradition of other ensemble morning shows, such as *GMA* or
Today, *The View* tried to mimic a family in which all the sisters got along
with their mom. On the second episode, Meredith turned to her boss and
asked, "Do you feel like a proud mama?"

"Yes," Barbara responded on TV. Asked years later about a maternal connection to her cohosts, she bristled. "No, I chose these women." She was their Svengali, and each costar, depending on her own background, had a different relationship with Barbara.

"My experience was like a fairy godmother," Debbie said. "She plucked me out of obscurity and put me in a world I wouldn't have been in." By picking someone so green, Barbara had set her up for failure. "I was so scared, so young, and so in over my head," Debbie said. ("*Maternal* isn't a word I'd use to describe Barbara," one producer snickered.)

Star wasn't intimidated, but she felt that she never got to see Barbara without her armor. "I was awestruck because of what she had accomplished," Star said. "She was tough." For Star, attending the Barbara Walters journalism school was like wandering through the Louvre. "I sometimes describe her as a version of the *Mona Lisa*. Most people don't realize the painting is very small, encased in feet of glass on all sides, so you can't really get to it. She was right there, someone I appreciated and loved. I wasn't sure if I could ever really see her."

Meredith, having worked side by side with Barbara at ABC, approached her as a peer. "When there was a big news story, you knew Barbara was going to take over," Meredith said. "Sometimes I would be frustrated because I'm a journalist, too." She relished knocking down the Barbara mystique by pushing her buttons, calling her Babs and bringing up sex whenever possible. "She's kind of a bawdy person behind the scenes. She told dirty jokes. I think she liked it because we humanized her."

The cohost who regarded Barbara most like an actual girlfriend was the closest to her age. "I've been able to tease Barbara," said Joy, who attended potluck dinners at Barbara's house. Barbara realized she wouldn't need to worry about an uprising, where Joy would steal the show. Joy wasn't a conniving rival, nor was she a wide-eyed ingénue. "I don't consider her some mother figure," Joy said. "I'm not afraid of her."

The View didn't catch on as a cultural phenomenon until much later. "When it came on, it was not a gung-ho success," Barbara said. The show only drew about 1.5 million viewers, a fraction of Oprah's or Rosie's numbers. That was due, in part, to the cold reality of daytime. *The View* didn't air in all the major markets, since the affiliates were making more money with their own local programming. Barbara, who hadn't been aware of this fine-print complication, rolled up her sleeves and used her star power to her advantage. She'd call up the station managers herself, pleading with them to try out her new program. She had no shame about going on the road, taking the Amtrak to Boston or Philadelphia, with a rolling luggage stuffed with VHS tapes to pitch *The View*. Who could turn down a face-to-face interaction with Barbara Walters? "I was a real pain in the ass," she said.

Every time a new station agreed to program *The View*, Meredith announced it on TV, to a roar of applause. "We were all aware of the numbers," Meredith said. "We all knew that the show would have probably gone away without her." Yet the prospect of an early cancellation didn't keep Meredith up at night: "It would have been okay with me one way or another. I don't want to be cavalier; I was just finding my way. After a few more years, then I was invested."

When Wendy Williams launched her talk show in 2008, with a shamelessly plagiarized opening segment called Hot Topics, she struggled to get celebrities to pop by. "If you're a new show, you don't get those guests you dream of," Williams told me. But Barbara overcame that barrier through her A-list Rolodex. "The first few guests I remember with great affection because they came on this cockamamy show," said Barbara, who wasn't above haggling for favors with actors she'd known socially or through her specials. The first week of *The View* featured an impressive lineup for the era: Sylvester Stallone, Michael J. Fox, Elle Macpherson, and Ray Liotta.

In September, a fifteen-year-old Ivanka Trump ventured over from boarding school to plug her modeling career. "I've had boyfriends before, but at this point, I don't expect anything serious," she giggled, when pressed about her personal life. Her dad, never one to turn down a chance for self-promotion, scheduled his first *View* sit-down in November. Barbara, in a tan suit with an orange sweater tied around her neck like a cape, asked the real estate mogul if he believed in monogamy. "I hope so," Trump said. "I love the institution of marriage. Someday, perhaps, I'll get it right." Two days later, "the trivia-spouting darling of daytime," Rosie O'Donnell, made a generous gesture to her competitors by doing an interview. She couldn't turn down an invitation from the icon she grew up watching on TV with her mom in Long Island.

"It was Barbara's name and reputation that we had to sell it on," said *The View*'s longtime booker, Donald Berman. That wasn't to say there weren't difficulties. *The View* had a different audience from Barbara's prime-time shows, which the staff learned the hard way when a full hour with Ringo Starr tanked in the ratings. Many publicists initially only promised their top clients on days when Barbara was confirmed to be there. "I think they felt it would be a little more prestigious," said Berman, who had come from *Entertainment Tonight* and focused on movies, music, and TV. Sue Solomon, a producer with a long TV career with Joan Rivers, Dick Cavett, and Montel Williams, pursued politicians and authors. "There would be no show without Barbara Walters," she said. "Her vision, her drive, her clout were key."

Even with such assurances, guests were nervous to appear on *The View* until they could see the finished product. "It showcased women with minds of their own," Solomon said. "They confessed a lot of things on the show that women are supposed to feel guilty about, and they said it out loud. There was a sign in the greenroom that said MAKE SPARKS."

That became the unofficial mantra backstage as well as on TV. Solomon and Berman bickered ("constantly," recalled one staffer) like a married couple in nearby offices.

"That's my booking," Berman would bark.

"That's my juice!" Solomon would shoot back.

Geddie sat in the studio audience, where the women occasionally threw the camera to him for a funny line. Fans came to recognize him by the nickname "The Viewmaster," as the neighborhood grump. "I'm much more comfortable on the floor than the control room," Geddie said. "I prefer to be hands-on."

The show was a work in progress. "In the beginning, the chemistry was not what you know the chemistry to be," said Mark Gentile, the director. "I remember thinking, 'We got to find a way to smoke screen this.'" As it creaked along, *The View* introduced a revolutionary idea—to mix news with opinion as the main attraction. Most talk shows had been shy about politics out of fear of alienating people with different ideologies. "I don't know too many shows where women are really allowed to express themselves politically the way we do," Joy said. "There are few repercussions. I could say the most scathing things."

When you talk to the producers, they point to two major events that gave *The View* its voice. On August 31, 1997, only three weeks into the show's start, Princess Diana died in a high-speed car crash in Paris while trying to escape a motorcade of paparazzi on a Saturday night. It was Labor Day weekend, and Geddie debated whether they needed to rush out a show on Monday, scheduled as a day off. "I'll never forget," recalled Jessica Stedman Guff, who was on vacation in Nantucket with her kids. "Do we run to the office? Bill made the decision that we do not respond to breaking news." *The View* addressed Diana's death two days later, on September 2, when the ladies gathered to reflect on her legacy.

"Today, there is only one story on everyone's mind," Meredith said somberly.

Barbara revealed that she'd met Diana several times, over private lunches and dinners, in the pursuit of an interview. She brought in letters and holiday cards that she'd received, showing off Diana's penmanship, which she called "large girlish handwriting."

Debbie remembered waking up in the middle of the night as a young girl to watch the royal wedding. "She didn't ask for all of this," Debbie said. "I feel like the media created her and killed her." As Debbie delivered this indictment, she started to weep. "Some people thought it was odd," said producer Stuart Krasnow. "Others thought it was fantastic." Although Debbie wasn't technically an anchor, women in news never showed emotion on air—this was years before Ann Curry's sobbing departure from *Today*.

By going all in on feelings, *The View* embodied a moment. Diana's death represented a milestone for women at the time. It was the dawn of a national conversation about the end of privacy. "We don't have a right to know everything about everyone," Star scolded during Hot Topics, after a clip of George Clooney at a press conference where he bashed the *National Enquirer* for its invasive practices. Many young moms in the nineties had grown up with Diana, and her death at age thirty-six felt intensely personal. "She was my contemporary," Star said over breakfast, twenty years later. "I couldn't imagine that this young, vibrant woman who had achieved what every little girl wants, as a princess, was dead. It made me face my mortality for the first time."

The other story that catapulted *The View* into the national spotlight was the Monica Lewinsky scandal, which broke five months later. "That was the gift that kept on giving," Geddie said. "It was the president of the United States. It was a young girl. There was the vindictive ratting out of a young girl. There was a scarred wife. It was a feminist subject involving a man many women had seen as a feminist. It was a real conflict because I'm sure everybody there voted for Bill Clinton. So it was interesting to deal with that."

The View was the lone perch in daytime that consistently took on Clinton, before the proliferation of talking heads on cable news. "You could click over—Regis wasn't talking about the stain on the dress," Geddie said with a laugh. "We were the only ones doing it. And we did it day in and day out for a year."

The story leaked on the *Drudge Report* on a Saturday in January, but because all the networks distrusted online reporting, *The View* didn't pick it up right away. The next Monday, the ladies spent Hot Topics yammering about the Golden Globes, where *Titanic* had won big, Christine Lahti was caught "in the potty" during her category, and Ving Rhames gave away his trophy to Jack Lemmon.

But once the mainstream press reported on the allegations, it was fair game. *The View* suddenly had its raison d'être. The show could offer sultry counterprogramming to the soaps, with the biggest sex scandal in US history unraveling in the White House. The ladies each picked their own heroes and villains. "I don't believe any of that," Debbie said on January 21, 1998, the first Hot Topics debate about the affair. She couldn't envision a scenario in which an intern named Monica—"What's her last name?"—bragged to her friends about sex with the president. Star reminded viewers that Clinton was innocent until proven guilty, while Meredith wondered if he could be impeached for obstruction of justice.

On January 27, all the cohosts were glued to an interview Hillary gave to *Today,* during which she tried to brush off the charges against her husband as a Republican witch hunt. "You got to hand it to her," Barbara said. "She looks wonderful."

While the story dominated TV, most news personalities weren't reporting on the first lady's fashion choices. What made *The View*'s commentary groundbreaking was that it took a major news event and dissected it through a female point of view. "The truth is that every woman in this whole scandal looks better now than she did in the beginning," Meredith observed the following summer.

"They all want Clinton to expose himself to them so they can get a makeover," chuckled Joy, who had nicknamed Linda Tripp "Mrs. Ronald

McDonald." "It's just not that important," Joy huffed on TV. "The Europeans are laughing at us. You cannot bring a country down to its knees because a girl is on her knees."

Despite soft ratings, *The View* coasted into its second season, primarily because nobody from the daytime TV team had the chutzpah to cancel Barbara. Then in November 1997, *The View* became infamous, thanks to a recurring skit on *Saturday Night Live*. Writers Tina Fey, Lori Nasso, and Paula Pell were amused with Barbara trying to pass herself off as a regular gal, with a group of girlfriends.

When Fey first arrived at *SNL* that year, she had made it her mission to write sketches for women. "And then I thought, 'Oh, this thing is new. We could do this,'" Fey recalled. "And there were parts for almost everybody." Cheri Oteri played Walters at a faux Hot Topics table, alongside Molly Shannon as Meredith and Ana Gasteyer as Joy. The celebrity hosts, from Claire Danes to Sarah Michelle Gellar to Cameron Diaz, took on Debbie. "Tracy Morgan was in drag"—as Star—"because there were no African-American women on the show," Fey said, with a sigh.

The first time they did the skit, "we were the only ones who had seen *The View*," Fey said. "The more dudely members of the staff were, like, 'What is this!?'" They thought the entire conceit had been made up. "No, this is a real thing," Fey told them. "I remember going to the wardrobe room after we had done it in dress rehearsal. And someone in costumes being, like, 'You're a feminist. Well, I hope you're happy making fun of women.'" Fey was surprised: "*Oh, no. I'm trying to give these actresses parts,*" she recalled thinking. "When Chevy Chase plays Gerald Ford, he's goofing on him. I was, like, 'We have to be able to goof on women, or we'll never get the women on.'"

Oteri agreed that *The View* was ripe for parody. "My take on Barbara was really funny," Oteri told me. "She would always ask a question and then bring it back to herself—like, 'I was at a make-your-own-sundae party with Madeleine Albright and a young Vladimir Putin.'"

The satirical portraits elevated the cohosts' fame. *SNL*'s Star was a talkative lawyer who doled out legal advice in situations that didn't call for it. Joy sputtered out jokes. Meredith came across as the straight one, who sometimes went overboard with personal secrets—such as her distaste for wearing underwear. "She just seemed like somebody who loved being a woman," Shannon said. "I said to her once, 'You seem like you like coffee and sex. You're sultry. You're Meredith!'"

"I loved it," said Meredith. "Being on the show meant that you had arrived."

One of the caricatures stung. On *SNL,* Debbie was portrayed as the village idiot who had to be put in a cage. The label didn't bother her. "They clearly picked up on the way I was being treated," she said. But her fish-out-of-water standing soon became so unavoidable, she took on the name Debbie the Dummy in the press.

Barbara knew the value of this kind of publicity. Rather than get mad, she cashed in. On April Fools' Day, *The View* invited the *SNL* cast to walk out onstage before the real ladies kicked them out of the chairs. *The View* had entered the zeitgeist, and awareness skyrocketed. There was just the question of what to do with the show's weakest link.

4

Death Becomes Her

One spring afternoon, Barbara raced into *The View*'s offices with a stop-the-presses scoop. She gathered the staff around her, informing them about an "important" discovery, which she'd just learned about at ABC News. "It's a big story," she declared. "It's going to change the world." She wanted it to lead the next day's show, telling everybody they'd forever remember where they were when they heard about this shattering breakthrough.

What the hell was it? "Viagra!"

"And then she went on to explain that erectile dysfunction would be treated with this drug," recalled producer Stuart Krasnow. "There was a lot of discomfort in the room. Here's this iconic newswoman who we'd all been so reverent to, just going on about erections." The memory still cracked him up. "What Barbara brought to *The View* was knowledge."

The View was located only three blocks west of ABC headquarters, but it was far enough so that none of the staff felt that they had to adhere to stuffy office culture. The producers at the mother ship had traditionally been gruff men. In the seventies and eighties, the network's news division had been rife with sexism, as some women tried to follow Barbara's example and entered the news business, which at the time resembled *Mad Men*. If the executives weren't ogling the new hires or barking at them after a three-martini lunch, they were dismissing them. Barbara liked to tell a story of how, when anchoring the evening news, the crew refused to talk to her because they saw Harry Reasoner as one of them and her as an intruder.

By the postfeminist nineties, the gender schism had balanced out. Shelley Ross, a tenacious producer at *Primetime Live,* had been climbing the ranks. "Diane Sawyer and I won an Emmy in 1990, for the first story we did together on the Menendez brothers," Ross told me. "It was sort of scandalous that we won for a murder story. Nobody called *In Cold Blood* a murder story, and that's what Diane and I had set out to do—to redefine it." In late 1998, Ross wrote an eight-page memo that earned her the job of executive producer at *Good Morning America*. She asked Sawyer to come with her to rebrand the morning show, which had been sinking in the ratings.

"I think you'll find that my time to do a morning show has come and gone," Sawyer, who was fifty-three, told Ross. "And I said, 'Don't believe it!' I felt like she was ageless, and she is." The president of ABC News, David Westin, took some convincing. "In a game of chess, you never expose the queen," Westin told a colleague about Sawyer. Ross didn't back down. "We would never expose Diane Sawyer," Ross said. "We'll make this great." Sawyer's move to *GMA* in 1999 eventually added more than one million viewers, as she followed Barbara to morning TV, with an expanded portfolio of crack-of-dawn scoops.

Over at *The View,* the cohosts could sleep in later and all bets were off when it came to decorum. There was no question that women, who made up at least half the staff, were treated as equals, a rare occurrence in the television business. But as daytime's stepchild, the office vibe sometimes felt like a college radio show, especially on the days when Barbara wasn't there.

For years, a married man carried on a public affair with one of the female staff and nobody blinked. A writer liked to flash his cock in the offices, as part of a running gag that made Joy laugh. The show's publicist, Karl Nilsson, would camp out on the premises, yet he seemed most interested in stirring up gossip.

"I always likened it to the book *Flowers in the Attic,* where the kids live in the attic and nobody grows because they don't get sunlight," said Alexandra Cohen, who became the second-in-command to Geddie around 1999. The only difference was all of *The View*'s producers lived in the basement. "There were no windows. You had to call up to security and go, 'Is it raining? Is it snowing?' You never knew," said Cohen.

The first floor of the Costco-like building housed the lobby, where tourists lined up outside for hours to nab a seat at the live tapings. The second floor held the dressing rooms for the hosts and the guests, as well as hair and makeup. The third floor was the studio, which included a greenroom (with watermelon and juice), where Geddie paced around if he wasn't in his seat. Finally, the control room sat on the fourth floor. A slow-moving elevator served as the artery, which had to be cleared out by security so the hosts didn't get trapped with camera-wielding fans.

For many of *The View*'s employees the main interaction with other human beings came through *All My Children,* the daytime soap opera that shared the building—it was split in half, with identical floor plans on each side. Sometimes, because Barbara was bad with directions, she'd accidentally roam down their halls, looking for her dressing room amid all the buff and tan bodies. Up-and-coming daytime actors such as Josh Duhamel would come over to sneak a look at the famous guests. Kelly Ripa, who started her career on the soap, took cigarette breaks on the loading dock shared by *The View,* wearing a coat over lingerie, in between shooting sex scenes.

Inside *The View,* there was order when Barbara came to work. She could be like a drill sergeant, pounding the pavement to make sure that the show adhered to her ethical and competitive standards. "I remember we wanted to book a psychic on the show," said Valerie Schaer, one of the ABC Daytime executives who worked on the show. "Barbara was very opposed to that. She didn't believe it. We'd say things like, 'Barbara, it really rates.'" So Barbara tested out the guest for herself in a private meeting. She was skeptical, until the psychic held up a hand over her eye, saying that Lou Walters wanted to say hello. "Barbara freaked out," Schaer said. "No one knew this, but her father had a glass eye."

Even if the ratings were still modest, Barbara had never looked better on *The View*. Roone Arledge, the ABC News boss, lodged one more complaint against the show because Barbara's appearances on other programs didn't have the same glow. "Bob Iger said to me, 'Roone feels Barbara is feeling tired on *20/20* because you're working her too hard,'" recalled Pat Fili-Krushel. "I go, 'That's not true!' I had brought in a theatrical lighting director to teach the television directors how to light. And we had theatrical hair and makeup. So then they tried to steal our people, and they didn't want to go to news."

Barbara only raised her voice if she felt that someone was trying to pull a fast one over her. For instance, she once turned on her TV to *The Wayne Brady Show*, the short-lived series that aired on ABC before *The View*. Barbara went apoplectic when she saw the guest was the same man waiting in their studio: celebrity event planner David Tutera, who had pretaped the episode in Los Angeles, thinking it would air later.

A voice on the underground speaker system, an artifact from the talk show set, paged him to report to Barbara's dressing room immediately. "I might have pissed my pants a little bit," Tutera said. "She starts going at me, *'How dare you do this?! You're not going on the show today. I want you to leave.'*" She eventually cooled down and let him tape a segment on how to entertain at the Oscars.

The cohosts cut loose on the days when Barbara was gone. During a Question of the Day in 1998 with Kenneth Branagh—"What's the craziest thing you've ever done for love?"—Meredith made up a story about how she got hitched to an Elvis impersonator in Las Vegas after a night of partying in her twenties. "This is a bit of a shocker," she said. Without Barbara there to force an immediate correction, the tall tale landed in the papers. Finally, days later, Meredith had to clarify she had been joking, an example of just how unruly *The View* got without its creator. "They hated when Barbara was on," Stedman Guff said. "She rained on their parade. It was like a bunch of sixth graders throwing shit around the room, and then the teacher walks in."

Even Bill seemed more at ease without someone looking over his shoulder. "Bill resented Barbara like nobody's business," Star said. "All I know is that he was happiest when she wasn't there. He made that pretty clear."

Geddie denied that characterization: "I would never take a shot at Barbara. There were some days that stuff happened, I said to myself, 'This show is so crazy and naughty, I'm glad Barbara wasn't sitting there.' She can be tough to be around. You've got to stay on your toes. It's a little more relaxed when she wasn't there. But in terms of Barbara's importance to the show, there would be no *View* without her."

Barbara was so involved, she even participated in staff negotiations. She blocked an attempt from Rosie O'Donnell to hire their director for her daytime talk show. "I meet with Rosie," Mark Gentile said. "She offers me more money than I'm making. And so I get this big deal, and I say at the end, 'I have to go back to *The View* and give them the dignity of responding.' Rosie was incensed with that."

Rosie called Barbara and told her that Gentile had come to her sniffing for a job.

"Well, we love Mark," Barbara said. "We want him to stay, but if he wants to go, that's okay."

She hung up and ordered that ABC raise his salary. "That's when I signed a contract," said Gentile, who had been living off his savings for six months because of his promise not to cash a single paycheck until *The View* had clicked into place. Rosie, who later became one of his biggest adversaries, helped prove his worth.

Something had to be done about Debbie. *The View* was a bold experiment, but it also at times felt like a revival of *The Odd Couple*. If Barbara excelled at facts and substance, Debbie was on the bottom of the Hot Topics totem pole with her vague non sequiturs. By her own admission, Debbie had no idea what she had stumbled into when she walked on the *View* set. She had no broadcast experience. She lacked a point of view about most subjects, from politics to world affairs. "I was a kid," Debbie said. "I had no clue." That wasn't entirely her fault—she'd grown up in Virginia and had been hired while she was still in college. It had taken years for Barbara to become a skilled interviewer, but Debbie wasn't afforded any room to fail. Instead, she was tossed into a rowdy vaudeville act, in which she fell into the role of the clown.

"How are you going to have an opinion if you haven't lived it?" Debbie said. "I didn't have the experience like the rest of them had. So I chose to really not say too much when they were talking about really heavy things, because I didn't know what to say."

Parts of her new job she liked. No wallflower, she was drawn to the spotlight, especially since it meant a steady line of bachelors asking her out on dates. Debbie and Star, the only other single cohost (who wasn't Barbara Walters), became instant pals. They'd attend movie premieres at the Ziegfeld Theatre and later even vacationed together in the Caribbean and Mexico. "We were thick as thieves," Debbie said.

"I do partnerships and relationships really well," Star said, agreeing that they had been close at one time.

But when it came to regular office hours, Debbie didn't have the chops to keep up with the fast pace of a daytime TV show. That became apparent as she stumbled on basic tasks such as reading from a teleprompter. "They sent me to a coach to learn how to do things on television—blah, blah, blah. That was a waste of money. In hindsight, they needed to sit me down and go, 'Here's the deal: you're too nervous.'"

Part of what made her so jittery was working in the shadow of a trail-blazer. With Debbie, Barbara was like an overbearing stage mom. After Debbie had gotten written up in Page Six for taking her top off at Hogs & Heifers, Barbara counseled her on not tarnishing her name as a public figure. It didn't matter that most twentysomethings in New York had ventured into the beer-soaked dive bar and done the same thing. Barbara was aghast that Debbie had disrobed in public. It was bad enough that she roamed the halls at ABC in a bra, as if *The View* offices were a college sorority house.

"She had her own Justin Bieber effect," said Krasnow, who was enlisted to help Debbie find her way because he'd worked for a young Ricki Lake. "All of a sudden she's famous and people are watching her, and she's still growing up."

Other catastrophes also made her bosses at ABC blush. Debbie recalled the time she got in trouble for wearing a skimpy outfit at a photo shoot. Barbara was scandalized when Debbie eagerly dished about her sex life to Howard Stern. Another morning on Stern's show, Debbie made a surprise cameo when a magician guest bragged about sleeping with her on the first date.

"What are we going to do?" Geddie gasped, running over to talk to her.

"That's not what happened," Debbie calmly responded, as she explained that she didn't sleep with him until the third date. She didn't seem to think that a guy discussing her sex life on the radio was *that* big a deal.

At the morning meetings, Debbie wouldn't offer much brainstorming for Hot Topics. She took detailed notes in her dressing room, decorated with a half-full water bottle drunk by George Michael that she'd swiped from MTV and a poster of the Bee Gees. But Barbara confiscated Debbie's crib sheet. "She'd take my cards and rip them up and throw them away," said Debbie, who received instructions not to sound too rehearsed.

Debbie's tendency to go way off script made her an easy target for critics. When a debate wasn't in her comfort zone, she knew she was blowing it, but she couldn't stop herself. "I was, like, 'What did I just say?' There was no taking it back because it was live."

Her unpolished style was magnified when her errors were being corrected in real time by you know who. When she wasn't crying about Diana, Debbie wondered out loud how the princess must have felt trapped in the wreckage, awaiting medical help, until Barbara snapped that Diana had been unconscious. On Martin Luther King Jr. Day, Debbie confessed her lack of knowledge about the civil rights leader. "I feel like I should know more about Martin Luther King," she rambled, blaming public school systems. Barbara just sat there, her lips tightening, unable to mask her disdain.

During the second-season premiere, Barbara teasingly asked if Debbie, back from a vacation in Greece, had a new boyfriend. "He's not allowed in the country—he doesn't have a green card," she mumbled.

During a lighter conversation about snooping houseguests, she interjected with a ridiculous tip that no housewife would try: "Hide marbles in your medicine cabinet. As soon as they open it—ding, ding, ding— they are looking at your stuff."

"You know Debbie will come up with something," Star said, rolling her eyes.

"One day, Debbie said something really stupid," said Stedman Guff, who watched the show from the control room, where she whispered into the cohosts' earpieces. "I said, 'Oh my God, that was so fucking stupid, I want to kill myself.' I didn't know the key was open and she could hear me."

Debbie scowled. "I can hear that, Jessica," she spoke to nobody in particular on TV.

"I couldn't believe she said that on air," Stedman Guff said.

Debbie had no regrets about shaming her. "I would have said it again," Debbie explained. "Why? It's probably one of the rudest things any producer has said to me. It probably was a silly thing. But as my superior, it would have been her job to take care of me and protect me, not to disparage me in front of all those people."

Krasnow tried his best to offer Debbie a crash course in broadcasting. He'd sit with Debbie before the show, carving out smarter takes on issues that she couldn't care less about. For a story about police brutality—"I don't relate to this," Debbie moaned—he suggested she tell a funny story about the time she was pulled over by the cops. "How did the police treat you?" he quizzed her, to get the wheels turning. "Did you get out of it because you were a pretty girl?"

Krasnow said, "One idea that I loved that never came to fruition was her and Barbara having sleepover dates. I remember really pushing for that." He thought that viewers would eat up the segment, especially if Barbara traded her uptown Manhattan luxury apartment for a tiny downtown studio for a night. Barbara, not willing to suffer that much for ratings, vetoed the suggestion.

Debbie wasn't shy about defending her honor. *The View* had a public email—TheView@aol.com—for fans to write in with their thoughts. "Nobody really knew what to do with their emails," said Krasnow. "Debbie, being a young person who had just graduated from college, was all about emails." She personally answered each one addressed to her, reveling in the chance to shame any haters.

"She'd write back, 'I'm twenty-two years old. Why don't you get on the show tomorrow and see how well you do?'" Krasnow recalled. She'd usually toss in a few expletives, just to get her point across.

"Debbie, you can't send those," Krasnow told her.

She did it anyway because she thought it was important for anonymous trolls to know that she was a real person hurt by their nastiness. "That was her therapy," Krasnow said. "It made her feel better." He paused. "Now I'm thinking she invented Twitter."

By the beginning of the second season, as *SNL* continued its vicious parodies, the damage to Debbie's reputation was permanent. Bill and Barbara had chosen her for *The View* in the hope that she'd bring viewers her age to the show. But according to internal research, Debbie was doing the opposite, scaring young women away.

"The audience just didn't like Debbie," Geddie said. "The older people were okay with her. They thought she was an idiot, but it was funny. Younger people didn't see themselves in Debbie. They thought by picking someone like that, we were talking down to them. It was never my intention for her to be a bad representation of young people. I thought she was a regular gal."

So Barbara decided that it was time to shuffle the deck. It was *The View*'s only chance to stay on TV, and Barbara never let sentimentality get in the way of ratings. "The only one who didn't succeed, although I thought she was adorable, was Debbie," Barbara reflected, years later. "I wanted someone young and funny. But on the show, it wasn't working."

Rumors started to swirl in the press that Debbie was getting axed, which the network kept denying. In late November, Geddie finally summoned her to his office and shut the door.

"We're going in a different direction," he told her. "We love you, but we don't think this is a good fit, so we're going to try to find someone who is more newsy."

"I remember sitting there and all the blood rushing out of my head," Debbie said. "Oh my God. I screwed this up so bad. All I wanted to do was be good for them. Of course I cried. I was so sad. These people were my friends. Here's the opportunity of a lifetime, and I blew it."

When Meredith heard about what had happened, she started bawling, too, and she went to Barbara to lobby on Debbie's behalf. "Debbie was like a kid sister to me," Meredith said. "I think of her as a puppy or a deer. I always felt bad because it was like they were trying to put words in her mouth. Her opinions were not as respected. I could have never done the show at her age."

Even though Debbie's time on *The View* had ended, ABC kept her on through the holidays, as they auditioned replacement cohosts around her. Then on January 6, 1999, the show abruptly addressed her absence, after the cohosts had squabbled about menopause, the Clinton impeachment trial, and "Is homework evil?" Debbie wasn't even at the table to say goodbye.

"We are announcing today that Debbie will no longer be a full-time cohost of *The View*," Barbara said, reading from a carefully worded statement. "She wants to spread her wings. She wants to pursue some new opportunities. She's looking into doing a situation comedy. Debbie herself is a situation comedy."

Barbara made it sound as if Debbie had initiated her exit, and that she could be back on the show whenever she wanted, which only fanned the public's interest. "When they fired me, the next day was like wildfire," said Debbie, who was bombarded with interview requests. "I was shell-shocked. I was not interested in talking to anyone." She made one exception, appearing on *SNL,* playing herself in a hysterical skit in which Debbie is so clueless, she still shows up to work after she's been canned.

She forgave Barbara, who sent her flowers as a peace offering. Yet Debbie had a falling-out with another TV pal, which she has never talked about. "Star, who was supposed to be one of my very good friends, didn't return my phone calls and emails," said Debbie, who wouldn't see Star again for seventeen years. "I was really hurt. I felt like she threw me under the bus. I felt super betrayed by Star."

Debbie would hear Star trash-talk her in other TV interviews. "She didn't need to use my firing to get press," Debbie said. "That really upset me."

When MTV's *Celebrity Deathmatch* asked Debbie to participate in an episode where cartoon versions of her and Star faced off in a boxing ring, she jumped at the chance. She told the writers to come up with the meanest lines possible. "That was my only way to get back at her for what she did to me," Debbie said.

Star evidently had her reasons for distancing herself from Debbie. "I became disappointed because she stopped working hard," Star told me. "She would stay out late and show up looking bedraggled. She gave rise to Debbie the Dummy. She is not a dumb person. It was difficult to see her not be able to right the ship."

Star believed that Debbie lost her job because she wasn't trying. "I don't think she fought hard enough to stay, and she could have done it," Star said, listing off what Debbie did wrong. "Less cute, more content. Young pretty blond girls quite often don't get over being young pretty blond girls. That gets you in the door. That doesn't keep you there. I thought Debbie needed to develop her own niche. She just wouldn't do it."

After trying to write a TV comedy series loosely based on *The View*, which she never finished, Debbie went on to hold twenty other jobs, ranging from red carpet coverage on E! to hosting CBS's *The Insider*. But no matter where she went, her notoriety from *The View* followed along. In the days before reality TV made public firings vogue, Debbie was a trendsetter.

"I was like the original 'Survivor' to be voted off the island," she said.

5

It's a Hit

I t was 1999, and *American Idol* had yet to democratize fame with the irresistible pitch that anybody could be a pop star. Nor had reality TV competition series such as *The Bachelor* or *America's Next Top Model* popularized the notion of chronicling the girl next door as she morphed into a pseudo-celebrity. In another three or four years, these shows and their copycats would dominate television, changing culture so that it looked a little bit more like Andy Warhol's vision for the future.

Barbara had always been ahead of the times as a journalist, but she had never received due credit for her eye as a pioneering producer. After dumping Debbie, she didn't let *The View* stay in the media's bad graces for long. Instead, she tactfully changed the narrative about her troubled talk show by unveiling a unique contest: a nationwide search for the next cohost.

"Back then, nobody did that," recalled Geddie. "I wish I made more shows out of it."

The View marked the first time that a TV series introduced a job interview that unfolded in real time. The lone prototype was the 1980s talent show *Star Search,* an incubator for discovering under-the-radar singers and comedians, including Rosie O'Donnell. Since nothing like this had existed, established TV personalities were scared about throwing their hats in the ring—they didn't want to look desperate. "It was tough, because once you said you were searching for a person on air, a lot of people said, 'I'm not sitting in that seat!'" Geddie said. "You were basically working with unknowns."

As *American Idol* later proved, that could be an asset. The anonymity of the competitors allowed viewers to see a version of themselves on TV. Almost overnight, *The View* morphed from an earnest coffee klatch into *America's Next Top Anchor.* The charade turned the show's reputation inside out. The novelist Jennifer Weiner, writing for *The Philadelphia Inquirer,* compared the cutthroat jockeying to rush week in a sorority. "Basically, what *The View* has done is give us a glimpse of something few viewers are ever privy to—the power shift," Weiner wrote. "Most TV successions happen behind the scenes: Leno replaces Carson . . . and if you, the viewer, want to figure out the hows and the whys, you're stuck combing the tabloids and trades for clues. Which might be why *The View* feels so compelling, in the same way watching the lions eat the Christians must have been compelling. The veil of secrecy has been shucked, the offstage shuffle has been shoved onstage."

By extending an invitation to smart career women, the Hot Topics table suddenly felt as approachable as Oprah's couch. Before the holidays, Geddie had gotten the word out to the major agencies that the show was testing new cohosts, so the young applicants arrived in droves. Viewers were encouraged to vote on *The View*'s website for their favorites. Yet the only opinions that truly mattered were Barbara's and Bill's, who personally vetted the contestants. Some had to pass a chemistry test, while others were allowed a shortcut. The rules were never spelled out because Geddie made them up as they went along. Adding racially diverse candidates helped, as did previous broadcasting experience, since the Debbie debacle had soured Barbara on total inexperience. The only other prerequisite, later adopted by *Idol,* too, was an age limit—you had to be younger than thirty to submit a tape.

The initial trial lasted two days for each applicant to give her time at the table with Barbara and without her. If the young woman shined during both attempts, she'd be invited back for more rounds. It was like speed dating—only with the understanding that you couldn't turn down a marriage proposal. All contestants were forced to sign a prenegotiated contract, tying them to *The View,* so that the winner couldn't trade on her newfound fame for a better offer. The starting salary was meager for TV, just north of $100,000. "The truth is, people would have done this job for free," recalled Amy Kean, one of the finalists, yanked from her desk as a columnist for the *New York Post.* "I think *The View* was the most important show in daytime television. It stinks that they didn't choose me."

The View suddenly became a media magnet as the tabloids trailed the contenders and TV critics ranked their favorites. The roster included two *Real World* alumnae (Rachel Campos-Duffy and Lindsay Brien), one of Colin Powell's daughters (Annemarie Powell), a local anchor from Omaha, Nebraska (Jill Cordes), and a Fox Sports reporter (Lauren Sánchez). By February, a *New York Post* story—with the headline "Star Search Without End"—noted that *The View*'s ratings had jumped to 2.8 million viewers, up from 2.3 million. The contest was extended indefinitely, which didn't thrill the regular cohosts. "For us, it was a little weird," Meredith admitted. "It threw off the rhythm of the show."

Joy was even less of a fan. "Those civilians," she sighed. "It was a gimmick. My recollection is, when people come on this kind of show who have not done it, it's not an easy thing to do. You have to have a certain amount of timing. You have to be succinct. You have to be informed. You have to get along with your siblings."

Cordes, twenty-nine at the time, made the cut after her agent secretly submitted a reel. She arrived in New York bewildered to join *The View* for forty-eight hours. Meredith, congenial even when the cameras weren't on, offered a heartfelt welcome. The other ladies weren't so warm. "I remember being terrified of Joy," said Cordes, who received a warning from a makeup artist not to step on Joy's punch lines, a particular pet peeve of hers. During a commercial break, when Cordes waved to a friend in the audience, Star told her, "We should be bonding." Cordes apologized. "I didn't mean to offend you by waving to my friend," she said, as the thought: "*I have no fucking idea why I'm here.*" Worst of all, a legend lectured her on TV for interrupting the other cohosts, a common mistake on panel shows. "I was chastised on air by Barbara Walters."

Cordes got into some personal trouble, too. During a Hot Topics debate about letting kids sleep in your bed—Cordes didn't have any—she tried to keep up by revealing how she and her boyfriend, Phil, cuddled with their cats. "I indicated that we were sharing a bed," she recalled. After the show ended, Cordes heard an irritated voice on the phone. "We have to have a major conversation," grumbled Phil. His religious family didn't know they'd been living together. ("My church ladies are appalled!" he gasped.) A big fight ensued. Cordes was relieved when she learned that she wasn't advancing. "It's the best job I never got," she said. "There was so much drama."

As a producer at ABC, Annemarie, who was Powell's daughter, knew Barbara. By testing her, *The View* started the trend of courting the offspring of politicians for TV news—a trajectory later followed by Chelsea Clinton and Meghan McCain. "My impression was they were trying to find a conservative voice and maybe falsely assumed I might be because of my father," said Powell, who struggled to get a word in at the table. "I'm not particularly aggressive by nature. I didn't have much to say." She was horrified when she watched her first appearance. She didn't look like herself; she'd worn a fuzzy pink sweater. The next day, she changed into a jacket and tried to speak up more. "I decided if I'm going back on TV, I'll look like myself and not Colin Powell's sweet daughter."

Two front-runners emerged. Rachel Campos-Duffy was the first true conservative to vie for a seat at *The View*. She checked a lot of boxes—as a Latina Republican who riled up Hot Topics with her pro-life stances. "I think conservatives have an idea that the women of *The View* are mean to conservatives," Campos-Duffy said. "But I was always treated very well."

She saw a clear opening, suggesting ideas in the meeting that would allow her right-wing ideologies to shine. "I would always remind myself that fifty percent of the audience believed what I believed, and they weren't going to be at the table or in the Manhattan audience. I could not tailor my point of view to get applause from this group because my group was somewhere in red-state America."

Until then, through the Clinton impeachment, conservative personalities were usually white men preaching to other men—from Rush Limbaugh on the radio to Bill O'Reilly on Fox News. By simply considering Campos-Duffy, *The View* tapped into a population that had never before been represented on daytime. "There was a lot of buzz in the industry that I was going to get it because it was going to be groundbreaking," Campos-Duffy said.

The other favorite was Lauren Sánchez, who would also have carried the mantle of the first Latina cohost. At twenty-nine, she'd had the most airtime, with a previous stint on *Extra*. She proved she could be good TV when she boldly declared that Hillary Clinton "knew she married a dog," a line that got picked up in the papers. "I was proud of that moment," Sánchez said. "It was what everyone was thinking." Backstage, her looks were scrutinized, as the wardrobe department gave her a stern warning to cover up her cleavage. ("You're talking to mom. Button up!") But Barbara, to her credit, opposed a makeover: "If you're going to get it, get it being you," she advised. After a few more practice rounds, Barbara was charmed. She leaned over one day and told Sánchez, "You pretty much got this." Sánchez was thrilled at the prospect of starting a new career on daytime.

There was only one problem: "I had a really big conflict with Star," Sánchez said. "She did not want me on the show—period." Star didn't hold back her venom. After one appearance, Sánchez recalled how Star pulled her aside and told her, "Don't think you belong here." Joy tried to calm the situation. "Don't you worry about Star," she told Sánchez. "You're going to be fine." It wasn't that Sánchez had necessarily done anything wrong. Star was determined to ice her out over something else—Sánchez was dating an African-American man. Star, single at the time, objected to interracial relationships, which she voiced to *Newsweek* in a March 2003 cover story. "There is a brother who is a popular actor who is marrying outside his race," Jones said, referring to another couple. "He was on the show, and so was the woman. I received hundreds of letters about this. Most were African-American women, and the point they made was 'Damn, we lost another brother.'"

～

As these temporary squatters passed through, *The View* got a face-lift. The Question of the Day was dropped, and the interviews with the celebrities took place with all the cohosts, a concept that came to define the show. Joy permanently joined the cast. "They put me on five days," she said. The latest research revealed that viewers were confused about why she and Barbara couldn't appear on TV at the same time, and they missed Joy's humor when she was off.

The rest of the segments were built around the hosts to help reinforce their different personas. Meredith's Guilt Trip had Meredith quizzing experts for parenting tips. Joy's Comedy Corner allowed Joy to invite over her stand-up pals for short sets—such as Mario Cantone, who cracked audiences up with his uncanny impersonation of Joan Rivers. Star Treatment featured Star as Miss Manners on etiquette and lifestyle. Barbara's Mailbag provided an excuse to solicit questions from Middle America.

Then in March 1999, *The View* received a late Christmas gift. At the age of sixty-nine, Barbara landed the greatest exclusive of her career—with a certain ex-intern that she'd been courting for months. "The interview to end all interviews," as Meredith later called it, was scheduled to air as a two-hour prime-time special on *20/20*. But since it wasn't on tape yet, Barbara had to tread carefully. "You should only know what it took to get Monica," Barbara told me. "I would call and call and leave messages." Barbara even managed to arrange for an off-the-record conversation with Lewinsky

to convince her that she'd be fair and compassionate, the best interviewer
to tell Monica's story. "We met in 1998, at my dad's house with my attorney
at the time," Lewinsky told me. "She showed a lot of compassion for the
situation I was in, which felt authentic. She also said something really
funny. My dad said I'd always been this good kid and never got into any
trouble growing up—that I didn't do drugs or shoplift. Without missing
a beat, Barbara quipped, 'Next time, shoplift.'"

Lewinsky felt a closeness to Barbara, the only reporter she personally
talked to about telling her story. "Humor has always been very important
to me and how I connect with people," Lewinsky recalled. "It's one of the
ways we all got through 1998. I was twenty-four when I met her, and had
grown up knowing Barbara Walters was one of the best. Barbara was one
of the most respected voices in news at the time. It felt appropriate to sit
down with her. I hoped that her being a woman meant there would be
more nuance and different angles to the conversation." She also hoped
that by talking to Barbara, she could get her old life back. All the while,
Barbara fretted that her rowdy girlfriends would derail these sensitive
negotiations. If Hot Topics veered bitchy on the days without Barbara, she'd
call up the control room in a panic. "Move on!" she'd huff at the producers.
"Don't kill the interview!"

As a master of self-promotion, Barbara used *The View* to tease her upcoming exclusive, and she soaked up the larger-than-usual spotlight on
her to advertise *The View*. She asked her daytime audience to submit
questions—they wanted to hear how Monica felt about Chelsea and Hillary, which made the final list. "Nobody knew anything about her," Barbara said. "They had no idea what she was like." Barbara secretly taped
the big exclusive on a Sunday in the *20/20* studios. The space was packed
with network suits and handlers. "It was terrifying for me," Lewinsky
remembered. "I'd never done an interview with a reporter, much less on
television and with such high stakes. The only interviews I'd done at that
point were job interviews and interviews with the independent counsel's
office. I remember very kindly she acquiesced to my request of the

room being cold, because when I get nervous, I often flop sweat. It was freezing."

Lewinsky spent four and a half hours with Barbara that day. "Barbara did a really wonderful job of putting me at ease as much as she could," Lewinsky said. "In some ways, I think what she's most famous for in interviews is not only her intellect, but her ability to create a space which is filled with so much empathy and compassion that people feel really comfortable to be vulnerable. And that's where she finds the humanity in these moments with the people she interviews."

Bryant Renfroe, Barbara's hairdresser, said, "I just knew I was watching history. It was such a big deal."

As soon as the interview wrapped, Barbara headed for the editing room to assemble a cut. "It was leaking and we couldn't take a chance," she said.

Barbara still managed to clock a visit to *The View* on March 3. "Forget about D-day. This is M-day," Meredith said, winking, as the screen filled with the words *Countdown to Monica*. Barbara was all too happy to squeeze in one last plug. "This is a very smart, very articulate girl who is in a lot of pain," Barbara said, as she introduced a clip. The guest that day— poor Ryan Phillippe, starring in *Cruel Intentions*—had to take a backseat to all the hype. (His girlfriend, Reese Witherspoon, who wasn't yet a huge star, stayed in the greenroom, briefly waving to America.) Barbara revealed that she'd just gotten off the phone with Lewinsky, who wished her interviewer luck and to "break a leg." In fact, Barbara told all the women at home, Lewinsky was watching *The View* right along with them. Barbara later had Meredith toss softball questions at her about the interview.

"Is it safe to say that a secret will be revealed?" Meredith asked.

"Yes," Barbara responded.

A few hours later, at 9:00 p.m., a pretaped Barbara introduced her opus with a triumphant glow. Watching the conversation back today, it still plays like a master class in journalism. No male broadcaster could have coaxed such raw answers out of Lewinsky, and Barbara covered a lot of ground. She meticulously sketched out details of the affair, asking about the first time Lewinsky kissed the president, if she was ever in love, and—in a carefully worded question—if Clinton had pleasured her back. Barbara even had Lewinsky define *phone sex,* for the few clueless viewers who couldn't follow along. Barbara saw the final cut as it aired live. "I remember my friends saying, 'I wonder who is going to watch this?'" she said. For years after, she loved to tell the story about how, during a commercial break, she'd peered over to the edge of her apartment. "I looked out my window, and there wasn't a car moving." The hyperbole was justified—a record 74 million Americans tuned in for at least a few minutes, the most ever for a news event.

The next morning, Barbara was back on *The View,* with her favorite clips and fresh commentary. "Y'all did not clap loud enough," Star told the audience before presenting Barbara with a diamond-encrusted crown on a purple pillow. "All hail to the queen!"

"I think she came across as quite bright," Barbara said, noting that Lewinksy's approval ratings had gone up by 11 percent, while the president's had gone down by the same amount—all because of Barbara.

"Only you can find a demure and nice, ladylike way to ask, 'Did you get off, too?'" Star said.

Joy poked fun at the euphemisms Barbara had employed. "She 'serviced' him. I thought she was working at Exxon."

They broke off the last part of the show so that Barbara—playing up her inner Phil Donahue—could take questions from the audience. One woman wanted to know, Was *The View* serious about hiring Monica? Barbara had spent the last day suggesting that Lewinsky could audition for the fifth seat. "Anybody who wants to apply for a cohost has to send a tape to Bill Geddie," Barbara said on March 4. "And Linda Tripp has a lot of tapes of Monica that she could send in." But Lewinsky, already worn-out by the invasive flashbulbs that had been stalking her every move, didn't take the bait.

They still stayed in touch and became friends. "She's always wanted to see my life move on, as many others have," Lewinsky said. "Barbara would joke about how she'd dance at my wedding. And every time I see her, she will say, 'Well, anybody I need to get my dancing shoes on for?' The last time I had lunch at her house, Icodel had brought us tea in these china teacups. I kept remarking how beautiful they were. Barbara scooted off in one moment and she had one wrapped up for me. I left her house with a teacup, which was so sweet."

The seasons changed. Campos-Duffy got married that spring to her boyfriend, fellow *Real World*-er and future pro-Trump Wisconsin Republican congressman Sean Duffy, and announced that she was pregnant. Yet *The View* contest kept trudging along, like a never-ending job interview. Geddie wasn't sure it ever needed to stop—maybe they could just indefinitely sift through new talent—but he finally caved to his impatient cohosts. The eighth candidate would be the last one: on March 25, Lisa Ling took a stab at *The View*.

The daughter of immigrants from China and Taiwan, Lisa, twenty-five, had grown up in a small town outside Sacramento, California, worshipping at the altar of Barbara. She had spent seven years as a correspondent covering breaking news at Channel One, a program that aired in middle and high schools. "Frankly, I had never watched *The View* because I was working all the time," Lisa told me. "I found out about the position kind of late." She was content with her life, but she agreed to throw her hat in the ring based on the pedigree of one name. "If Barbara Walters is attached, I'd love to try," she told her agent.

Lisa's debut was relaxed, which worked in her favor. She wore a jean jacket with chunky red heels, projecting a laid-back California vibe. Meredith introduced her with a grand gesture that was meant to encapsulate all her reporting abroad: "You have been to the Balkans and back again, baby."

"I actually have never been to the Balkans," Lisa, the studious reporter, corrected her.

"You're calling me a liar already!"

"I've been to some very contentious parts of the world, like Afghanistan and Algeria and Colombia."

"I have a better question," Meredith replied. "Are you a virgin? Let's get to what's important for *The View*."

"I'd rather go to Kosovo than answer that question."

Joy couldn't let her off the hook so easily: "How many times have you been a virgin? This is part of the initiation." Three minutes into her audition, Lisa was already at a loss for words, knowing that her dad was watching.

"I was completely stumped by that," Lisa recalled. "I sat at that table, thinking, 'What do I do?' I have a conservative Asian family." Despite all her hours in the field, the prospect of trading barbs with these women intimidated Lisa. "Sitting in front of that live audience and trying to generate a reaction was super challenging," she said. "It was a realm I was unfamiliar with."

Her knowledge ultimately won out, and she advanced to the last round. *The View* narrowed down the contenders to three finalists: Campos-Duffy, Sánchez, and Ling, in a knife fight to the finish line. Real news events shaped each of their performances. On the morning after the Columbine High School massacre, April 21, Meredith confessed her terror: "I didn't think that the places where my kids go to school are dangerous." Lisa, who'd been booked that day, kept the conversation moving with a story about how she was bullied by jocks in high school and the animosity that comes from that. When Star complained about the ease with which the killers could look up instructions online to build bombs, Lisa took a hard stance. "I don't think we should blame it all on the internet," she pushed back, sounding like a sensible young person.

Barbara and Bill needed to make sure that Lisa could also showcase a lighter side. "Growing up in an Asian family, I was always told to keep my private life private," Lisa said. "These women had a forum to talk about everything, including their personal lives." On one of the last competition shows, Lisa volunteered to get her belly button pierced, which *The View* advertised as a big spectacle. "It was something I wanted anyway," Lisa said. "I said, 'Why not do it on national TV?'"

The stunt paid off. 'I thought, 'Wow, you must really want this job,'" Meredith said.

After that, Barbara called Lisa into her dressing room to officially offer her the cohost seat. "I felt like I was in a dream, and I was pinching myself," Lisa said. "I said yes right away." Since the outcome wasn't public yet, Lisa was forced to pack up her belongings quietly without saying goodbye to her coworkers at Channel One. "I had to move to New York City to start a job on a national talk show in secret," said Lisa, who left behind the house she'd just bought in Los Angeles. "It was not easy to do."

Barbara phoned the runners-up to break the news. Sánchez, who was in a car, had to pull over. "I just remember bawling," she said. "It was devastating to me." She wanted to know if she lost the job because of Star, and Barbara insisted that Jones wasn't the reason. ("In my opinion, there was no competition," Star said, years later. "It was Lisa Ling's job.")

Campos-Duffy was equally devastated. "Lisa is a great talent; I don't want to disparage that," she said. "But I feel like I'd done really well. I think they had their mind set on a single girl, which never made sense to me. I was much more of a viewer when I was at home with my kids."

On May 3, it was finally time for the big reveal. "Yes, we have milked this for all it's worth," the show's announcer said.

Meredith tried out her best Ed McMahon voice—"We have picked our cohost," she said—as the stage filled with a high school marching band. Although Lisa's name had leaked early in the press, the show treated it as a full-blown surprise.

"This has been quite a competition," Barbara said, as Lisa joined the table with a big smile. "And I must say, as we all know, it was very close." Barbara assured viewers that the runners-up would have distinguished careers on TV, in case some of their fans were disappointed.

Meredith said, "Listen, Lisa, we may seem supportive—"

"But the witches of Eastwick could come out at any moment," Star howled.

For some time, Lisa kept the drama dialed down. She found a way to relate to all her new colleagues. Joy was like her adopted Jewish aunt—Lisa loved to sprawl on Joy's dressing-room couch and vent about boy trouble. Lisa gained Star's trust enough to receive an invitation to Star's fortieth birthday bonanza in Jamaica. Barbara could see a younger version of herself in Lisa. Barbara would invite her to fancy dinner parties at her home, and Lisa easily impressed foreign dignitaries and ambassadors.

However, Barbara wasn't entirely pleased by her new hire's expansive career goals—she told Lisa not to shrug off her home life. "She felt like she neglected hers because her struggles as a woman in the industry were so challenging," Lisa said. "I think she had regrets about that." Lisa paused. "At the time, I kind of rolled my eyes."

Lisa was so ambitious, she got to work at around 7:30 a.m., an hour before the other cohosts. She made it clear that she was there to learn. "When we picked Lisa, she was exactly the cure for everything that ailed us," Geddie said. "She was smart. She had a great vocabulary, and a presence about her that said, 'I'm only twenty-five, but I have a voice, too. I'm no Debbie Matenopoulos.' That changed so much for us."

Geddie, who credits the contest with saving *The View,* was worried that viewers would stop watching after it ended. "But that wasn't the case," he said. "The numbers went up after that."

Lisa still clung to hope that she could play the part of the hard-hitting broadcaster. "The one thing that was hard for me, I don't think people ever wanted me to show my journalistic credentials," Lisa said. "Anytime I talked about my reporting overseas, it fell on deaf ears, which was a bummer. I really wanted to prove that young people shouldn't be cast in this one-dimensional light."

The producers were much happier when she dished about movie stars. *The View* had finally cemented its status as a stage for top guests, including George Clooney, Sheryl Crow, John Travolta, and Tom Cruise, who didn't leave until he'd signed autographs for every single member of the audience. "You're what a movie star should be," producer Alexandra Cohen said, beaming at him. "He gave me a huge Tom Cruise grin." The sudden burst of star power at *The View* created backstage tensions of a different kind. Mariah Carey never wanted to sing live. "A lot of lip-synching," Cohen said. "A lot of stopping and restarting. Then she'd do it and her people would call and want fixes."

Nobody on staff will ever forget the day an Oscar-winning actress visited, with a list of outrageous demands. "Did anybody tell you about Faye Dunaway?" said senior producer Mark Lipinski, laughing. "She wanted a gym and a bed. We actually didn't have that. We moved an office and we made a bedroom and an exercise room for one appearance. She was only there for a couple of hours. The funniest thing was, her assistant's name was Christina. And you could hear her yelling down the hall, 'Christina! Christina!' It was just like the movie," he said, referencing 1981's camp classic *Mommie Dearest,* starring Dunaway as a formidable stage mom with a daughter also named Christina.

Outside of all the celebrities, *The View* needed to bank on other daytime staples. Lisa scored points when she took up challenges, such as agreeing to a haircut on TV. "That was a big regret, because I hated it," said Lisa, who started to choke up. "After it was cut, I was, like, 'What the fuck did I just do?'"

On the whole, the show's makeover—with Lisa at the table—was a success. With the addition of its newest cast member, the *SNL* parodies stopped, as the show claimed its place as the Mensa of daytime TV. Lisa can only remember one time where she put her foot in her mouth. "Did I ever get in trouble?" she asked musingly. "I think I may have said *tits* on the air once." She didn't know the word wasn't allowed on TV. "I got a little hand slap."

6

The Star Diaries

Before she was a household name, Star Jones used to talk about herself as if she were already famous. She dished that she had two mentors in her life: Johnnie Cochran, from her time covering the O. J. Simpson trial, and Barbara Walters. But as Star actually achieved stardom, she could feel an odd vibe from the leader of *The View*. Star first noticed tension when she showed up to a dinner party on the Upper East Side. Barbara was there, too. When she tried to present Star to the guest of honor, Prince Andrew, he brushed off the introduction. The Duke of York already knew Star through his ex-wife, Sarah Ferguson, and he bypassed Barbara to give Star a hug.

"Star's favorite song is the 'Thong Song,'" Prince Andrew quipped, referring to the raunchy R&B hit. He'd picked up this tidbit from a previous exchange.

"I can't believe you're saying that!" Star laughed.

Not only was this unladylike, but Barbara had become the third wheel in a conversation with the royal family. "Barbara looked like she was going to die," Star recalled. "She was mortified. Maybe I didn't appreciate boundaries enough: I'll take responsibility for that. But I was having a good time. What I should have seen was, I penetrated her world in a way that she never would have. She's Barbara Walters. She's not going to have these conversations."

Throughout her career, Barbara had perfected the art of knocking down women—and men—who tried to upstage her. Now she had to worry about a homegrown rival. If Barbara expressed early concerns about fending off an *All About Eve* situation on her talk show, she wasn't entirely wrong. Only one cohost had the guts (and the moxie) to play a modern-day Anne Baxter. It shouldn't have been a total surprise: Star's name practically called out for its own marquee. After *The View* finally took off, Star became the second-most-popular black woman on TV, after Oprah Winfrey. And Star lived for the applause.

Star was smart enough to leverage her fame into a series of businesses—all under the umbrella of Star Inc. She signed a deal with Payless shoes as a spokeswoman to hawk their affordable footwear in TV commercials, created her own line of wigs, and traveled around the country giving speeches, collecting substantial fees. When *Newsweek* featured Star on its cover in a roundtable about issues facing African-American women, the other participants were Beyoncé Knowles, the rapper Foxy Brown, and the ABC journalist Deborah Roberts. Star was the most outspoken in the group—and probably the most recognizable, too, at the time.

She admitted that it went to her head: "I think I got too big for my britches. My ego started to take over, and I didn't know how to pull back. I didn't know how not to be larger-than-life."

On TV, Star was widely adored. "We got to our first focus groups," Bill Geddie said. "They would say, 'I like the fat black lady.' She was extremely important in getting people interested in the show. Daytime audiences found their way in through Star Jones."

Part of her appeal was that she was a churchgoing woman of faith who talked about God. She spoke to audiences in an informative yet down-to-earth way—with the Oprah touch. When Senator Hillary Clinton finally visited *The View* for the first time in 2003, to promote her memoir *Living*

History, Star asked whether she'd run for president in five years. "I've told the audience I'm going to do a leave of absence and join your campaign, but I need to plan," Star said with a twinkle in her eye.

"Well, that doesn't put pressure on me," Clinton said, laughing. "I've got a Senate campaign coming up in '06. You don't have to quit your job for that." She clutched Star's hand. "But I will need your help."

Star grew up in New Jersey, as the older of two girls to a single mom from a modest family. In her self-help book, *Shine: A Physical, Emotional & Spiritual Journey to Finding Love,* Star writes about how she decided to pursue law at eight, after watching the soap opera *Another World*—her grandmother Muriel told her that a lawyer could have helped a character who was always in trouble. At nineteen, just after high school, Star underwent a complicated surgery to remove a tumor from her thymus gland. "I never really thought I would die, even though the doctors said it was a possibility," Star told me. "They had to crack my chest to get it out."

After law school, Star worked her way up to assistant district attorney in the Brooklyn homicide bureau. Between crime scenes, she popped up as a legal expert on NBC's *Today,* on the same stage that had launched Barbara. The trial of the century put her on every producer's radar—she was a constant presence on *Inside Edition.* When *The View* rang, Star was making a run for her own talk show at NBC. "I learned something there," Star said. "The news division shouldn't be doing entertainment shows."

Star lived in a one-bedroom apartment on the Upper East Side, which she referred to as "the penthouse," even though it wasn't on the top floor, nor was it bigger than the other units in the building. Something grandiose was inside, though: a humongous portrait of Star that hung in the foyer. "Her bedroom had three television screens," said celebrity event planner David Tutera, who later organized her wedding. "I had no idea what it was for. I think, in her head, she was watching different programs for the next day. But it wasn't like she was Brian Williams."

Once *The View* exploded, there was no turning back from the dueling-divas narrative between Star and the rest of the cohosts. "The bigger we got, the more the show started to change," Star said. "It was almost like a reality show: the first season always starts out, you're fascinated because you don't know these people. Then the next season, they think they're stars and it goes to pot."

The irony is that Barbara wanted *The View* to represent empowerment, not to reinforce the traditional clichés about women attacking each other over petty arguments. "It's funny," Geddie said. "When we started out, we were trying to show that women could work together. And we were going to be this beacon of light against the stereotypes of women, backbiting and vanity. And in the end, we proved all of that. But I think it's really not so much about being women. It's about being famous."

The View suddenly started to feel like *Mean Girls*. Many of the problems backstage revolved around Star versus members of the staff. When the show went to Disney World to shoot a week of episodes, Star called up publicist Karl Nilsson with a complaint. She wanted to know why her hotel suite didn't overlook the ocean. Nilsson had to gently explain to her that Orlando was surrounded by land in all directions.

There were two versions of Star. She could act like the woman you saw on TV, the curious and sarcastic girlfriend with no shortage of useful advice. "Star was nice when she wanted something," Tutera said. During the Season 2 cohost contest, she took Campos-Duffy under her wing, inviting her to a posh Bible study. "Star Jones was always extremely kind to me," Campos-Duffy said. "Those stories mean nothing to me."

Her other persona came across as daytime's own Miranda Priestly from *The Devil Wears Prada*. After the morning meeting, producers would drop off the final Hot Topics to all the cohosts. They weren't allowed to make eye contact with or speak to Star; they'd been told to deliver the note cards on a bookshelf by the door and run. "She was the nastiest," said one employee, who recalled how Star had made a producer cry on her first day of work as a way of showing the woman who was boss.

Another day, a producer had his family visiting. "Star, this is my wife and son," he said, passing her in the hall.

"Pleasure," she mouthed, without stopping.

Unlike the other cohosts, Star stayed in touch with the actors who appeared on *The View*. She turned many of them into personal friends, a trick out of the Barbara Walters playbook, as she vacationed in the Hamptons with Vivica A. Fox and Kim Cattrall. If a celebrity was in distress, Star always came to the rescue. Take Michael Douglas ("my favorite guest, because he's the first man on television that made me feel sexy and pretty," Star said). Just before his wedding to Catherine Zeta-Jones in 2000, Douglas rang up Star in a panic.

"I know you're a lawyer, but are you a judge, too?"

"Michael, what are you talking about?"

"I had one assignment from Catherine. It was to get a judge to marry us, and I didn't do it."

"She's going to kill you!" Star cracked. She told Douglas that she had someone who could help, hung up, and dialed her pal Judith Kaye, a celebrated judge on the New York Court of Appeals. "So Judge Kaye performed the ceremony," said Star, who attended the glitzy affair at the Plaza Hotel in November. "It was really wonderful."

As she quietly struggled with body-image issues, Star put on a brave face. She masked her insecurities by talking about her fabulous wardrobe and career. Even though she was single, she liked to imagine the kind of wife she'd be. "Star and I had different points of view about being female," Joy said. "For someone who is a lawyer and so educated, to hear her say something like 'I like to come home to my man and let him be the boss' . . . It's so antifeminist. We used to spar about that."

For all Star's old-fashioned ways, she wasn't exactly neat. Her dressing room looked as if it were out of a *Hoarders* episode. It was stacked with clothes and shoes. That made it the perfect hideout for vermin. One night, the janitor complained to Joy that he'd just swept up the carcass of a crushed mouse from the floor of Star's dressing room and that Star must have stepped on it and killed it without knowing. Joy had grown to detest

Star so much, she gleefully spread the story to some of her friends on the show. "Can you believe it?" Joy would ask, thrilled. ("Who told you this?" Joy said, when asked about it, with a guilty expression on her face.)

On her summer vacations, Star loved to visit outlet malls—she kept a comprehensive list of the best around the world. "I went to Florence with her on a cruise," Joy said. "The boats dock. Instead of going to the Uffizi Gallery, she goes outside of the city to the outlet center." However, nothing could beat the best deal imaginable: freebies. Many producers never forgot the day her sister was visiting the show for a baby shower segment. They said that the two of them raided the studio early, clearing out the rest of the products that were supposed to be sent back to the manufacturers and that Star then had a van pull up to the loading dock, and they made away with all the merchandise. Star denied that she did such a thing. "Not true," she said. "Every cohost took the leftover merchandise."

For all her bravado, Star was suffering on the inside. She couldn't stop overeating. Despite all her career achievements, she felt a void—an inescapable loneliness. "I was unhealthy," Star said. "I can't emphasize that enough. I had put up so many beautifully built walls to mask a problem, an addiction. I gained the most weight on my most financially successful year. I couldn't accept that the success was mine."

She'd lose her breath just walking out to the studio set and wheezed between sentences. Since viewers at home could hear it, the crew had to lower her microphone so that it wasn't too close to her mouth. Star had so focused all her energy on becoming famous that it was destroying her. She'd absorbed a pearl of wisdom from one of her first meetings with Barbara, who gave all the ladies advice for career longevity: "Don't let anyone sit in your seat." As a result, Star never took her eye off the pedestal. "I remembered that," Star said. "Half of being successful is showing up. Unless I'm deathly ill, I'm going to be here every day."

By the time George W. Bush was elected president by 537 ballots in Florida, *The View* had become a legitimate force in daytime TV. Yet it wasn't such a political vehicle yet. Meredith wouldn't reveal whom she voted for in the 2000 election, only saying that she picked the candidate who she thought would keep the country the safest.

On September 11, 2001, the four cohosts (minus Barbara, who was off that day) were chatting in their daily Hot Topics meeting when they heard that a plane had crashed into the World Trade Center. Geddie thought it must have been an accident. "We kept talking, and the second plane hit, and it was clear something terrible happened," Meredith said. They all evacuated the studio, trying to locate family or friends.

"The journalist in me wanted to go down there," Meredith said. "The mother in me wanted to get the hell out." She told her driver to go to her kids' school. "It was a very telling moment in where I headed," Meredith said. "I don't regret my decision, because for me it was the right one. Had I been working at ABC News, I would have been sent down."

Lisa was a hysterical wreck. "My boyfriend"—the actor Rick Yune— "had just flown back to LA that morning," she said. "He was actually supposed to be on one of the planes, but he ended up getting on an earlier flight." As she recounted it, the memory still gave her chills. "I'm sitting in my makeup chair at work, thinking I may have lost my boyfriend. I could not find him for hours until his plane got grounded in Wisconsin."

The show went dark to around-the-clock hard news, just like all other entertainment programming. Six days later, on the morning of September 17, *The View* returned to TV—before David Letterman, Jay Leno, or any of the nightly talk shows. Nobody could imagine delivering a comedic monologue. The studio was only half-full because producers couldn't find enough tourists to fill the seats.

"We want to get back to normal, but it's very difficult," said Meredith, who—like all the cohosts—wore a loyalty ribbon as a sign of solidarity.

Barbara had been reporting all week from Ground Zero, conducting interviews with New York mayor Rudy Giuliani and families looking for their loved ones. "We're not really calling them victims because we're still hoping they'll be found," Barbara said on TV. "I think we're all grateful to be alive and realizing that the difference between life and death is seconds."

The show's tone was somber, a reflection of a nation under a cloud of grief. *The View*'s signature theme song didn't play over the opening credits. No celebrity guests were at the table. Instead, Geddie invited New Yorkers to tell stories of the relatives and friends they still couldn't locate.

"I remember the first time we made a joke and people laughed," Meredith recalled. "That's not to pat us on the back, but people needed a reason to feel good again. And because we were in New York, it was really important that the show came back."

The Bush years brought transformative change to the nation, with US troops invading Iraq under the guise of the war on terrorism. On TV, the biggest hits were still *Friends, CSI,* and *ER,* but they were about to be displaced by *American Idol* and *The Apprentice. The View* was feeling stale. Three years after Lisa had joined the show, the ratings dipped as large patches of the country couldn't relate to five liberal women in Manhattan chatting about their privileged lives. Geddie was concerned that *The View*'s cohosts were too homogeneous.

Although she helped stabilize *The View,* Lisa didn't seem like the right cohost for the long haul. Because of her news background, her arguments were too sensible to provoke outrage. And she wasn't that invested in pop culture, except for the time NSYNC's Justin Timberlake gave her dance lessons. "Honestly, I just didn't enjoy interviewing celebrities," Lisa said. "If someone was doing something interesting that I connected with, okay. But for the most part, it was really surface conversation about whatever project they were working on—very lackluster. I was just not very good at faking that."

During Hot Topics, she tried to offer glimpses of her daily routine as a single woman. "My boyfriend, at the time, I talked about his penis size," Lisa said. "I was very complimentary, by the way." Even when she offered something so revealing, it was never enough. "We had one problem with Lisa," said producer Jessica Stedman Guff. "She never talked about her personal life on the show." They wanted all the dirt—Ling had privately confided to the other cohosts that Yune had been cheating on her. "Now nothing is more relatable to the women of America than a guy who is fucking around," Stedman Guff said. "She refused to talk about it. And we would beg her."

Lisa didn't think such requests were fair: "I felt like I was doing as much as I could. But at a certain point, it would upset people in my life when I would talk about them without permission." She got into a tricky situation when she revealed that her prom date had been gay, outing him to his parents. "I felt so bad," she said. "I didn't think twice about it because I have always been a fag hag."

It was time for a shake-up. *The View* needed another firing followed by another contest, to freshen up the cast. In a twist this time, the new cohost would be a conservative. "That was very important to Bill, who was a Republican," Barbara said. "He used to complain that the show was too liberal, especially Joy. We thought it was important to have a mixture."

The youngest cohost would once again take the fall. But unlike Debbie, who faced a public execution, Lisa's dismissal would be handled quietly. Geddie called Lisa into his office and told her she was being let go, but that they'd give her time to find a new job. Lisa wasn't too broken up—she had always seen *The View* as a stepping-stone, not a life term. "Quite honestly, it was not a hard job," Lisa said. "Our hours were not that difficult. I was done by one or two o'clock. I did feel unfulfilled."

Lisa would announce she wanted to return to what she loved the most—field reporting. "We said she had another job," Barbara said. "She didn't. But later on, she did."

Lisa told viewers that she was leaving *The View* to host *National*

Geographic Explorer, a series that allowed her to cover hard-hitting stories from around the world. Her final day on the show was on December 5, 2002, more than a year before her contract expired. When asked about what really happened, she still described the parting as mutual. "I had known there was a conservative voice missing," Lisa said. "I went out and started talking to people well in advance of them telling me they wanted to find that person."

She treasured her three and a half years on a show that made her a household name. "I owe a lot to my time on *The View,*" said Lisa, who still gets introduced by that credit, even after starring on her own TV series for the Oprah Winfrey Network and CNN. "Not only did I learn about how to be better on television, but I became a much more open person. I would say I'm a lot more liberated."

7

The Republican

Star Jones always knew how to talk herself out of tricky situations, but no amount of legal expertise could rescue her from her current crisis: she was morbidly obese. She'd tried countless diets, and they'd never worked—she just kept getting larger. To avoid feeling embarrassed, she stopped weighing herself. But she knew her health was in peril, as her size prevented her from getting around the way she used to. On airplanes, she couldn't buckle the seat belt without asking for an extender—or the strap wouldn't reach over her waist.

As *The View* entered its summer hiatus after Season 6, Star consulted with her doctors and decided to have gastric bypass surgery. It was her only hope of leading a normal life again. Although her TV job required her to dish about all her adventures, she saw this as a private matter, one that she never intended to reveal to strangers. She'd confided in Barbara Walters about the operation before going under the knife. "I had a legal obligation to tell the executive producer," Star said. "I was going to have life-threatening surgery. With gastric bypass, people die."

She also told Barbara that it would *not* be fodder for *The View:* "I specifically said, 'I just can't talk about it.'"

On August 19, 2003, Star quietly checked into a hospital. Surgeons cut her stomach into two pouches, which restricted her eating, and reconfigured her small intestine so that it would absorb fewer nutrients. She came home in tremendous pain, with immediate restrictions on her diet. "I was very weak," she said. "For several weeks, I could not eat anything solid. It was a lot of pressure on my body."

When she returned to work in September, she was so frail that the stage manager, Rob Bruce-Baron, had to wrap his arms around her to help her off the set, but she didn't let any of that show on TV.

Star says her initial silence came from her fear that the surgery wouldn't work: "It was very scary. I had never been successful at any diet my whole life."

Other patients experience similar doubts. When Al Roker, the jolly weatherman on *Today,* underwent the procedure one year earlier, he explained his absence by telling colleagues he needed to have his gallbladder removed. After a few months passed and viewers noticed he'd slimmed down, he shared his whole story, knowing that weight loss was a home-run topic for morning TV. By coming clean, Roker became more relatable—and more famous. However, it may have been easier for him to do that because his career wasn't so tied to his looks. And he was a man.

On the day that Star checked into the hospital, she forced herself to step on a scale: it registered 307 pounds. She wasn't sure if that was the heaviest she'd been, but it was the biggest number she'd ever seen. Her goal was to melt away a third of herself. The other two-thirds would be the foundation for the new Star, who practiced more discipline and avoided fatty foods.

Within six months, she'd shed seventy-five pounds because of the surgery. "It was just a jump start," Star said. To keep up the progress, she needed to stick to a structured diet. She swore off her favorite sweets and decreased how much she consumed at each meal using portion control. (The first time I had breakfast with her, in July 2007, she ordered a single scrambled egg with cheese. When the waiter brought her two by mistake, she squealed, "That's too much," before shoveling half of the entrée to the side of her plate, where it remained untouched.) Her sedentary routine had changed, too. "I was under an intense physical regimen," said Star, who began to enjoy regular exercises such as Pilates and tennis. "I would work out every day." Eventually, she pulled off a miracle transformation, as she thinned down from a size 26 to a size 8. Yet she never once discussed how she got there on *The View,* only saying that there had been "a medical intervention."

The tabloids started to write snarky articles about how Star had gotten a gastric bypass, and that the show's producers were furious that she wouldn't address it. Behind the scenes, Barbara, Joy, and Meredith resented her for making them act as if she'd lost the weight on her own, which created an impenetrable wall between Star and them. They believed she was forcing them to lie. "I think that bothered me the most," Star said. "Each one of us had something that we were not comfortable talking about. Barbara had surgeries that we were not talking about on air"—cosmetic procedures. "Meredith's husband had MS. We knew it from day one. We did multiple stories about MS, and she did not want to talk about it, and we respected that until she was ready. I always felt it was our obligation to protect each other. And I don't think they did the same for me."

Barbara, who liked to dissect all hardships under the antiseptic light of the cameras, couldn't bear the silence. She thought that Star was coming across as out of touch. But Star felt that something else was going on. From her vantage point, part of the reason her relationships with the other women had turned bitter was because she was no longer the token fat girl. "Bill Geddie said something to me after my weight-loss surgery that I didn't hear at first," Star explained. "He said, 'The things you were able to say and do when you were the big girl at the table, you won't be able to do now. *You're now competition.*'"

In hindsight, she understood the backlash over her refusal to share her secret: "I admit years later, having lost the weight, having kept it off, I wish I had been strong enough to handle it a different way. I wish I had been able to say, 'I'm going through a health issue, I can't talk about it yet. But please trust me and let me get through it.' But I couldn't."

For a long time after, when she looked in a mirror, she still saw the old Star—the one entrapped by 307 pounds. "I needed to actually lose the weight in my head as well as on my body," Star said. "I had to sit down with the therapist and analyze what was going on, and why I was so closed."

She remembered having a breakthrough: "I would go to therapy in full makeup and lashes." Her therapist asked her, "Why do you come in here as the full Star Jones?"

"This is who I am," Star insisted. That explanation didn't cut it with the therapist. "She asked me to strip it down and come in a tracksuit and no lashes and see how I felt about it. I remember walking down the street, and people would smile. They just saw me. I realized I got far too much satisfaction in what others thought. That's why I was so scared to bring people into my process. But it was bullshit, because I was unhealthy. I can't emphasize that enough. It was an addiction."

Two years later, in 2005, as she was working on *Shine,* her entire team—including her lawyer and publicist—tried to convince Star to finally disclose the details about her gastric bypass. The book, positioned as a self-help guide for women, would have been the perfect platform to open up about a lifesaving medical procedure. Even then, Star couldn't imagine doing that. She still wasn't ready. "No way," she said. "If you ever bring it up again, you're all fired."

If Star had been more forthcoming, she would have kept her fans. She told me an endearing story about how, after her surgery, she donated fifty boxes of oversize clothes to a charity—including the red suit that she wore to her *View* audition. "I sort of fantasize all the time that there's a woman starting out in a new career and she walked into her destiny because she was wearing my suit," Star said. "It was a magical suit." She even left a note in the pocket: *I hope it's as good luck for you as it was for me.*

⁓

The next *View* cohost wasn't going to be a shrinking violet. With Lisa Ling gone at the end of 2002, Geddie was free to execute his vision, to scout out a conservative to join the Hot Topics table. Throughout 2003, as celebrities filled in, producers vetted more than a thousand tapes, searching for female Republicans eager to back George W. Bush's policies—a group that was invisible on TV outside of Fox News—in yet another competition. This time, *The View* narrowed down the finalists to Rachel Campos-Duffy, who had just missed out on the Debbie Matenopoulos seat; Erin Hershey Presley, an actress from the ABC soap opera *Port Charles*; and Elisabeth Hasselbeck, a shoe designer from Rhode Island.

The last applicant's résumé included unconventional TV experience, as a contestant on the second season of *Survivor*. On the Australian outback, Elisabeth (who went by the last name Filarski) was a spitfire who took on the mantle of the fan favorite. She couldn't be broken by the harsh outdoor conditions, although she did cry after reading emails from her Catholic parents. She exuded plenty of charisma—think Sandra Bullock on the prairie—even as she lost patches of her hair due to a vitamin deficiency. Through her alliance with a schoolteacher named Rodger Bingham, Elisabeth finished fourth on the show. Her edition of *Survivor* was the most popular TV series of 2001, drawing an average of 30 million viewers a week.

Elisabeth kept up the girl-next-door act during her post-*Survivor* press tour. Late-night talk show host Craig Kilborn called her "America's new sweetheart."

"I don't know why they say cute, you're beautiful," he said, as he flirted with her.

David Letterman asked her if she'd had any secret flings on the show. "That's why your hair is falling out," he told her, after she confessed that she hadn't.

Elisabeth's addition to *The View* would be groundbreaking for several reasons. "The controversial part about Elisabeth was not that she was conservative," said Brian Frons, who headed ABC Daytime. "In the US, we were not used to really taking people off reality shows yet." Elisabeth was the first reality star to extend her fifteen minutes of fame into a real occupation. She became a shining beacon for a generation of wannabe celebrities who wanted to stay famous after a few episodes of *The Amazing Race* or *Big Brother*.

Reality TV had become so pervasive by then that *The View* introduced their new cohost with some help from the genre. On November 24, 2003, Joy Behar started the episode with a pretaped skit with the guest of the day, *Bachelor* star Bob Guiney, fresh off his final rose ceremony. Joy joked that *The View*'s contest had different ground rules than the dating orgy that he'd just escaped from. "Listen, we didn't have to tongue kiss any of them," she said. "We don't do group sex on this show. Well, I can't speak for Barbara."

That prompted Barbara to perk up as the cameras flickered on her. She stressed the great pains involved—again—in choosing a single winner. "We decided to take a vote," she said. "Before we reveal who our new cohost is, let us set the mood." As the *Survivor* theme song filled the studio, the cohosts all raised sheets of parchment with the same name on it. By a vote of four to zero, this tribal council elected Elisabeth onto their island.

Wearing a big grin, the twenty-six-year-old took her spot at the table. The daughter of liberal parents, she'd been a nomad ("I'm kind of living on United Airlines right now"), hosting a little-seen show from Los Angeles on the Style Network called *The Look for Less*. Her husband of just over a year, Tim Hasselbeck, couldn't be in the audience because of his new contract as a quarterback for the Washington Redskins. (In one of the trial episodes, Behar had switched into initiation mode, asking Elisabeth if she ever worried he'd cheat on her with a cheerleader. "No," Elisabeth stammered. "He's such an honorable man.")

Elisabeth instantly made herself comfortable at the table, like the cousin who had no trouble interjecting her opinions at Thanksgiving dinner. Her first episode ended in a group toast, but not all the viewers felt like celebrating. The second rejection stung even harder for Campos-Duffy.

"Elisabeth was conservative but not necessarily an activist," she told me, listing off her accomplishments as a college Republican. "I thought I was going to get it. I was pretty depressed for a couple of days."

The View had invited Campos-Duffy back after she stayed in touch with Barbara by sending holiday cards with pictures of her growing brood, yet producers never saw her as a front-runner for the seat. Initially, Geddie liked Presley, based on her upbeat personality and faith-based values. But Elisabeth overtook her as the favorite. "I think we just found Elisabeth the least polarizing of everybody," Meredith said. The other applicants were too focused on espousing their conservatism and couldn't keep up with the show's interest in pop culture and casual girl talk. "There was a bit of showboating," Meredith said. "Elisabeth seemed to listen."

Barbara was drawn to Elisabeth's strong screen presence and her counterintuitive views. For example, Elisabeth rejected abortion, but revealed her more complicated emotions about same-sex marriage, which was far from legal yet. "I totally struggle with it because I'm a Christian woman," she said on TV. "Biblically, that's not how things are supposed to be. But for me, it really boils down to love."

"Here's what I liked about her," Geddie said. "She was the entire package. She was smart. She was brash. She was fearless. She really wasn't afraid of anybody—Barbara Walters, or me, or anybody at the table. And she looked like a million bucks. I used to go to focus groups, and they'd say: 'Please don't fire her. I hate everything she has to say, but I can't wait to see what she's wearing every day.' They loved her fashion sense."

Elisabeth's addition to *The View* was a defining moment of change for the show. "That's when we were hitting on all cylinders," Geddie said. The conventional wisdom was that entertainers should steer clear of partisan issues—even Oprah didn't wade into that sphere until the 2008 election cycle, when she vociferously backed Barack Obama before he was even a candidate. "I did not want us to become a political show," Barbara said.

By taking sides with erudite discussions about the war in Iraq, *The View* struck gold, as it predicted the future of America. The show re-created a society where one of its members was constantly at odds with the rest of the group, and there was no hope of ever bridging the political divide that separated her. Of course, squabbling talking heads were a fixture on shows targeted to men, such as CNN's *Crossfire*. But they hadn't dominated all corners of TV yet, and there had never been an all-female panel arguing—with their fists up in the air—about politics. Yet Elisabeth's arrival on the show also had an oddly familiar quality to it, a nod to *Jerry Springer* and its intense family feuds.

In the latest iteration of *The View,* no topic from the political world was off-limits. Elisabeth had a megaphone to present an assortment of Republican ideas, from health care to taxes, as when she viciously fought with former professional wrestler and Minnesota governor Jesse Ventura in 2009 about waterboarding (she supported it; he didn't). That stay-at-home moms were exposed to a heady altercation about torture, as opposed to a fluffy cooking segment, proved that *The View* had changed the mold. Elisabeth morphed into a polarizing figure, constantly generating press for *The View.* In the seasons ahead, other entertainment shows would cover her battles with liberals such as Melissa Etheridge and Michael Moore. Fox News, which later employed her, frequently showcased Elisabeth's arguments about a hot-button topic, asking their viewers to weigh in about what she'd said or done.

Elisabeth ascended as a star for a portion of the country that felt that they didn't have a voice at the table. There wasn't another Republican heroine like her (Ann Coulter or Michelle Malkin didn't hold a prominent spot on a network TV show). Elisabeth's reach extended far in her access to political heavyweights, thanks to the Barbara Walters brand. She had face-to-face interactions with Democrats in a way that most Republicans on TV didn't, as *The View* started using its new political relevance to land major players from Washington, DC.

During Hillary Clinton's first visit—"You guys have such great chemistry," she told the group—Elisabeth, who was still auditioning, proved that she was ahead of the curve. She asked the US senator if she was concerned about a new trend of celebrities jumping into politics after Arnold Schwarzenegger's recent election as California governor.

"I think a lot of people worry about it," Clinton said, not realizing she should be one of those people. "But it just depends upon what they do if they get elected. Some are successful, and some aren't."

As Elisabeth became more popular, she felt more emboldened to push her views. She started out as an amiable colleague who would rather talk about crafts than public policy. But her costars say that she changed. "Elisabeth came into the show as the sweet girl who had been on *Survivor*," recalled Joy. "Within several months, she became this rabid Republican. It was quite shocking."

Elisabeth and Bill would often huddle in his office with the door closed after the Hot Topics meeting, which annoyed the other cohosts. They thought he was using her as a puppet. "She was literally Bill's mouthpiece," Star said. "He's so Republican. So he would go and feed her information. She would regurgitate it." Star leaned in closer as she shared this detail. "You know I'm not lying."

Geddie pushed back against the notion that he was coaching Elisabeth: "I think a lot of people thought I was giving Elisabeth talking points. We just happen to be two Republicans in the room. I felt it was important that she speak up, speak her mind. I gave everybody ideas about a lot of things."

As Elisabeth's profile grew, she gave Star a run for her money in the drama department. She had a penchant for tears in the makeup room if something didn't go her way. She threatened to quit often, sometimes even telling Barbara to her face (or behind her back) that she was over *The View*. During a contentious 2011 interview with Bill Maher, Elisabeth monopolized most of the airtime to shame him for a mean-spirited, sexist joke he'd once made (Maher had suggested that we send Elisabeth to Egypt in exchange for CBS News reporter Lara Logan, who had been assaulted overseas). There was reason to be angry, but maybe not on TV. Most viewers didn't remember the Maher joke.

Barbara was so displeased that Elisabeth had hijacked an interview to shame a guest, she took her aside the next day to tell Elisabeth that she'd crossed a line. Elisabeth refused to back down. She instead yelled back, questioning why she was being reprimanded and threatening to leave *The View*. In the end, she always returned—as soon as she'd cool down enough to remember the value of her seat.

To those who were close to her at work, it was as if her Republican role took over her identity. "I grew to believe that like Debbie, but in a different way, she was being force-fed her positions," Meredith said. "I'm not sure that I always felt that it rang true. It almost felt like a caricature. It was heat for heat's sake."

Elisabeth's arrival marked another evolution in the chemistry of the show. The backstage interactions among the cohosts—while pleasant— never again felt the same. There was no longer the illusion that the cohosts were friends. They were now actual adversaries. "It wasn't as political as people think because Elisabeth wasn't hard," Star said. "She had opinions, but she didn't have facts. It wasn't as if she was the most well-read human being on the planet when it came to those opinions. And that's typical of right-wing conservatives. They just spout stuff. So bless her heart."

8

Bridezilla!

It was a chilly morning by Las Vegas standards. *The View* had come to the desert to shoot a week of episodes in an outdoor studio at Caesars Palace outfitted like the Roman Colosseum. On February 16, 2004, four of the ladies, all bundled up in sweaters and parkas, hiked to the stage. But one cohost received a more spectacular introduction—riding on top of a caravan, carried by four black men dressed as gladiators.

"Move over Cleopatra, Barbara Walters has arrived in Vegas," Meredith Vieira said, laughing.

Talk shows will sometimes travel to new locations during sweeps month for a spike in the ratings. (ABC will frequently use this as an excuse to milk free screen time for Disney World or other theme parks owned by its parent company.) Yet on this day, a change in venue wasn't really necessary, since viewers had another reason to tune in. The night before, Star Jones had finally seen her number one dream come true, as her boyfriend, Al Reynolds, popped the question. This wasn't a private exchange. He got down on one knee at the NBA All-Star Game in Los Angeles and said into a handheld microphone, "Star Jones, will you marry me?" The unabashedly romantic gesture was met with cheers from twenty thousand fans. Even Denzel Washington, seated next to the happy couple, broke out into a grin.

As the image of Star covering her face in pretend shock filled the JumboTron, the flashiest *View* cohost found herself back in the tabloids—this time for good reasons. Her fandom, though lessened by her weirdness over her gastric bypass, knew how much she had always yearned for a husband. She'd talked about it on *The View* relentlessly. However, back at work, the other cohosts sounded like ambivalent bridesmaids.

"Star Jones got engaged last night," Meredith said.

"She's got the ring!" Elisabeth Hasselbeck chirped. "Show off the bling, Star."

"Al popped the question in the middle of the NBA All-Star Game," Star said.

"How understated can you get?" Joy Behar said.

"Did you cry?" Elisabeth wanted to know.

"I know you never expected it," Barbara added, sarcastically, about the spectacle. "Very private."

"I knew it was going to happen this weekend, because on Thursday, Al asked my parents for my hand in marriage."

"How about the rest of you?" Joy poked.

The camera zoomed in on Star's glistening diamond ring, as she gushed about how hard it was to patiently wait for it.

"So at the top of the fourth, you got five carats," Meredith said, before changing the subject.

Joy had a story to tell about how she took the same plane to Vegas as Barbara, which calmed Joy's fear of flying. (True to form, Barbara was the star of this adventure, after she accidentally knocked over a glass of water before takeoff, wetting herself "on the crotch.") Elisabeth talked about how her husband, Tim, was late to a dinner because he'd gone gambling, a habit she didn't appreciate. These tales were hardly comparable to Star's life-changing moment of bliss, but they received equal airtime.

It wouldn't stay that way for long, as Star Jones's wedding of the century soon hijacked *The View.* Star had grand expectations for her big day. She didn't just envision a lavish ceremony. She wanted to host a star-studded event that would feel like the US version of a royal wedding, where she'd play the part of Lady Di. "That's how she perceived it to be," said David Tutera, who orchestrated her wedding. And she wanted *The View* to help foot the bill.

After the trip to Vegas, Star sat down one afternoon with Barbara and Bill. She told them that she wanted the planning for her wedding to be a recurring theme on the show, via segments in which the viewers could follow along. This would allow Star to ask for things for free. Such personal product placement was good for Star, but it violated a golden rule of TV. As one high-level ABC executive put it, "You don't give advertising away; that's not how it works. And there were so many conflicts. What happens if you upset a sponsor by promoting a competing brand?"

Star wasn't concerned about any of that. "I said, 'It might be something fun for us to do on the show.'" She came up with the idea to extend giveaways to the audience, so that everybody could benefit from the freebies. Star pointed out how Oprah and Ellen DeGeneres did the same thing in the years that followed. "It's now the coolest thing in the world," Star said.

As the boss, Barbara could have vetoed this scheme. Yet the journalist inside her was terrified of losing an exclusive. When Star made her pitch, she presented it with a crafty ultimatum, saying that she'd take the story of her wedding to another entertainment show—such as *Extra* or *Access Hollywood*—if *The View* didn't want it. So Barbara went along with the plan, afraid that she'd lose out on buzz for a program that, in Season 7, was approaching the television equivalent of middle age.

"In retrospect," Geddie recalled, "I should have said, 'Take your wedding somewhere else! Just don't talk about it here.' But it seemed stupid. It was a big event and we wanted to make the most of it. We were caught in the middle."

To avoid fines from the Federal Communications Commission, the show had to list in the closing credits every brand that Star hawked. "We were completely aboveboard about it," Geddie said. *The View*'s place in daytime, as opposed to news, allowed some wiggle room. But it also caused confusion, because Barbara was still a member of the news division, where an anchor wouldn't be caught dead shilling for free food or flowers. "These things were done on a lot of different shows," Geddie said. "They were *not* done on shows with Barbara Walters on them."

Although ABC executives later feigned ignorance about what was going on, the network had been kept in the loop. The show even assigned a producer, Dana Goodman, to ring up the companies on behalf of the bride, pursuing her outrageous demands. Staffers recall hearing Star brusquely place orders for one product after the next as Goodman scrambled to keep up. "It wasn't as if everybody didn't know what was going on," Star said. "I love how there was all this talk about how Star got freebies. The show made those calls. I was never allowed to legally plug anything on ABC without it being disclosed. And they went back to every piece of tape; there was not one time that we did not give written disclosure that there had been some consideration."

Whatever the legal implications, ABC had a rule that forbade employees from accepting gifts worth more than $75—even Disney/ABC Television Group president Anne Sweeney made a point of returning jewelry presented to her on overseas trips. At *The View*, the staff felt as if they were watching a car wreck in slow motion. "You're allowing this lady to get married and use us to get everything for free," said one prominent producer. "It was so sketch. We all hated it and knew eventually the viewers would catch on and say, 'This is tacky and disgusting.'"

It wasn't hard to connect the dots because Star's every move had purposefully been choreographed for millions to see. When it came to her decorations, Star had high-end tastes. "Star loves crystals," said Tutera. "She loves opulence. She loves everything big and glamorous. I refer to it as *more is more*. That was really the vibe of her wedding." However, on daytime TV, where a host is supposed to present herself as relatable, all that bling created a chasm between her and the stay-at-home moms.

"I'm so giggly, I can't stop!" Star gushed in a segment about her engagement party, alongside the other ladies (who looked miserable) and Tutera. She'd poached her enthusiastic companion—a younger version of Martin Short in *Father of the Bride*—from *The View,* where he had appeared as an expert on entertaining. As Star went on about herself, Barbara rolled her eyes. Next came a shameless plug for TheStationeryStudio.com, an online vendor that Star had used for cards. After that, she fawned over a series of over-the-top candelabra settings.

On another day, Star could enlist only Elisabeth to stand by her side for the hyped debut of her official wedding invitations ("She had so many invitations," griped one producer). Tutera rolled through a few of the cheaper options before he revealed Star's choice. Rather than a paper stuffed inside an envelope, Star would be sending out a box packed with a magnolia leaf and a satin pillow, tucked with pearls that carried her save-the-date card.

"You better get another job to pay for this invite," Elisabeth wailed when she learned that each one cost $85. (For a wedding the size of Jones's, with 450 guests, that meant $38,250 on invitations alone!)

But Star didn't need a second job. "Thanks to Alpine for all those invitations," she said, beaming, as she cut to a commercial.

Months before all this, Stephanie Guillen, a thirty-eight-year-old construction worker from Longmont, Colorado, had been watching *The View* one morning with her mom, who had diabetes. The show had done a segment about the disease, with additional information available on its website. When Guillen logged on to learn more, she stumbled upon a contest, a chance to win a Star Treatment. Guillen had submitted a photo and details about her long days of physical labor in overalls and a hard hat. A few weeks later, Star personally called her to tell her she'd been selected for a makeover on national TV.

Guillen flew to New York in November 2003, where she was given a shopping spree at Saks Fifth Avenue, a massage, a facial, and her first-ever manicure and pedicure (with Star, in a fur coat, accompanying her, as a fairy godmother who shared in all the perks). Star, who could be generous when the mood struck, invited Guillen to her apartment, showering her with free boxes of Payless shoes. After that, Star took her new friend out to dinner, where they commiserated about being single. "You could tell something was missing," Guillen recalled. They attended a party for Alicia Keys's new album (*The Diary of Alicia Keys*), where both women ambushed the unsuspecting pop star as a camera crew from *The View* chronicled their adventures.

"She introduced me to all these people," Guillen said, including music mogul Clive Davis and Pink. "The whole thing was a grand experience."

After Keys belted out a few songs, Star felt some eyes on her. "We were standing in the center watching Alicia, and there was a gentleman in the back of the room to the right," Guillen said. "We're trying to be pretty cool. She said, 'Do you see him?' I said, 'Yeah, he's cute.'"

Star went over to get a better look. "She left me with Pink," Guillen said. "And they chitchatted." Star came back with a spring in her step; the man's name was Al Reynolds and they had an immediate connection. In *Shine*, Star remembered that moment with Al: "This handsome man with skin the color of cooked butter, this man with the most beautiful lips I'd ever seen, a Clark Gable jawline, and the deepest brown eyes on the planet . . . I was charmed out of my wits." She heard a bell ring. "It was a bell of exultation, not warning," she wrote.

Star dropped Guillen off at her hotel and that was the end—for the time being—of a dream night out in Manhattan. "The next thing I know, they are engaged," Guillen said. "I couldn't believe her. She moved quick."

Reynolds impressed Star with his charm, good manners, and career as an investment banker. The two found themselves in a whirlwind courtship, filled with dinners, lengthy phone conversations until 4:00 a.m., and tickets to Broadway plays, such as *The Boy from Oz,* a musical about a closeted songwriter named Peter Allen who marries the fabulous diva Liza Minnelli.

Star talked up Al to the *View* staff, telling them about how quickly they'd bonded. The *View* team got their first glimpse of Reynolds at the Christmas party. Several staffers snickered that something was off.

"He's totally gay," they whispered. (In November 2017, Reynolds came out as bisexual.)

The gossip eventually got to Star. But she was focused on a prize. Just three months after meeting Reynolds, Star was flashing a sparkling engagement ring. "I wanted the parade" is how Star put it. She didn't believe the rumors, anyway. Since they were both religious, they decided to take a celibacy vow before they got married.

Her wedding hoopla started to eclipse the other cohosts. Meredith and Joy protested to Barbara that they didn't like how Star's bridal planning—which would last for the next nine months—was holding *The View* hostage. "There were some issues," Joy recalled. "It became a lot about the wedding, which really changed the format of the show. I guess we were not thrilled with that."

Instead of siding with them, Barbara issued a surprising mandate. She told them to shut their mouths and go along with it.

"You're paid to be actors!" she snapped. "Act!"

Barbara's defense of Star didn't mean Barbara approved of what was happening. She'd agreed to this circus, and it was too late to put the lion back in the cage. Meredith felt that Star's wedding had irreparably tainted the show. The Hot Topics were no longer the show's selling point with the public. Instead, *The View* was all about her cohost's endless march down the aisle. "I certainly didn't like the idea of the show revolving around one person," Meredith said. "I thought that was dangerous territory. But the show let that happen. I can't fault Star."

In retrospect, Star agreed with Meredith's assessment. "She is right. It did become about one person." In an interview with me before the 2016 election, Star compared the nonstop press about her wedding to the way the networks were covering Trump during the presidential campaign. "It's ratings gold, but it's ticking a lot of people off."

The former leader of the free world was on the phone for Star Jones. "Hi," purred a familiar voice. Bill Clinton may not have regularly watched *The View*, but even he knew about the wedding. Clinton wanted to let Star know that he'd received the details about her special day (the box with the pearls must have done the trick), and that he would have loved to be there. But, unfortunately, he'd just had heart surgery and was under strict orders from doctors to stay in bed.

"He called me to tell me he couldn't attend my wedding, which cracked me up," Star recalled. "I was at the dentist. I said, 'Mr. President, you need to take care of yourself! You don't need to worry about this.' And he said, *'Hillary is going to be there.'*"

Star's guest list was a checklist of Manhattan's rich and fabulous for 2004. The crowd of 450 felt like a cross between the Oscars and the White House Correspondents' Dinner, with celebrities galore—among them, Chris Rock, Kim Cattrall, Angela Bassett, Samuel L. Jackson, Spike Lee, Lorraine Bracco, and Kelly Ripa. The rehearsal dinner was a meal of chicken, ribs, and sweet potato pie prepared by P. Diddy's mother, Janice Combs. Even some of Star's twelve bridesmaids emitted wattage, such as Natalie Cole, Vivica A. Fox, and Holly Robinson Peete. And, of course, it wouldn't be a true New York event without Donald Trump, who knew Star through *The View*. He brought along his fiancée, Melania, as his date.

The *National Enquirer* called it "the biggest celebrity wedding fiasco of the year," but it was more than that. Star had blabbed about her day so much that she'd turned the event into an over-the-top extravaganza, earning the name "bridezilla" in the tabloids. Even among the jaded East Coast set, the impression was that to be at Star's wedding meant having a cocktail story that you could tell for years. "You could barely walk," Meredith said. "That's what I remember. Her parents were nice. It was like a showbiz wedding. I don't think I'd ever been to anything quite like that."

Many people weren't even allowed through the door. "No, I wasn't invited to the wedding," said Anne Sweeney, laughing, despite her position as the highest-ranking executive overseeing *The View*. A lot of the producers at the show, who had helped Star plan for her big day, didn't make the cut either, and they were all outraged. "We were not included," said one person who worked at the show. At the eleventh hour, an email was sent out, telling some of them they could come to the church service, but not the party at the Waldorf Astoria. This move was particularly offensive because Star had made a big deal of asking the other cohosts on air if it was okay not to invite everybody from her inner circle to the wedding. Barbara, who'd survived three marriages, told Star she could only get away with that if she had a small gathering.

"She invited me to the shower," said producer Jessica Stedman Guff. "I got her this suede wedding album from Tiffany. And then she didn't invite me to the wedding. It was very rude."

Star managed to ruffle more feathers at *The View* by making good on her initial threat to Barbara. Because she didn't feel that the show was promoting her wedding *enough*—short of turning over the entire hour to her every day, nothing would have sufficed—she booked a series of segments on *Access Hollywood*. It was the quickest way to squeeze in plugs for her bachelorette-party gift bags. "This irritated me to no end," Geddie said. "That Star, who was only a star because of *The View*, would be on another show."

As the wedding day approached, the press seized on Star's freebie crusade, peddling the narrative that she was using *The View* as her own cash register. *Saturday Night Live* brought out a sketch that took place on Star's last night as a single woman. ("Our wedding is going to be off the hook," the Star caricature said to a fake Al, whose vows included mock shout-outs to Lady Speed Stick, Continental Airlines, and Quiznos.) The *New York Post* published a scathing story that Star, in addition to stock-piling merchandise, was searching for corporate sponsors to help finance a wedding-day spa.

Yet, contrary to what the public read in the gossip pages, Star paid for most of her wedding herself. "The reality is, she honestly didn't get that much for free," Tutera said. "I know what she spent. But the assumption was she was getting *everything* for free. I think people believed she was asking for more than she deserved. I personally think she was unfairly handled."

Tutera provided some specifics. He said that Star covered her own flowers, food, and bar tab. "Did her friend Natalie Cole's uncle Freddy sing at her wedding for free? Yes. That makes sense. There might have been other small things. But let me tell you. It was far from what was portrayed."

Even if she kept a tight RSVP list, Star made sure that her new friend made the cut. She phoned Guillen to tell her to get back on a plane. "You were there when we met," Star told her. "You've got to come." Star even covered—probably via her corporate connections—travel and lodging. "Star is a very gracious woman," Guillen said. "I was not anticipating attending something like that."

On November 13, 2004, Star Jones finally found true happiness—as Manhattan's own Cinderella. On that morning, the entrance to St. Bartholomew's Church was swarmed by gawkers and paparazzi. Part of this had been Star's own fault. She told everybody on TV exactly when and where her wedding would be, which caused a mob scene: an immovable line of chauffeured cars and photographers clogged the streets. To keep the area secure, the New York City Police Department, working with two private security firms, had to shut down a stretch of Park Avenue, which for Star gave the procession an aura of even more exclusivity.

The gown, from celebrity designer Reem Acra, came with a train twenty-seven feet long. That number wasn't chosen at random. "It was two feet longer than Princess Diana's train," Tutera explained. Before the service, as the crowds gathered in an unruly mess, Tutera made a suggestion. He asked Star to go into the doorway of the church and wave at them. Even the royal family would have acknowledged the little people. "A great photo opportunity," Tutera said. "It makes her connected to her fans. She wouldn't do it, which I think bit her in the ass."

Star had laid out specific instructions for how the day would proceed. The highlight of the ceremony (beyond the kiss) was supposed to be Patti LaBelle belting out a rendition of "My Love, Sweet Love" at a perfectly scripted moment. "As a gay guy who is obsessed with Patti LaBelle, I was already freaking nervous," Tutera said. Then he couldn't locate her. "She got lost in traffic." Those street closures had claimed their first celebrity victim.

Instead of enjoying the festivities, Tutera found himself pacing at the front of the church. Through a set of headphones, he instructed his staff to reshuffle the entire program, without telling Star. "Patti finally shows up," Tutera said. "The ceremony has started. At the foot of the steps was every news outlet you could possibly think of. Patti gets out with a big cape, as she normally would, and instead of running up the steps, she decides to take interviews with all the news outlets."

What did Tutera do? "I said, 'Patti, this is not the time for interviews! I need you to run up the stairs, get on the altar, and *sing*.'" And she did. "Star never knew this," Tutera said. "I flipped the order of her ceremony."

Barbara and Bill took their reserved seats near the front. Meredith and Elisabeth sat in the back. Joy snuck into the balcony of the church for an aerial view. "If I get married, will you come to my wedding, too?" Joy quizzed Hillary Clinton later on. As the priest asked the guests if anybody objected to the blissful union, Chris Rock scuffed his feet against the floor, and the entire room erupted into laughter.

Star had devised a special exit from the church. A tunnel of fabric was built outside a back door, so that when she got into her car, her dress still remained a mystery to the public at large. For the second time, Tutera broached the idea of waving to the minions camped outside. "She didn't want anyone to see her," he remembered. She'd sold the first images of her gown to *People*.

The Star Jones wedding was ahead of its time. It capitalized on the illusion of the celebrity dream nuptials, just as glossy magazines had started to fork over millions for portraits of famous brides and grooms. At the Waldorf, Star banned all cell phones—a rule that wouldn't seem surprising now, but it was unheard of in a pre-iPhone age. Star wanted to keep all the rights to all the pictures from her party. Just try to tell that to Barbara Walters. When an assistant asked her to check her phone, she declined and walked right in. "Let's just say it didn't happen," Tutera remembered.

The dinner at the Waldorf took place in a ballroom at the hotel. After three courses, the guests were escorted to another sprawling space for an all-night dance party. The dress code had been described as white-tie. "She didn't want anybody in pants," said Guillen, who had bought an expensive dress to fit in. "I remember looking at Joy, and she came in a black pantsuit. I was taken by that. I don't know if anybody else noticed or if it was just me."

Joy later admitted to this fashion violation. "I wore a dressy black suit, and Star didn't like that," Joy told me. "She wanted us to wear dresses only. I wore pants. I don't understand rules like that at a wedding. I guess I'm just a rebellious kind of gal."

Guillen saw something else that bothered her. When the minister blessed the food, Joy was snickering and whispering jokes to her longtime boyfriend, Steve. "That's not what you do during prayer," Guillen said. "I was offended by that, and I was disappointed in meeting Joy. I thought she was kind of rude."

Star and Al had their honeymoon trip planned to Dubai for a later date. She couldn't leave the country until she finished her press obligations, sitting down with *People* in a sparkling sweater embroidered with the words *Mrs. Reynolds.* She resumed work on Monday to share all the memories from her magical weekend.

At least one of her famous guests was moved by the procession. In the days after the wedding, Tutera got a call from Trump requesting a bid on his upcoming ceremony, set for January 2005. He wanted a carbon copy of what he'd seen, and long before Melania plagiarized from Michelle Obama's Democratic National Convention speech, she borrowed something from the *View* bride. "Melania and Donald copied my design and hired someone else," Tutera said. "That's the God's honest truth. Look at the photos of their wedding versus Star's. It's the exact same thing! The way the flowers were set up, the layout, the whole thing."

Star had accomplished what she'd set out to do. She had staged her own royal wedding—complete with all the dysfunction that would haunt Charles and Diana. "I had a fabulous wedding and a horrible marriage," Star said. "It just didn't work. Sometimes, it doesn't."

9

Meredith's Great Escape

For almost a decade, Meredith Vieira played the nice and normal one on *The View*. This wasn't simply an act for the TV cameras. Of all the ladies, she was the one who changed the least after the show became a phenomenon, never letting fame get to her head. She didn't raise her voice, create any unnecessary obstacles, rock the boat, or make life hell for any of the staff.

But in the middle of Season 9, which ran from 2005 to 2006, Barbara Walters sensed that something might be wrong. It was time to renegotiate Meredith's contract, yet her agent, Michael Glantz, hadn't moved forward with a new deal.

One morning, Bill Geddie approached her to see if he could figure it out. "Why haven't you signed your contract?"

Meredith shrugged off his question. She had a window to meet with other suitors, but she didn't bring that up.

Geddie tried to convince her to stay. "He sort of referenced the fact that at my age"—she was fifty-two—"it might be hard to get work," Meredith recalled. "The implication was it wasn't easy to get another job. And I'm thinking, 'Yeah it is!'"

Meredith had been harboring a big secret, as a game of high-stakes dominoes was about to commence. It all started with Dan Rather's forced resignation from the *CBS Evening News* in November 2004, after running a story believed to be factually inaccurate about George W. Bush's Texas Air National Guard service on *60 Minutes*. Bob Schieffer filled in as the temporary anchor until the network could find a true star. And we all know who CBS CEO Leslie Moonves wanted. Hiring Katie Couric would be a glass-ceiling-breaking moment, since no woman had ever held solo duties behind the desk of a nightly news broadcast.

Over at NBC, the prospect of losing Couric made executives panic. At that time, *Today*—a cash machine—had successfully fended off *GMA* in the ratings for more than ten years, despite Diane Sawyer's attempts to chip away at their lead. Couric, who had been appointed coanchor in 1991, was a big factor behind the popularity of *Today*. She'd built a crisp and peppy chemistry with Matt Lauer, who acquiesced to whatever Katie wanted. If she decided to bolt, it wasn't clear that *Today* could keep winning.

That's when Jeff Zucker, the president of NBC's Television Group, where he oversaw the news division, made a risky bet. Instead of promoting from within the *Today* family (following Couric's and Lauer's trajectory) and elevating Ann Curry, he wanted to steal from next door. This would be a first. Every modern anchor of *Today* had climbed up the news ladder. Although Meredith was an experienced journalist, having spent twenty years doing news stories, that hadn't been what turned her into a star. Instead, she'd carved an unconventional path through *The View,* on which she effortlessly juggled the latest national tragedies, self-help trends, and celebrity fads on Hot Topics. (Moonves's backup plan for the nightly news, if Couric turned him down, was also Meredith, a sign of *The View's* reach.)

Meredith had toyed with the idea of leaving *The View* once before. When her initial contract was up in 2002, she pondered an offer from CBS to do a morning news show. Yet a concern held her back. "I'm not really a morning news person," she told me. "The more we talked, the more I thought, 'I don't think this is really for me.'"

At the time, Barbara helped Meredith land a bigger paycheck at ABC so she'd stay. *Who Wants to Be a Millionaire,* the quiz show that Regis Philbin had built into a prime-time smash, was about to be spun off for syndication. The first choice to host it, Rosie O'Donnell, turned them down, expressing a desire to retire from the limelight after ending her talk show in May 2002. "Meredith wanted more money," Barbara said. "In order to get her to stay, I talked to ABC and gave her *Millionaire.* I was responsible for that happening." The second job on *Millionaire* roughly doubled Meredith's salary.

Flash forward to the end of 2005. Zucker, who had started his career at NBC as the savant news producer who had morphed *Today* into a ratings juggernaut with big news stories, live concerts, and snappy celebrity interviews, knew how to play hardball. His reputation for always getting what he wanted meant that he wasn't timid about prying talent from Barbara's tight grip. He arranged a private meeting with Meredith. There were no witnesses because he picked her up in a chauffeured car one October afternoon from *The View,* and they drove in circles on the way to *Millionaire,* which taped later in the day.

People don't know this yet, but Katie is going to leave and I'd like for you to be her replacement, he told her.

"I remember saying, 'You're skewing a little old,'" Meredith said. "It was the weirdest conversation." Rather than offer her the job, Zucker asked her to meet with Lauer because she wouldn't want to do it unless they got along. It was a smart way to keep her engaged, so that she'd at least entertain the idea. Meredith had dinner with Lauer at his apartment. "They knew I'd like Matt," she said. (This interview was conducted before NBC News fired Lauer in November 2017 for alleged sexual misconduct with colleagues.)

Suddenly, despite her aversion to the crack-of-dawn hours, this job didn't look so bad. "I started to think about, 'You can have this opportunity at the *Today* show. It's the number one show. It's iconic. It's been around forever. Will you kick yourself if you don't do this? Will you always regret it?'"

It wasn't as if she would be leaving an ideal work environment, since morale at *The View* was at an all-time low. Star's wedding had ended, but it left a permanent stench on the show that couldn't be scrubbed off. The bad press had taken its toll. In the aftermath, Brian Frons, the president of ABC Daytime, held an all-hands-on-deck meeting, outlining what producers later referred to as "the Star Jones rule": they were all forbidden under any circumstances from accepting any gifts.

"I was literally asked to be off ABC," said David Tutera, who was banished to doing shows on cable TV. The network heads worried that the mere sight of Jones's wedding planner would give viewers PTSD.

Another unpleasant situation bubbled up around the time of the wedding. *The View* had scheduled a home renovation segment for Meredith, who would redo her kitchen on TV, with a national retail chain covering the expenses. But the story got back to the network that she was getting a free kitchen, and ABC wouldn't allow it. In protest, Meredith's agent, Glantz, went all the way up the chain of command to Disney's then-president Bob Iger, who upheld the ruling.

"Meredith was doing her house. Somebody or another complained," Barbara said, recalling the tale about the free kitchen years later.

"I was never going to be given a free kitchen," Meredith said. "I think they used me as a scapegoat, because I never got anything. It was a really obnoxious period. I had seen somebody take a lot of things, and it was fine. I worked with a producer and that was it. It never happened. It's also interesting that Barbara perpetuates that story. I don't think that's right."

One staffer recalled how during the meeting with Frons, all the cohosts had been dressed in costumes for a Halloween episode. Meredith, who was the Wicked Witch of the West from *The Wizard of Oz,* believed she was being unfairly targeted. "She starts crying, with the green face, and she rips off her nose," the employee recalled. "It was an absolute nightmare."

"I felt like I played out *The View* in my own head," Meredith said. "The show was evolving. It didn't feel the same way. If you don't feel the same way, you should go. The vibe was getting weird. There was just a lot of stuff in the air. I felt it was becoming a little bit more about acting than connecting."

Zucker had made Meredith a hefty offer, but he sweetened it by letting her keep *Millionaire*, resulting in an estimated income of $10 million a year. That way, he knew that ABC wouldn't be able to come even close to matching her salary.

"There were conversations about, 'Does ABC News want to write her a holding check or use her in another way?'" said Frons. The decision came back not to do that. "So it became a no-brainer. It was 'Okay, she's going to go.'"

Barbara still mounted an effort to keep her moderator. "Barbara pulled me aside and said, 'Do you know how hard it's going to be? And you have to get up early,'" Meredith said. "In her own way, she was trying to talk me out of it. That's human nature. Somebody is going to leave, and you say, '*What are you, nuts!*' I understand what she was doing."

When Meredith finally accepted the *Today* offer, she was a mess: "I was crying. I was scared. But I knew it was the right time to do it. I felt like at *The View* I wasn't growing anymore. And that wasn't a good thing."

Barbara Walters never thought that *The View* would outlive the departure of one of its stars. In 2002, after Frons came to ABC Daytime, he remembered a stark prediction at a lunch at Trump Tower in Columbus Circle.

"Barbara can be very prickly," Frons said.

"You know," she told him, "when Meredith, Star, Joy, or I go, this show is over."

Frons pushed back. "I said, 'No, you've actually created something that's a franchise just like *Good Morning America*.'" If one of the cohosts left, they simply needed to find the right replacement.

"I'm not sure about that!" Barbara responded, as she was prone to do if someone questioned her judgment. Now that theory was about to be tested. The future of *The View* depended on what happened next.

On *The View*, Meredith had done a lot of heavy lifting. As a young girl growing up in Rhode Island with three older brothers, she had learned from an early age how to navigate a big family. It was a tricky tightrope that she had to balance on TV. She was in charge, yet she also had to defer to Barbara at the drop of a hat. Viewers loved that she could be equally serious and irreverent—her shticks included dressing up like Bette Davis or Johnny Depp for Halloween episodes, tap-dancing in a hot-dog costume during baseball season, and making out with her cohosts as pretend lesbians. "We just did it to piss off Barbara," Meredith said, laughing.

After she decided to go, Meredith said that Geddie apologized to her for his earlier comment. "I have no recollection of making any issue with her age," Geddie told me. "If she said I said it, maybe I thought it was a ploy. I was trying to get her to stay. I certainly wanted her to stay." He'd been worried that Meredith would get poached: "I warned Barbara early on that Meredith was going to be scooped up by the *Today* show. If you looked at the landscape, there was nobody else for it. She was perfect for it."

The crew members were all devastated to hear that Meredith would be leaving. For many of them, she was their favorite cohost. She told them, in a sob session backstage, that she'd be taking all of them to NBC with her in her heart.

"When Meredith left, I cried," Joy said. "I loved Meredith. We got along really well on the show."

It was time to bite the bullet and announce to viewers that *The View*'s beloved moderator was out. ABC wouldn't release Meredith from her contract early, so she had a few months left on the show through the summer.

On April 6, 2006, Meredith's departure became a Hot Topic, just hours before NBC had scheduled a press conference to show off their latest star.

But, quite strangely, it didn't open the show. "Hello, everybody, and welcome to *The View*," Meredith said. "Big news. Big news. That always feels so good, doesn't it? After months of speculation, Katie Couric made it official yesterday. She is leaving the *Today* show to become the first female solo anchor for a network evening newscast."

That was Barbara's cue to take over: "I called Katie last night to congratulate her and to tell her I thought she did the right thing. In part, I had to go back to my own feelings. Because, I can't believe it was that long ago, but many years ago I left NBC to come to ABC to be the first female coanchor."

"How many years ago, Barb?" Star asked devilishly.

An awkward pause hung in the air.

"It was 1976," Barbara continued. Then, improbably, she showed a series of vintage clips of herself doing the news, as if she were the one about to make a giant leap forward in her career. As she cut to a commercial, Barbara dangled some intrigue. "And when we come back," she said, with a twinkle in her eye, "we have some news of our own to make."

Seven minutes into the show, it was finally time for Meredith to take center stage: "I sat down last night to write what I was going to say to you all today. I couldn't do it. And I realized it is because I'm having trouble finding the right words to express how I feel right now. . . . I've reached a point where I have to veer off my path. I'm very honored that NBC has asked me to cohost the *Today* show.'"

The audience showered her with a standing ovation. "I'm miserable that you are leaving," Joy said. "I have to say, I feel as though I'm losing a sister. I'm an only child. This has been an experience of siblings for me."

Barbara, annoyed, said, "Joy always has to be first. And everything you said, we welcome and echo."

"Well, Joy is a dear friend," Meredith replied, trying to protect her.

"It's all right. I'm not picking on you," Barbara said to Joy.

"Yes, you are," Joy said.

"We promise that we will be new and fresh," Barbara said a little later, as she tried to reassure viewers that nothing would change.

"As opposed to old and worn-out!" Meredith grinned, pointing to herself. "Speaking about new, Melania Trump has a new baby, and we'll be right back."

Sure enough, every time something big happened on *The View*, a member of a certain family seemed to be in proximity. Only seventeen days after giving birth, the future first lady granted her first interview about her son, Barron Trump. The segment promoted her website and ongoing modeling career.

"Everybody is fantastic," cooed Melania. "We have a great time, to have somebody at home, somebody very mini."

Barbara, always the journalist, lobbed an important question. "Are you breast-feeding?"

"Yes."

"It certainly looks like it," Joy quipped, as she eyed Melania's abundant cleavage.

"I wake up every three hours."

"Tell Donald to stop waking you up!" Joy said mockingly.

The interview closed with Barbara. "We are very happy," she said about her guest's milestone. "As you gathered, this is a very special and emotional day for us."

"I know," Melania said, turning to Meredith. "We will miss you here at *The View*. But we will watch you on *Today*."

⌘

Barbara Walters didn't want just *anybody* to take over for Meredith at *The View*. In the same way she had chased after the biggest subjects for an interview, she was obsessed with landing a huge name—she wanted to make a massive splash with her announcement. The new cohost had to be a game changer. Inspiration struck one night when she went to a screening of an HBO documentary called *All Aboard! Rosie's Family Cruise*. The movie chronicled Rosie O'Donnell's life outside of fame, as the retired talk show host had started a first-of-its-kind cruise ship for gay parents.

Boy, if I could get Rosie back to daytime, that would be great, Barbara thought.

A few weeks after that, Barbara invited Rosie to a dinner party at her home. In the midst of the crowd of newsmakers, Rosie won over the group by belting out show tunes behind a piano. Barbara was beyond charmed—and also desperate. She cornered Rosie after and offered her the *View* job.

"Come try it," Barbara said.

Rosie accepted on the spot. She was feeling restless, and she'd even filled in several times as a guest cohost on *The View*. She had nothing else to do, outside of spending her days holed up in a crafts room of her house in upstate New York. That spring, a *New York* profile titled "Rosie O'Donnell Lets Her Freak Flag Fly" captured her years in seclusion. "Six years of megastardom, that was intense," she told the magazine. "I needed to refuel myself with real life."

The way Rosie saw it, she couldn't turn down this offer. She had too much respect for Barbara as a trailblazer for all women on television. "Ro's reaction was, when Barbara asks, you say yes," said Cindi Berger, the power publicist who counts both Barbara and Rosie as her clients.

As Meredith packed up her office, Barbara revealed in a small meeting with a few key staff members that Rosie was coming to *The View* as the new moderator. Star was offended. In the *New York* interview, Rosie had painted Star as a phony for not owning up to her gastric bypass (which Star still hadn't publicly admitted). Star's protests fell on deaf ears. A plan was in motion that she didn't know about: ABC was getting ready to cut her so they could clear the stage for a reboot in Season 10.

Star's firing had been in the works for some time. "We started to get feedback in focus groups that was sort of mind-bending," Frons said. "We actually had people in Atlanta"—regular viewers that were meant to measure impressions of the show—"come in and say, 'Why is she lying and saying she lost all that weight with Pilates? She obviously had a tummy tuck.' And then someone else goes, 'Yeah, and her fiancé is gay! What the hell is going on with her?'"

Barbara tried at first to shield Star because she had been such an important factor in *The View*'s early success. But once Meredith decided to abandon ship, and ABC turned over the binders of negative research, Barbara caved. If they pooled both Meredith's and Star's salaries, they could afford Rosie, who only agreed to a one-year contract for reasons that would later become clear.

Nobody at ABC had the courage to tell Star to her face that she was getting fired. Instead, an ABC executive called her agent that spring after the Meredith news, during a few days when Star was away at a women's conference in Phoenix. Her agent then played a game of telephone with Al Reynolds, who flew to Arizona to break the grim decision.

Star recalled returning to her hotel room in Phoenix and seeing her husband's suitcase in the hall. Her heart stopped. *Why is he here?* "Then my assistant, who had traveled with me, came to the door of the suite, closed the door, and went back to her room," Star said. "I saw my then husband come out." Her mind imagined a dark tragedy: "I started to cry because I thought my mother had died. He came and he took my hand. That's when he told me they weren't renewing my contract. And I remember going, 'Oh!'"

Wasn't Star mad? "Not initially, when you thought your mother had died," Star said. "I breathed. I really exhaled. And then later, I was like 'What???' For about thirty seconds, I was grateful it was just that. I can handle business setbacks."

She was about to prove that in a way that would eternally wound Barbara Walters.

Meredith wasn't going to vacate her home at ABC without a proper send-off, so she asked for a comedic roast on her last day, June 9, 2006. It was one of the stranger episodes *The View* had ever staged, with the set reshuffled and a theme song reminiscent of *The Price Is Right*. Meredith sat side by side with her cohosts and guest comedians, who included Mario Cantone, Kelsey Grammer, Gilbert Gottfried, and Joan Rivers. Her first choice, George Clooney, wasn't available.

"Meredith, you are a wonderful and also highly emotional person who can break into tears at the drop of a hat," Barbara said as the master of ceremonies. "But I can tell you from personal experience that once the alarm clock goes off at four in the morning, you'll really have something to cry about."

Rivers prompted the most uncomfortable moment. "I love the whole panel," she said. "It's going to be very hard to do *The View* without you and without Joy . . . oh, I'm sorry. That's next week."

Barbara followed suit: "I'm sorry you had to find out this way," she said to Joy.

Everybody chuckled, including the cohost—Star—who had actually been secretly fired. She had continued to show up to work as if nothing were wrong.

The singer Michael Feinstein belted out the tune "Rhode Island Is Famous for You," which Meredith had said she'd been listening to when she felt anxiety about her decision to leave. Meredith's husband, Richard, and their three young children were in the audience, although maybe they needed earplugs: most of the routine sounded like a racy nightclub act, not a family-friendly show that aired at lunchtime.

With the hour winding down, Joy had to show her undying love for her television soul mate. "I just don't know how to express it. I thought to myself, 'What would Rosie O'Donnell do?'" And with that line, Joy started to passionately make out with Meredith.

"Here's your gum back," Meredith said. "My poor daughter is sitting there thinking Mommy is a lesbian." Meredith looked up. "This is it. This is my farewell tribute. I did two thousand shows with these bitches in nine years."

10

Scandal

S tar Jones would depart *The View* with a tasteful farewell scheduled for later that summer. Her goodbye episode had been choreographed with all sides signing off on it. She'd announce in late June 2006 that she was exiting, in euphemistic language that she felt comfortable with, to pursue other opportunities. A few weeks after that, producers would throw her a divine going-away party, and everybody would separate without any hard feelings. It would be, to the relief of Barbara Walters and the staff at ABC, a clean and amicable breakup.

But Star had a different idea. She wanted to draw blood. Contrary to public perception, *The View* cohosts weren't perpetually at one another's throats—at least, not according to Star. "Everybody thought it was catty," she told me. "It really wasn't. Nobody plotted on Debbie, that's the honest to God's truth. Nobody plotted on Lisa. I think the first real time there was a plot was against me."

Star saw her firing as something more sinister than losing a job. "In reality, they could have just said that with Meredith leaving, we are going to change the direction of the show. I would not have been happy with that, but I would have respected it. People get fired all the time. I get it."

Star was enraged by the character assassination of her in the press, and she blamed Barbara for all the nasty gossip items about her gastric bypass. Star believed the show was leaking these stories to ruin her. "You don't get to hurt my career when you know damn well that I helped make the show," Star said. "That's not fair. What I did not like was a concerted effort to destroy me professionally—Bill and Barbara, specifically. And Joy helped.

"They all fed stories to the media," Star insisted. "I've learned all of this subsequently. They were attacking my marriage, but more importantly, they were feeding stories about me not wanting to talk about my weight-loss surgery." She cited an unlikely ally as one of her sources. "They actually fed Rosie things about me that were private. She told me, so I absolutely know it happened." (Asked about it later, Rosie told me, "What I knew was this: She dug herself a hole, but they gave her a shovel. They allowed things and then called foul afterwards.")

As the one who always got the last word, Star wasn't about to slink away quietly from this fight. "She was very professional," Geddie said. "She didn't break down crying or anything like that." Her hard-edged lawyer training had taught her how to keep up a poker face. However, she was feeling wrecked on the inside. "They wanted me to stay for three months, and initially I was going to be okay with that, until they started the trickle effect," Star said, about the series of articles that appeared about her departure, which she hadn't announced yet. "It was hurting me. It was really devastating my psyche. It was just mean."

She quietly sought outside counsel. Although no one ever found out, her last day on the show was designed by crisis management publicist Judy Smith, later the inspiration for Shonda Rhimes's TV show *Scandal*. According to Star, she had a secret meeting with Smith.

"What do you want?" Smith asked her.

"I want this to be over," Star remembered saying.

"No. What do you want in ten years?"

Star thought about it for several days before settling on an answer. "And then I told her, I want to be able to walk in the rooms of professional women and have them respect me for my choices and be empowered to take control of themselves and their careers."

With that in mind, Star hatched a scheme. "I did exactly what the plan was. It was not to be nasty to my colleagues. I had no reason to be nasty. You take control of it. Don't lie to the public. Don't say I'm going off to do bigger and better things. Just simply look into the camera and say, 'I'm not going to be here.'"

She contacted *People* for another interview, under less auspicious circumstances. Star wanted to tell them that she'd been fired from *The View*. The conversation would be under embargo, meaning that it couldn't run until after *The View* had aired on June 27.

At work, Star had agreed that she would make her official announcement about leaving two days later. Yet there were a few clues at *The View* that morning that something big was about to happen. Star wore a glamorous pink suit. She carried a page of handwritten notes that she didn't show to anybody. And her pastor was sitting in the audience. She mysteriously asked one of the show's producers to tell director Mark Gentile to cut to her after the show's first commercial.

Barbara was in an upbeat mood. It looked as if *The View* would have longevity despite losing Meredith. Even better, the moderator's chair was finally hers—at least for a few weeks until Rosie started. Barbara held court with pizzazz, injecting as much sex into Hot Topics as possible. One of the guests that day was a serial sperm donor, and she quizzed the other cohosts if they'd ever let a child conceived from a donor meet the man who was technically the child's biological father. After that lively discussion, Barbara asked if a wife can press rape charges against her husband, based on a recent plot from the Denis Leary show *Rescue Me*.

"Oh, absolutely," said Star, who kept looking down, vaguely distracted. "If a woman says no and you force yourself, it is rape."

Once the show returned from a commercial, Star took over, interrupting Joy. "Excuse me one minute. Something's been on my heart for a little bit. After much prayer and counsel, I feel like this is the right time to tell you that the show is moving in another direction for its tenth season and I will not be returning as cohost next year."

"It's shocking to me," Joy mumbled. Barbara looked dazed. Elisabeth, for once, was speechless. They all knew that Star was finished, but they hadn't been prepared for her to blurt out her departure like that. It was a stop-the-presses moment in pop culture, as *The View* went off the rails as gripping reality TV. Better yet, Star had one-upped *The Real World* by blindsiding the executive producer of her own show in front of millions.

Still not knowing what exactly was behind this reveal, Barbara composed herself and asked the crowd to get on their feet for Star. "We have read rumors," Barbara said. "This is a surprise that this would come about this way."

Geddie bolted from the studio to try to figure out what to do next. "That was the angriest I've ever been in my career," he said. "I'd gotten a call right before the show from a woman who worked with her, telling me all the things she wanted for her final show. It was fully orchestrated. When you let someone go, you ask, 'Do you want the easy way or the hard way?' She chose both, which I think is dishonest."

On TV, the show went on. ABC News anchor Charlie Gibson dropped by to discuss his final week on *GMA*, but no one could concentrate—what he had to say didn't seem to matter. The sperm donor granted an interview with his new wife. Star kept her distance from Barbara between commercials, and there was still confusion about what had prompted her to change the date of her announcement. Just as the show wrapped, the *People* article went live online, and Barbara realized the full extent of Star's coordinated attack.

The story portrayed Star as a loyal employee who had been pushed out the door. "What you don't know is that my contract was not renewed for the tenth season," Star told *People*. "I feel like I was fired." That quote was like throwing a match on gasoline. The story was picked up by every news outlet in America.

"Terrible," said Barbara, when asked about how she felt that day. "I think she was furious, and she felt she was maligned and she was going to say, 'Screw you!' The show became far more provocative as time went on."

Joy recalled the mood on the set. "We were surprised that day. She pulled that out of her brassiere. *What!?* That did not go down well with the administration."

Star slipped away, without saying goodbye to the crew. ABC went into crisis mode. They had to hit back hard, so viewers wouldn't shun *The View* and blame Barbara for kicking Star off the show. Barbara's reputation was on the line. Star had specifically planned her attack to destroy Barbara's image as a reputable journalist who could be trusted to tell the truth. To deal with the fallout, an emergency meeting was held with Barbara, Cindi Berger, Geddie, and several ABC employees. *What the fuck are we going to do?*

"I was so furious," Geddie said.

A decision had to be made about Star's fate. On TV, she'd said that she would be on the show through the summer. Barbara, still reeling from the *People* article, was concerned that banishing Star from *The View* would appear coldhearted and could do more damage.

"Barbara doesn't like conflict," Geddie said. "She doesn't want to look mean. I don't care if I look like I'm being mean. I'm a producer."

Geddie felt strongly that Star could never again return to *The View*. "Who knows what she'll say or do? It's a live show. She's already made us look like an idiot." He pointed out that if she continued to play the victim, she'd inflict more harm on the show every day. Berger sided with Bill, and Barbara relented. "We told her not to bother coming back," Geddie said.

Star didn't expect to stay on *The View* after her takedown: "I knew exactly when and how and what I was going to say. I knew that I would never come back again. Barbara was absolutely floored because it exposed the way things are done in television and it had not been done before." She felt the most betrayed by Geddie. "I resented more than anything that he didn't tell me the truth."

Not that Star needed *The View* for more airtime. Hundreds of reporters were banging down her door for quotes. The news media ran with the story—it was the most epic fight (so far) in the history of daytime TV.

Barbara had to do damage control by getting on the phone that afternoon with journalists to tell her side of the story. In this area she naturally excelled, and she managed to successfully put her own spin on the saga. "They had done a great deal of research, and her negatives were rising," Barbara dished to *The New York Times* about Star. "The audience was losing trust in her. They didn't believe some of the things she said." When asked why she lied in a previous interview that Star would not be fired, Barbara answered, "I was trying to protect Star."

Meanwhile, Star appeared on *Larry King Live* that week, peddling the narrative about all the ways she had been mistreated. She followed up *The View* with a series on Court TV that was canceled after one season, and she and Barbara remained estranged for years. Star doesn't believe it was wrong to speak her truth, and she understands why people still talk about it: "Somebody took control of their own destiny and blindsided the greatest female broadcaster on television. It was planned completely—by the real Olivia Pope!"

The View desperately needed Rosie O'Donnell to hurry up and get there because the show was coming undone at the seams. "And then there were three," Barbara said the next day, as she appeared with a downsized panel of only her, Joy, and Elisabeth.

Star's exit escalated tensions that had been building on the show. On August 2, just as *The View* was about to go on hiatus, it almost lost another cohost in a scuffle that registered as a 10 on the Richter scale of meltdowns. The full details never made it in the papers, outside of a few reports about how Elisabeth looked distraught after a fight with Barbara on TV.

On this quiet summer day the singer-songwriter Lisa Loeb—"Stay (I Missed You")—was the celebrity cohost. Earlier that morning, Rosie O'Donnell, in a burst of excitement behind the scenes, stopped by to sit in as an observer on the Hot Topics meeting. "We could barely keep her off the set today," Barbara explained on TV. The show was getting a make-over because Barbara wanted to keep up with Meredith on *Today,* even though *The View* wasn't on at the same time. In the makeup room, Rosie couldn't just sit back and observe. She hijacked the discussions about re-modeling the set, which she had started managing right down to the new paint colors for the walls.

Animosity was in the air. As Rosie kept talking, she championed all the other cohosts except Elisabeth. The producers had to get around to the headlines they were going to talk about on TV, including a news story about how the FDA was considering the morning-after pill for over-the-counter consumption. As Elisabeth defended her anti-abortion views, Rosie piled on, fighting her in a debate that Rosie wouldn't even be par-ticipating in. Barbara and Joy took Rosie's side. Elisabeth got so worked up that she started to bawl because she felt that everybody was ganging up on her.

Rosie hadn't even started yet, and Barbara's rule about saving argu-ments for the camera had already gone out the window. But at least this was only a minor tiff—or so it seemed. Rosie left the building, and it was time to do the show.

"Our audience is all here because we're air-conditioned," Barbara said at the top of the program. "It's hot outside. It's hot inside."

"I love the heat," Elisabeth responded in a bit of unforeseen foreshad-owing.

The Hot Topics dug into Mel Gibson's apology for his anti-Semitic ti-rade after getting arrested. "He needs to be welcomed into the Jewish community by a public circumcision," Joy said. "Talk about a lethal weapon!"

Then it was time for the controversial story about the morning-after pill. No sooner had Barbara brought up the subject than Elisabeth got worked up again: "My heart is, like, almost out of my chest right now. I feel very strongly about this. I don't think I'm alone. I believe that life begins at the moment of conception, and when that egg is fertilized—"

"This prevents the fertilization," Barbara tried to clarify.

"It's taking away that environment for that egg to develop, which it would develop most of the time into a baby," Elisabeth said. "To me, it's the same thing as birthing a baby and leaving it out in the street."

"I think that is so extreme," Loeb said.

Elisabeth wasn't having any of it, as she started shaking.

"Elisabeth, calm down, dear." Barbara sounded like a Sunday-school teacher who had to control an unruly student.

"I can't. This makes me so upset, Barbara."

"But everybody has strong opinions," Barbara admonished her. "There are many other arguments that other people could give you. I think the most important thing, which is what we see today, is we've got to be able to have these discussions and listen to other people's opinions and not go so crazy that you don't listen."

"I heard everything you said."

"I barely started," Walters snapped. "There are many other opinions. We have to have a way of discussing this without exploding, because people have to understand each other."

Elisabeth tried to interject again.

"Could you stop now?" Barbara was mad. "We have to go on and we have to learn how to discuss these things in some sort of *rational* way."

The last adjective felt like a slap to Elisabeth's face. As the show cut to a commercial, Elisabeth ripped up her note cards and stormed off the stage. Joy went after her. Since all the ladies were still wearing microphones, their conversations were audible in the control room. I reviewed a recording of what happened next.

"Fuck that!" Elisabeth screamed in a narrow corridor behind the stage.

"I'm not going to sit there and get reprimanded on the air. It's not okay to sit there and get reprimanded on the air."

"I know," Joy said, trying to soothe her.

"What the fuck! I'm not going back out there."

"Come into my office here," Joy said.

"No! I'm not going back out there. You know what? I can take it in the meeting room," Elisabeth said, referring to the earlier exchange. "I'm not taking it out there on air. I'm not taking it."

"Okay, honey. I hear what you're saying."

"What the fuck! I don't even swear. She has me swearing. This woman is driving me nuts. I'm not going back. I can't do the show like this. She just reprimanded me, and she knew exactly what she was doing. Good-bye! I'm off. Write about that in the *New York* FUCKING *Post*!"

Elisabeth stomped off, racing down the stairs to her dressing room.

Barbara and Bill were huddling on their own, on another side of the stage. "I think Elisabeth might be furious," Geddie said. "You just shut her down and told her she was a maniac."

"I did not!" Barbara protested, as she blamed a producer in the control room for forcing her to stop the conversation. In frustration, she started to mimic the producer: "'Wrap it up! Wrap it up! Wrap it up! Wrap it up!'"

Another producer ran over to tell them there was an emergency. "Elisabeth has just walked off the show," Joy calmly announced as they joined her.

"Well, that's ridiculous," Barbara said.

"Where is she?" Geddie asked, as it dawned on him that *The View* would be back from a commercial in three minutes. Barbara tried to follow him down the stairwell, but Geddie wasn't sure if that would be helpful. "You have to go, Barbara," he said. "Because you have to start this show if I can't find her." Barbara made a U-turn for the stage.

In all this havoc, only one person wasn't breaking a sweat. As producers were running around wildly, Joy looked at herself in a mirror. "I hate this color," she said about her lavender blouse. "How am I supposed to get pregnant in a color like this?" It was an inside joke because she'd already revealed on TV during the birth-control debate that she'd entered menopause.

Barbara approached several other staffers, relitigating what had happened and arguing that she wasn't in the wrong.

Downstairs, Geddie found a hysterical Elisabeth in her dressing room, telling another producer that she was done with *The View.*

"I quit," Elisabeth said with tears in her eyes. "I'm quitting. I don't need to be reprimanded on the air like that by this woman. I will take it in the meeting. I will not take that on air. I'm leaving." She looked at Geddie. *"Barbara just fully reprimanded me live on the show to everybody in America!"* she screamed. "Bill, I don't want to go out there."

Geddie knew he had only seconds to turn this around, or the entire debacle would be breaking news. Since this was all unraveling live, the show might return with one of its cohosts missing from the stage. It was life-or-death for *The View,* which was looking more and more like *Survivor.*

"I've already beat up on her about it," Geddie said. "You are a professional. You've got to go back out there."

Elisabeth was mortified at the thought. "She reprimanded me like a child! I can't even breathe right now."

"I said something to her," Geddie begged. "Everybody said something to her. You have to go on because you're a pro, so come with me." He physically moved her back toward the studio, speaking to her like a small child. "I said, 'How could you do that? You tried to humiliate her for thinking what she thought.'"

"Not even that, Bill." Elisabeth was most outraged by Barbara's tone. "To talk down to me and say, 'We have to learn how to discuss this.'"

"You were not crazy," Geddie said, as they quickly sprinted up the stairs. "Everybody feels the way you feel. Every producer weighed in on it. They thought it was horrible."

"You know she can get someone here who is going to sit there and not be passionate. I don't even have my cards. I chucked them. I'm sorry, I've never done that before." Only forty-five seconds were left before airtime.

On the stage, Barbara was frantic. She tried to shoo Loeb away, so that viewers wouldn't wonder why only one cohost had vanished and not the others. Barbara thought they could perhaps pretend that they had evacuated the entire couch for Sally Field, who was waiting in the wings for an interview about her new show, *Brothers & Sisters*. Just as Loeb had been told to leave, she was ordered to return, because someone announced Elisabeth was coming back. Barbara, always a steady producer, knew that she needed to keep a loose cannon under control, and she commanded that Elisabeth sit next to her.

With mere seconds left, Elisabeth took her seat.

"This is why we shouldn't have done it," Barbara whispered to her. "Because you're so emotional."

"I don't want to be scolded for being emotional," Elisabeth sniffled.

"You weren't scolded," Barbara shot back.

There isn't a faster remedy for a broken friendship than TV cameras. When the lens focused, a tearful Elisabeth and Barbara were sitting with their arms around each other, acknowledging that they loved each other despite the squabble viewers had just seen.

One of the questions for Field had been about the new morning-after pill, but Barbara quickly cut it, and the interview had an almost meditative vibe. No one would have guessed that Elisabeth had almost ended her *View* career that morning. But in many ways, this was just a preview of the hysteria that was about to engulf *The View*.

As Joy stood in front of the mirror during that insane commercial break, she muttered to a few producers, "She gets excited. The other one is going to get just as excited," Joy said, referring to Rosie. "I've got news for you. This is the beginning."

Part Two

Rosie's View

11

The Queen of Nice

From the beginning of *The View*, Barbara Walters had leaned on Rosie O'Donnell for support. Even though they headlined competing talk shows, there was never a hint of jealousy between the two TV superstars. How could there be, when Rosie was so nice to Barbara? On September 12, 1997, Rosie played the Motown classic "I Can't Help Myself (Sugar Pie Honey Bunch)" to bring out Barbara as a guest on *The Rosie O'Donnell Show*. Barbara had interviewed Rosie before, but on this morning, they switched roles. Barbara answered questions about attending Princess Diana's funeral in London, an eventful trip that had included a night in Paris with Michael Jackson (sans surgical mask) for a primetime special. Barbara happily promoted *The View*, but she almost forgot to mention her cohosts, naming them at the end.

"This is the most adorable show," Barbara said. "I've been watching it backstage. It's so lively!"

Rosie returned the compliment, telling Barbara how much she enjoyed *The View* during its second month on TV. "I think it's a great format," Rosie said. "It's wonderful for women at home to see themselves and their perspectives reflected back in the four different people."

"Four different bigmouths and me," Barbara said. "Would you mind coming on every day?"

"Every day?" Rosie asked, as though she'd been cornered. "All right." Rosie tried to find an excuse. "But you're not there every day."

Barbara expressed gratitude to Rosie because *The Rosie O'Donnell Show* was the lead-in for *The View* in New York, giving it a bump. "Barbara always said the reason her show stayed on was because of me," Rosie told me. "And we had huge ratings."

Before Jimmy Fallon, Ellen DeGeneres, James Corden, or Andy Cohen adopted the persona of the talk show host as the superfan, there was *The Rosie O'Donnell Show,* which aired from 1996 to 2002. For six seasons, Rosie took on the title of the world's utmost expert on movies, TV shows, musicals, and crafts, without uttering a cross word. She averaged 5 million viewers on her best days, nipping at Oprah's heels and clobbering her at the Daytime Emmys. On TV, Rosie offered a ray of sunshine; it was not for nothing that *Newsweek* dubbed her the Queen of Nice. Rosie was so popular, she stepped in as host of the Grammys and the Tonys, making her Hollywood's emcee of choice after Billy Crystal.

Her show was the place to go if you loved talking about pop culture, celebrities—and Rosie O'Donnell. Instead of engaging in normal banter with her famous guests, many of her questions revolved around Rosie's own obsessions: *All My Children, Ally McBeal,* Ring Dings, decoupage, Tom Cruise, and Barbra Streisand. No star, no matter how big, could escape Rosie's rabid interests. On February 3, 1997, Hillary Rodham Clinton participated in an interview that was unlike anything she'd previously done on TV. Rather than discuss public policy or health care, the first lady played a round of trivia about *The Mary Tyler Moore Show,* kissed Oscar the Grouch, and belted out a duet of "The Telephone Hour" from *Bye Bye Birdie.*

"We'll be here all week," Rosie said, waving a hand. "Gimme a high five!"

When she'd conceived of her talk show, Rosie told her agent she wanted to do a modern *The Merv Griffin Show,* from the 1960s. It was a stark departure from the typical fare then offered in daytime, where other hosts encouraged their scandal-ridden guests to fight. But viewers were ready for something new. With the O. J. Simpson trial airing during the day, no family feud could keep up with that saga. Rosie's pitch was simple counter-programming: "A lot of Broadway, a lot of singing, and no celebrity gets hurt," she recalled. "It was a celebrity safe zone, just like Merv was." She remembered watching his show as a child. "I thought afterwards that Merv, Tony Bennett, and Sammy Davis were going to get something to eat and have a drink. I wish I was at that restaurant."

The formula for Rosie's success was that she was your thirtysomething best friend. She was famous, but not so famous that you couldn't imagine hanging out with her. She seemed genuinely humbled and excited to be around entertainment legends, from Elaine Stritch to Celine Dion. That enthusiasm came across in the show's opening, which featured an animated Rosie soaring through the streets of Manhattan, a wink at the credits of *Bewitched.* In public back then, Rosie was America's favorite kid sister, cousin, and daughter all rolled into one. Off camera, like most comedians, she was different. At the mall, she'd notice how strangers would come up and ask why she wasn't smiling the way she did on TV. Rosie demanded a lot from her army of producers. She could be aloof and exacting. If they failed to deliver precisely what she had envisioned, from elaborate games with the audience to off-the-cuff musicals, she tended to lose her temper.

"She did hold people to a very high standard," said her friend Janette Barber, who eventually became the head writer on the show. "The way I used to say it was, 'If you fuck up, you're gone. If you make a mistake, then you have a chance to fix it.'"

Rosie was born in Commack, Long Island, as the middle child—the Jan Brady—of five kids. Show business was always an escape from the bleak reality of her youth. She watched soap operas with her nana and took the train to Manhattan to catch Broadway matinees, collecting all the *Playbills* under her bed. One of her fondest memories was coming home from school to her idol Barbra Streisand's albums. Her mom, Roseann, adored Streisand, an infatuation O'Donnell clung to in the pit of her heart. After her mom died from breast cancer in 1973, ten-year-old Rosie used to imagine what it would be like if Streisand had gotten sick instead. Rosie thought that Streisand's fame and wealth would have unlocked a cure.

Rosie was expected to pitch in around the house and care for her younger siblings. But she was dealing with another darkness. As a little girl, Rosie was sexually abused by her father, Edward Joseph. Although she'd identified herself as a victim in her 2002 memoir *Find Me,* she never publicly named her father as the perpetrator until now. "It started very young," Rosie said. "And then when my mother died, it sort of ended in a weird way, because then he was with these five children to take care of. On the whole, it's not something I like to talk about. Of course, it changes everyone. Any child who is put in that position, especially by someone in the family, you feel completely powerless and stuck, because the person who you would tell is the person doing it."

Rosie wasn't the best student, but she had a knack for comedic timing. In high school, she started playing clubs on Long Island. In 1984, she scored big as a contestant on the second season of *Star Search,* on which she became a semifinalist in the comedy round. That led to acting opportunities, and a stint as a VH1 VJ; she wrote her own riffs between music videos (excellent training for any would-be talk show host). By the early nineties, Rosie boasted a formidable movie career, with roles in *A League of Their Own, Sleepless in Seattle,* and *The Flintstones.* (The less said about *Exit to Eden,* the better.)

Between films, in 1994, she starred as Rizzo in the Broadway revival of *Grease.* The show's musical director, John McDaniel, auditioned her at his home in Los Angeles, with the song "There Are Worse Things I Could Do." It was an apt choice. "She's not a great singer," McDaniel said. "She's an enthusiastic singer." He fibbed a little. "I called the producer in New York and told her that Rosie was fantastic, and we've been great friends ever since." The production was a smash. Rosie returned the favor a few years later by making McDaniel the bandleader on her show.

What made Rosie so relatable on TV could sometimes backfire. Her honesty could hurt others or herself. In a profile in *Cosmopolitan* around the time of her stint in *Grease,* she revealed to the writer Patrick Pacheco that she was single but open to dating women. "I wasn't ever lying to a gay reporter," Rosie said, looking back on that day. "I know he's gay. He knows I'm gay. And we both knew that we were in a culture that wasn't allowing you to talk about it." Her publicist at the time, Lois Smith, had to do damage control, calling *Cosmopolitan* editor in chief Helen Gurley Brown to get the quote extracted from the story. Rosie followed Smith's advice not to walk with her girlfriends down a red carpet. "Listen, this was not done out of homophobia," Rosie said. "It was done out of love and protection."

Rosie's original career plan was to continue to make films and eventually transition into the director's chair, a bold dream for a young woman in Hollywood. Her role models were Nora Ephron and Penny Marshall; Rosie had been directed by both. By her midthirties, she was pulled in another direction after she adopted her son Parker. On the set of the Nickelodeon film *Harriet the Spy,* in which she played the title character's nanny, she only saw Parker for an hour a day because of the hectic shooting schedule in Toronto. "I took my maid," Rosie said. "And when I came home from work, he wouldn't go out of the maid's arms and come to me. I called my agent and said, 'You need to get me a job where I can stay in New York City. I'm not doing another movie. He needs to be in his own crib. He needs his family around.'"

Rosie had filled in as a guest cohost on *Live with Regis and Kathie Lee.* She was intrigued by the more laid-back lifestyle of a morning talk show host, so she could have afternoons and evenings free to spend with her son. Kathie Lee Gifford was rumored to be about to step down (she didn't until five years later, in 2000). "I said, 'If that's really true, tell them I'll

do it!'" Rosie said. "Then she decided to stay." Rosie figured she could try
it on her own. Did she really need a cohost?

In addition to *The Rosie O'Donnell Show* being a safe haven for stars,
Rosie wanted it to feel like a late-night show that aired during the day.
"Nobody had done this yet, so it seemed like a far-off thing," Rosie said.
She promised not to stoke any controversies. "I was not really known for
anything political at the time as much as I was just a truth-telling comic,
who was funny and round."

The pitch attracted widespread interest around Hollywood. "A lot of
people were after her," said Hilary Estey McLoughlin, the former president of the production company Telepictures, who met with Rosie. "I guess
we talked her into it." The company's leader, Jim Paratore, was an enter-
prising producer who later created talk shows for Ellen DeGeneres and
Tyra Banks, among others (and also launched *TMZ*). Rosie's contract stip-
ulated that she wouldn't trash-talk like on *Jerry Springer*. She negotiated
an up-front salary of $1 million and potentially much more through sig-
nificant ownership of the show, which would be syndicated and sold to the
networks. "I said, 'I want the Oprah deal,'" Rosie remembered. "And, yeah,
I got a lot of money. More money than a human needs in a lifetime."

Rosie had only one choice for her executive producer. When she had
appeared on *Late Night with David Letterman* to do stand-up comedy, she
felt safe with a young producer named Daniel Kellison. "I think you'd be a
perfect fit for it," she told him. The Telepictures executives thought he was
too green, but they flew him first-class from New York to Rosie's home in Los
Angeles for a meeting. "Jim and Hilary are there," Kellison said. "Jim starts
in and says, 'You're too young. You don't have much experience. We're
talking to a lot of people.'"

Then Rosie strolled into the room. "I already told Daniel he's my choice.
I hate everyone else."

"And Jim and Hilary looked sick," Kellison said. "All of a sudden, their
negotiation went out the window."

Kellison's agent, James "Baby Doll" Dixon (who went on to represent

A-listers such as Jon Stewart and Stephen Colbert), urged him to play hard-ball. "He goes, 'Rosie is going to call you. Don't call her back.' Ugh. Okay." It worked exactly according to their plan. "They are going crazy." Within a few days, Kellison had been offered a massive deal. "It was a pretty outra-geous amount," he said, laughing. He also received a stake in the show, which vested over time. When Kellison told Letterman about the offer, the late-night host gave him his blessing. "Letterman was my hero and I hadn't been planning on leaving." Kellison had worked on *Late Night* for eight years right out of college. "I remember when I left, there was a case of wine on my chair. It was a Château Lafite Rothschild from 1982, worth more than one hundred thousand dollars."

The hiring spree for *The Rosie O'Donnell Show* resembled that for a buzzy internet start-up. Producers arrived through unconventional routes. Some came from magazines, with the (flawed) thinking that journalists could help pre-interview guests. Others were comedian friends that Rosie had met on the nightclub circuit. Caissie St. Onge, who served as Letterman's assistant, went to see Rosie in Manhattan on a rainy afternoon. "I was wear-ing a silk skirt," St. Onge said. "I got splashed by a truck on the way over. I went to my interview covered in mud."

Rosie didn't care. She was playing a video game on her computer. "I have to finish this or else it will make me crazy," she told St. Onge. "Plus, I'm a little nervous meeting new people."

Rosie broke the ice by complimenting St. Onge, telling her that she reminded her of her little sister Maureen. "We got into a talk," St. Onge said, "about how people would say to her, 'Not to insult you, but you look like Rosie O'Donnell.' I said, 'I would not be insulted to be told that I looked like her.'" And just like that, Rosie had a new assistant.

Rosie was up-front with her colleagues about who she was. "Being gay was never the hardest part of my life," Rosie said. "My childhood was. This is 1995. Nobody's out." She felt a financial responsibility to disclose her sexual orientation to the executives at Telepictures. "I said, 'I want you to know, before you invest this money in me,'" Rosie recalled. "'I don't want you to come to me in three months and go, "Oh my God, the *National Enquirer* has this thing."'"

Rosie had clear guidelines for how she'd talk about her personal life. She never pretended that she was sleeping with men. Even when she discussed her crush on Cruise, she made it clear that she had no sexual interest in him. She'd blush as she described her ultimate fantasy—she wanted him to come over to her house and mow the lawn with his shirt off. "It's one thing to say that I am," Rosie told Barber. "It's another thing to say, 'I'm not.' And that I won't do. If I'm not going to tell my truth, I'm sure as hell not going to tell a lie."

On the morning of June 10, 1996, at 10:00 a.m., Rosie O'Donnell made her grand entrance through a blue curtain on the eighth floor of 30 Rockefeller Center, in the same studio that Phil Donahue once occupied. "Hiiiii!" she welcomed viewers in a casual black pantsuit matched with a red shirt. "I felt like Jerry Springer," she said on TV, after the audience gave her a standing ovation. "You ever notice, his show, they stand up every day? My show is going to be different. It is! Today on *The Rosie O'Donnell Show,* women who sleep with their in-laws. Kidding! Hahaha. Just a joke."

The atmosphere on *The Rosie O'Donnell Show* resembled that of the world's happiest kindergarten class. Her wooden desk looked on TV as if it were designed by Toys "R" Us, with a collection of action figures, PEZ dispensers, and Koosh balls that she flung into the audience. The tourists in her studio were bribed into clapping with free gifts (books, CDs, Broadway tickets) and snacks—such as the Ding Dongs and chocolate milk under their chairs to keep them caffeinated. In later seasons, the prizes got bigger. "We would give people cars," said McLoughlin, who later took over as the second (of four) executive producers on the show. "People would not like the cars they got; it didn't have the specs they wanted. She would tell us to go back and get the car they wanted."

Each morning, three producers checked her desk, to make sure all her props were in order. Rosie had a digital music player, before the iPod had been invented, that allowed her to cue to some of her favorite songs (her playlist included Streisand's "People," Savage Garden's "I Want You," and Ricky Martin's "Livin' la Vida Loca"). She loved to mouth along to the words whenever she felt inspired. Each episode began with an introduction from a member of the audience. Rosie had a knack for improvising with strangers, which she'd developed from her years on the road. After a few minutes of that, she took a seat, to dish about what she'd done the previous night or to share stories about her kids. Rosie called this part of the show *chuffa*, a term she borrowed from director Garry Marshall that referred to actors filling in their dialogue on the day of a scene. Finally, it was time for the interviews—a roster of three or four guests that ranged from genuine stars to nostalgia TV. She launched her first show with George Clooney (after calling in a favor to Warner Bros., which produced her show and *ER*), Toni Braxton, and Susan Lucci.

Just as *The View* did a year later, *The Rosie O'Donnell Show* debuted in the summer so it wouldn't face stiff competition. However, unlike *The View*, Rosie didn't need to worry about her initial ratings. She was an overnight hit. "I always say, arrogantly, it surprised everybody except for me," Barber said. "I had seen her at the mall. I saw what happened with her and people." On the set of *A League of Their Own*, for example, Madonna originally drew the biggest cheers from the two thousand extras in the stands. "By the end of the month, Rosie would walk out and it would be like the second coming of Christ," Barber said. "Joan Rivers was like that, too. She would take that extra minute; she would remember them. They felt they were her."

Rosie's show changed daytime TV. It made networks reevaluate what the stay-at-home moms wanted to see. "I don't think we had established definitively that a daytime talk show was for women," said the comedian Judy Gold, who took a job as a human-interest producer on the show. "That was the result of Rosie." She cleared the path for a wave of celebrities to test the waters with their own family-friendly vehicles, from Roseanne Barr to Tony Danza to Bonnie Hunt. Even Oprah had to rejigger the content of her show, covering fewer tabloid stories and more celebrity interviews—and products, such as her annual Christmas list of favorite things. If it weren't for Rosie, DeGeneres might not have followed suit, with her dance moves and shopping trips to CVS with Michelle Obama.

Rosie wasn't just an influencer. She was also a tastemaker. After she showed her audience a Tickle Me Elmo doll, it became the sold-out holiday toy of 1996, fetching thousands of dollars on eBay. She sang songs about getting a mammogram for breast cancer month, which saved lives. She conducted one of the first interviews in the US with J. K. Rowling, after Rosie discovered *Harry Potter* before the rest of us. At the end of their talk, she gave Rowling a home computer (a Mac desktop) because Rosie felt bad that the future billionaire wrote her novels in longhand.

Even if Rosie didn't say the word *gay* out loud, *The Rosie O'Donnell Show* had its host's identity proudly on display. "I remember saying to John McDaniel, 'My God, if anybody knew how gay this show was,'" Gold said. "I mean, it was the gayest show ever!" On any given day, there was never a shortage of chorus boys or interviews with the likes of Richard Simmons or Liza Minnelli. McDaniel had a partner at the time, but he wasn't allowed to mention him on TV. "I had been out since I was in elementary school," he said. "It was weird to be in a situation where we weren't allowed to talk about it."

DeGeneres came out in 1997, which marked a turning point in the culture. "I remember thinking, 'Well, she's going to ruin her whole career,'" Rosie said. "And then she came on my show, and I said, 'I got to figure out a way to stand next to her so that everybody in the know is going to know I'm not leaving her out there alone.'" Rosie devised a clever exchange, in which DeGeneres revealed the character on her sitcom is Lebanese. ("Maybe I'm Lebanese?" Rosie retorted.) "Every time I'd watch Matt Lauer accuse somebody of sexual impropriety, I thought to myself, 'You hypocritical fuck,'" Rosie said. "I never wanted to be a hypocritical fuck."

Despite all her success, Rosie couldn't ease up on the gas pedal. "It was a shit ton of pressure on Rosie at all times," Kellison said. She arrived in the studio at 6:00 a.m. each day to prepare. So did the people around her, which could be grueling for a staff largely composed of nocturnal animals. "I was in my early thirties and I'm tasked with running this multimillion-dollar corporation," Kellison said. "There are a hundred-plus employees, and I had never managed anything like that before."

His father-in-law—who worked as a partner in a Boston bank—sent him a stack of management books. His favorite tidbit of advice came from *How to Win Friends and Influence People*. "This thing Dale Carnegie said, if there's one magic sentence to stop someone in their tracks and have them be sympathetic with you, it's this: 'I don't blame you for being mad at me. If I were you, I'd be mad at me, too.' I remember going to Rosie's office. She was really upset about something."

Kellison used the line. "It's okay, Daniel," she said. "You've got to be more careful about these things." Its effectiveness eventually wore off as he kept getting things wrong for her.

Some of Rosie's biggest clashes were with her directors. Even as she hosted a live TV show, she kept an eye on the monitors behind the cameras at all times, calling out which shots she wanted with her own unique hand gestures. "Bob I yelled at every day," Rosie said about one of her directors. "I'm admitting it. I couldn't believe I'm watching TV and there are little kids doing an Irish jig and he's not on their feet or their faces." She didn't like another director she remembered now as "this really old man" who used to work for Merv Griffin. He kept telling her, "You guys are reinventing television." But he couldn't keep up with Rosie's pace.

She cycled through four directors in her first seven months. "At a certain point, it's diminishing returns," Kellison said. "There are only so many people who can do this sort of work, and it's an imprecise art."

Rosie was furious one day when a producer patched in a call from the mayor of Philadelphia, who was supposed to offer her the keys to the city. This turned out to be a prank. The voice on the other end was Captain

Janks from *Howard Stern,* who berated her. "Howard Stern said you were a fat pig," Captain Janks said on live television. "Oh, really?" Rosie responded, as all the blood drained from her face. She was devastated that her team had let the call through without properly vetting it.

Megastardom had other drawbacks. Rosie couldn't appear in public without creating a mob scene. The paparazzi would stalk her on vacations. "I went to Florida for my birthday and they got pictures of me on my Jet Ski," Rosie said. "I was with some lesbians I knew from LA."

When she returned to work, Kellison pulled out a tabloid that had run the photographs. "They got you," he sighed. "What are we going to do?"

"I said to myself, 'I'm going to get a new executive producer,'" Rosie recalled. She fired Kellison and replaced him with McLoughlin, who lasted a year before going back to Los Angeles to Telepictures. Next arrived former *View* producer Roni Selig, who also didn't work out. The duties of overseeing the show finally fell to Rosie's longtime manager Bernie Young, a former police detective. That's how tough you had to be to keep Rosie protected. "It just came down to one day, she said, 'Look, man, you take the job,'" Young said.

If an employee met Rosie's standards, she could be a selfless and giving boss. Rosie told St. Onge that she stressed her out as an assistant, but Rosie eventually let her audition as a writer, where she thrived. To accommodate her mostly female staff, Rosie built a full day-care center in the corner of her studio, so that parents could bring their kids (age one and older) to work as she did with Parker. The babysitting services were free of charge. When St. Onge couldn't find her son there one morning, she was told he'd gone to the stage to watch Destiny's Child rehearse. "Tell your mom what I told you how to say," one of the singers said. St. Onge's son responded with glee, "Beyoncé is my fiancée!" Hugh Jackman stopped by to play blocks with the kids. "I think everyone wanted to see it because it was such a curiosity and so unheard of," St. Onge said.

The list of celebrities who needed Rosie to promote their latest projects never diminished. Rosie got in early on the careers of Britney Spears,

Jessica Simpson, Ricky Martin, and Justin Timberlake. They appeared alongside Hollywood titans such as Cher, Madonna, Julia Roberts, and Tom Cruise, whose arrival was marked by a cardboard countdown clock as the day approached. But nothing compared to her ultimate interview.

On November 21, 1997, Barbra Streisand received a whole hour on *The Rosie O'Donnell Show,* more time than Hillary Clinton. Rosie wanted to air the interview without any commercials, but Telepictures wouldn't allow it; they needed to pay the bills. Rosie burst into tears the moment Streisand walked onstage, saying that she felt as if her mother had come back to life. "I'm always wary about doing an interview with someone who is a big fan of mine because I don't want to disappoint them," Streisand told me. "I don't want the reality to step in, like, 'Am I a real person? I'm not twenty feet high and on a movie screen.'" Streisand was charmed by Rosie. "She's adorable."

Streisand likes to be shot from the left side of her face, so Rosie flipped her entire set so that Barbra would be seen from her best angle. Rosie even did it a few weeks early, to hide the true motive behind the redesign. Streisand admitted it years later: "She changed the chair to give me my good side."

"Listen to me," Rosie said, laughing. "I would do anything for her. She wanted it, and she wanted it covered up so you didn't know she was vain. I was, like, 'Done and done.' What else?" Rosie told me a story about how she caught Streisand's appearance on *Ellen* in 2017. Rosie was aghast that her hero had been relegated to the second guest spot, behind the actress Sofia Vergara. "I will never talk to Ellen again," Rosie said. "Such disrespect." She sent a message to Andy Lassner, DeGeneres's executive producer, who had worked on Rosie's talk show. The email read, *Go to hell.*

Every interaction with Rosie O'Donnell is a high-wire experience. When I first met her in 2006, she offered me a tour of her movie-star house on the Hudson River. She was especially proud of her kids' adjoining bathrooms, reminiscent of *The Brady Bunch*, and she didn't fuss with dressing up for a photo shoot. She cracked open a cupboard of snacks as she speculated about a celebrity guest that Rosie thought had come late for an appearance on live TV because she was on drugs. (Her wife at the time, Kelli, who was listening in from a nearby room, interrupted, "This is off-the-record, right?")

In 2007, Rosie attended a book signing at a Borders in Manhattan, and she electrified a crowd of housewives from New Jersey and Long Island. In 2009, over a phone call, she seemed touched when I told her I used to do my algebra homework in front of her show in high school. She asked me where I went to college. "You must be supersmart," she said. "What did you get on your SATs?" In 2014, we met at a restaurant on the Upper East Side, where she seemed hopeful about a number of things related to *The View*. When I saw her a few weeks later, she'd already changed her mind about everything she'd said.

In the spring of 2018, after months of sending me emails written in haiku about how she couldn't meet me, she agreed to a lunch. She arrived wearing a baggy hoodie from the musical *Hamilton*, offering me so much information in the first two minutes, I had to race to turn on my tape recorder. Even as she spoke freely, she was worried because of what happened to Donald Trump's former strategist Steve Bannon after the scandalous tell-all *Fire and Fury* hit the internet. "I don't lie," she said. "So I'm going to tell you too much and it's going to be bad for me in the end."

Her stories were packed with kaleidoscopic asides that overtook her original points. She was candid and raw, especially when she talked about her crippling depression: "I was watching *Homeland* last night, and I was, like, 'I wish I had bipolar.' It's so much more treatable with medication. It's so much more receptive to serotonin and dopamine. It's so much better than when you're just depressed and your body basically shuts down. It's like you're under the water and you can't find your way to the surface."

In 1999, at the height of her talk show fame, Rosie had a breakdown.

She traced the cause to the Columbine High School massacre that took the lives of twelve students and one teacher. "I went on medication, antidepressants," Rosie recalled. "I had always had depression, but I did the Irish thing of having some beers and put your boots on, girl. And then I fell through the ice. I was finally famous and powerful, and in my world that came with a magic wand for justice. I was going to cure a lot of diseases. I was going to call all the famous billionaire women; we were going to form the Justice League of Women. We were going to go around like Emily's List on steroids and fix these social ills. That's what I thought came with fame."

She understood that this notion about fame, which she'd carried with her since childhood, was an illusion. "When I realized I could do nothing about children being murdered in school and their bloody bodies flip-flopping out of the second floor, I had some sort of break. I couldn't sleep. I couldn't eat. I couldn't stop crying. I had dreams that there were people in my house. I woke up every twenty minutes. I was a mess. In hindsight, I probably should have been hospitalized."

She went to see a psychopharmacologist, who prescribed her the antidepressant Effexor. "I said, 'How long am I going to take this?' She said, 'The rest of your life.' I said, 'That seems harsh.'"

Rosie struggled to pretend to be happy on TV each day. She finally erupted on May 19, 1999, during an interview with Tom Selleck that turned into a discussion about the National Rifle Association. He was there to promote his movie, the romantic comedy *The Love Letter,* and she tried to ask him about gun control.

"You can't say that guns don't bear a responsibility," Rosie said, in a debate that still feels relevant twenty years later. She wanted to know why the NRA supported assault rifles. "This is a gun that can shoot five bullets in a second."

"I can't speak for the NRA," Selleck huffed.

"But you're a spokesperson, Tom. You have to be responsible for what they say."

"Now you're questioning my humanity."

Rosie's confrontation turned into breaking news, a window into an activist persona that later defined her on *The View.* "There were personal attacks on me and my family," Rosie said about the NRA. "They are a terrifying group, and they know how to shut people up."

As her talk show entered its later seasons, Rosie tried to stretch in different directions. She was less interested in celebrities and more focused on how to make a difference. She invented the segments Super Kids, in which she spotlighted young people from disadvantaged backgrounds; Chub Club (weight loss); and one on adoption. Feeling burnt out, she told her producers that she spoke with Oprah, and the two had decided to merge their talk shows, so they could each take half a year off. The idea never came to fruition because *The Oprah Winfrey Show* was owned by Harpo, a different production company.

In 2000, Rosie proudly endorsed Al Gore on TV, despite her promise to Telepictures not to get wrapped up in politics. The week of the election, she intervened on behalf of Streisand, who got into a dispute with Barbara Walters. "I went on her show the Friday before the election," Streisand said of a conversation that aired on *20/20.* "I remember saying, 'There are three reasons to vote for Al Gore. One, the Supreme Court. Two, the Supreme Court. Three, the Supreme Court.' And when I saw it on television, I was so deeply disappointed because it was edited." Walters blamed ABC for the cuts. "She said, 'Channel Seven made her do it,'" Streisand recalled. To help, Rosie aired a political PSA that Streisand had created. When the network tried to stop her, Rosie put her career on the line, threatening to not sign her contract extension and to end her show.

She'd stay only two more years. Paratore kept offering her more money, but Rosie knew that six seasons was all she had in her. She wanted to retire and take the spotlight away from her kids. "When I left my show, I had enough money that I never had to work again my entire life. I don't look at the money. I don't know how much I get paid," she said, referring to her acting roles.

The final curtain on Rosie's talk show would come down in the summer of 2002. In March, as her days on daytime were dwindling, Rosie came out of the closet to protest a law in Florida that banned adoption by gay couples. She gave the interview to Diane Sawyer, choosing her over another eager colleague. "Barbara is a legend and that can never be taken away from her," Rosie said. "But she's older than Diane." Barbara, never one to tolerate losing a scoop, revealed on *The View* on February 14 that she'd always known Rosie was gay and that she supported Rosie. Since Sawyer's prime-time special wouldn't air for another month, Barbara managed to insert herself in the story.

To replace Rosie, the producers at Telepictures looked everywhere, hoping that her program could continue with a new host the way that *The Tonight Show* had. On the short list was Joy Behar, who had subbed for a couple of days when Rosie had been sick. But Joy declined the offer, and the comedian Caroline Rhea took a shot at it. She was canceled after one season because "she didn't connect in the same way," McLoughlin said.

Looking back, Joy wished that she had made a different decision: "When Rosie O'Donnell left her show, Hilary wanted me to take over. I said, 'I'm on *The View*. I've got a steady gig. I don't know if I feel like bothering with that.' And I didn't do it. I regret it. I wish I had jumped in. I think I would have done a pretty good job."

12

All Aboard!

After a blissful four years of soaking in the Miami sun and spending time with her kids, Rosie O'Donnell isn't sure why she agreed to return to daytime TV. "*The View* was a laughable program," Rosie told me. "They had no respect and no one thought anything about it." As evidence, she pointed to a never-released documentary she made about producing the Broadway musical *Taboo,* with Boy George. It was filmed in the days after she exited her talk show. "There's a part," Rosie said, "where someone says, 'Cut to you in ten years. Where will you be?' I go, 'Probably a host on the fucking *View.* Can you imagine that!' Guess what? I have it on tape from 2002."

Like the other women that came before her, Rosie was sold on *The View* strictly because of Barbara. But Rosie became the first A-list cohost to board the daytime talk show. Rosie didn't need money or fame; she had both in abundance. She was after something else. She saw Barbara as a mother figure, which is how she pictured every older female celebrity— from Bette Midler to Joni Mitchell to Florence Henderson—whom Rosie remembered from her childhood.

Barbara needed help, so Rosie switched into martyr mode. She couldn't say no: "I loved her and I wanted to work with her. I never, ever, thought for a moment that Barbara Walters didn't love me. But sometimes my big love overwhelms people."

But Rosie and Barbara had different ways of looking at the world. Barbara characterized their relationship with more hesitation. "Rosie O'Donnell is a great talent," she told me. "She also has, shall we say, emotional problems."

Rosie's arrival at *The View* was marked by turbulence from the start. And not only because producers learned that she was the new moderator while they were in the air, flying from New York to Los Angeles for the Daytime Emmys in April 2006. The idea was that Rosie would appear with Barbara onstage at the awards show as presenters, where they'd make the surprise casting reveal about *The View*'s fall season. But the story got leaked a few days early. As the *View* staff reclined in their seats, teetering above the earth, they saw a breaking report on Fox News. "This is how we find out?" they gasped, scurrying back and forth in the aisle to discuss the latest development.

After they landed, Geddie called an emergency meeting at the hotel. Since they couldn't go to the bar, for fear of eavesdroppers, he assembled his team in a vacant parking lot for a pep talk. Geddie acknowledged that Rosie was notorious for being difficult ("We had all heard horror stories," one staffer recalled), but he tried to reassure them that she'd turned a corner.

He'd taken a long meeting at her apartment in Hell's Kitchen, where he'd been up-front about his concerns. "I had friends who worked for you," he told her. "They said terrible things." She responded convincingly that she had changed: "I was a different person then. I am on different meds now."

"And I believed her," Geddie said.

Only a small group of people knew about Barbara's plan; the cohosts were in the circle, but they had all been sworn to secrecy. In Los Angeles for the Daytime Emmys, Joy stopped at a gifting suite in the Renaissance

Hotel, where she inadvertently confirmed the news. "I was told, 'Don't tell anyone Rosie O'Donnell is coming on the show!' They said it a hundred times. But when I'm shopping, I lose consciousness," Joy confessed. A camera crew from *Entertainment Tonight* ambushed her, and Joy said she was thrilled to be Rosie's coworker. "Five minutes later, Barbara came over—she's shopping also—and says, 'Don't say a word about Rosie O'Donnell!' Oh my God, what did I do?" Joy begged *View* publicist Karl Nilsson to get the clip killed.

"What's going to happen?" Joy asked him.

"We're all going to die," Nilsson replied.

"I go back to my room, practically saying the rosary, even though I don't believe it," Joy said. "I get a call from Barbara."

Entertainment Tonight had already reached out to tell Barbara that they knew that Rosie was the new cohost. "And guess who told them?" Barbara hissed.

"Meredith Vieira?" Joy said with a lump in her throat.

"No, Joy! I want you to know I'm not renewing your contract." Barbara hung up.

"I was, like, 'Okay,'" Joy recalled. "'I'll get another job.' But then she changed her mind ten minutes later."

By the time Barbara and Rosie appeared onstage on the night of April 28, their announcement was the worst-kept secret in Hollywood. They were TV's newest power couple. Barbara, acting maternal for a split second, helped Rosie pick out her outfit—a black suit with scarf-length golden-striped lapels that looked like something the students at Hogwarts would wear. Later on, Joy, Meredith (who was about to leave for *Today*), and some producers met in a hotel room for drinks. "What is Rosie going to be like?" they asked, with fear and curiosity in their voices.

It was a fair question. In her four-year break from show business, Rosie had become an enigma. True to her word, she'd shunned the spotlight and kept a low profile. "I was drinking a lot of beer," Rosie said. "I was smoking joints in Miami when I was down there; going on my boat, looking at dolphins. It was a fucking perfect existence. It was glorious. And everybody in my world got to enjoy it." Her only interaction with the public was through her blog. Before Twitter, Rosie kept in touch with her fans by posting photos and answering their questions in late-night insomniac sessions.

Rosie was so under the radar, ABC was initially cold to the idea of hiring her. "I don't know," said Brian Frons, the president of the network's daytime division. She'd done a few stints as a guest cohost. "We had her on," he recalled. "She seemed a little flat." He asked to talk to her on the phone. "I was blown away," Frons said. "What was so amazing about her is that she was a host, but she talked like an executive producer. She said, 'When I sit on that stage, I'm going to make every one of these people better.' And then she proceeded to say how."

Rosie decided that Joy looked too disconnected and bored. She wanted her to dive headfirst into the Hot Topics discussions instead of simply delivering punch lines. Rosie was determined to find a way for Elisabeth Hasselbeck to grow. "It can't just be opinion," Rosie told Frons. "It can't just be arguing. I'll make her better. I'll be her friend," which wasn't expected, given their differing political views. Above anything else, Rosie wanted to shield Barbara.

Something had gotten lost in translation during the negotiations. Barbara and Bill thought they were hiring a new moderator, who'd be part of the group. Rosie, who agreed to a single-year contract, had a different vision. She thought Barbara needed to be rescued. Or, to use another metaphor, Rosie was the guest you invite for cocktails who decides she's going to renovate your entire kitchen.

"You should never really go into someone else's house and tell them how to rearrange their furniture," Rosie said. "And that's something that was very hard for me to learn because I had been an actor in an ensemble, and I knew how to do that. I've never had a negative word about me on the set of any single show involving acting. But when I'm in charge, as I was in my household as a little child with a dead mother, I try to get it done. I knew how to fix the show. And part of it was getting Bill Geddie to shut up and take a step back."

Despite their earlier chat, Rosie quickly turned on Geddie. She thought he was riding on Barbara's coattails for fame and a paycheck. "He was an idiot," Rosie said. "He was this guy who had got on this legend and had never done anything on his own that was in any way notable. He was this misogynistic alpha male who thought he was better than the women. That's my feeling. He never fired anyone and bought their loyalty, like they were cult members. And the show never got to progress artistically."

Rosie's biggest clashes were with the director. Just as she viciously argued with whoever held that job on her own show, she and Mark Gentile quickly took opposite sides. On a quiet morning in August, Gentile was making preparations for Season 10 when he got an unexpected visitor. "The door opens on the side, and in walks Rosie with one of her little lieutenants," Gentile said. "She barks out her first words—not *hello*, not *hi*."

"Who said it should look like a house?" Rosie berated him about the set. "It shouldn't look like a house. It's a TV studio." With that, she left.

Gentile was shocked. "We all sat there. I was, like, 'What the hell was that?'"

Rosie was now managing every detail of the latest makeover by herself. "It looked like a nanny's living room," Rosie said about the beige paint on the walls. "So we had a set designer come in and they made it blue, and I thought it looked beautiful." She rearranged the chairs in the audience in a U-shape, which made the *View* stage seem more intimate. She insisted on regular giveaways for the audience, and she had a machine installed to drop confetti on the stage.

In her last daytime venture, Telepictures had urged her to stay away from politics. But on *The View*, the out and proud Rosie wouldn't be holding back. The country was divided at the time, after George W. Bush had invaded Iraq under the false pretense of weapons of mass destruction. "I had a little kid I was picking up at school every day, and every mother was talking about what was happening with Bush," Rosie said. She was determined to bring those conversations to daytime TV.

~

On September 5, 2006, Rosie O'Donnell reinvigorated *The View* as the show's next moderator. "Like it or not, here I come," she declared in a pre-recorded clip before the opening credits. She walked out onstage, her arms locked with Barbara's, as if they were long-lost girlfriends. In the weeks ahead, the gap between them during their entrances would grow wider apart.

In the minutes before the show, Rosie paced backstage. She'd secured Jessica Simpson as the first guest, a big celebrity in 2006. But Gentile had reshuffled the audience so the teenage groupies were all seated near the stage to watch the musical performance by Simpson. Rosie was worried the crowd was too young to root for her. "Where are my people?" she asked Gentile. "Where are the fatties?" He didn't know what to say. "Of course, I never even thought of that," he said, remembering the exchange.

There was no need for alarm. As soon as she walked out, Rosie was met with rock-star applause. "I ask you, for heaven's sake, what is all the fuss about?" Barbara said, already looking uncertain about her new hire.

"Well, it's about our new set," Rosie said, quickly channeling her lovable daytime-TV persona. "What do you think?" This led to more clapping.

"Do you think we should introduce you?" Barbara said, not able to repress her controlling nature. "Or is that unnecessary?"

"Okay. My name is Meredith Vieira, and welcome to *The View*." Rosie chatted about how she was wearing heels to fit in and why she let her hair grow out, after a bad buzz cut scared all of America. Rosie then pointed to a big bouquet of flowers displayed on the stage, which had been sent to her by her old crush.

"We have so much to talk about today, so we should put Tom for to-morrow," Barbara awkwardly interrupted.

Rosie stayed true to her word about what she'd accomplish on *The View*. She coaxed out stories from Elisabeth about potty training her kids and from Joy about her daughter's engagement, all the while cracking jokes. Rosie then enthusiastically talked about her own gay family. ("It was a vivid contrast to Ellen DeGeneres, who never alludes to her sexuality on her talk show," the *New York Times*'s TV critic at the time, Alessandra Stanley, wrote in a glowing review.) Rosie's then wife Kelli was in the audience, and Rosie had her four kids to rely on for endless anecdotes. The ladies even addressed a tabloid report that Barbara had spotted a mean haiku on Rosie's blog and they were already feuding.

"I have never read a blog," said Barbara.

"I was saying that I felt powerless and that I was a little scared to come on *The View*," Rosie confessed. "I was just being dramatic and emotional."

Barbara asked how Rosie felt four minutes into her new gig.

"Really excited to be here and kind of ecstatic!" Rosie blushed. "I'm just happy that we're all here together."

So was the rest of the country. That premiere for Season 10 of *The View* landed 4.2 million viewers, the most-watched episode in the show's history (a considerable jump from the 2.7 million viewers it attracted the previous season). In the months ahead, Rosie would bring a 17 percent increase in viewership. With numbers like that, Barbara and Bill had their hands tied. Regardless of their personal feelings for Rosie, ABC wasn't about to let its new star slip away.

Rosie's edition of *The View* was appointment TV. She continually opposed Bush's policies, defended LGBTQ rights, and advocated for feminism, more than a decade before #MeToo and Time's Up. Other TV outlets from *Access Hollywood* to Fox News started covering *The View* nightly. "I went in there being me," Rosie said. "Like, the Michael Jordan of daytime is going to come in and help this team. I tried to fix the show, and many would say I did."

Politics aside, Rosie still relied on many of her old producing tricks, which worked like a charm. She had the cast of Broadway's *Beauty and the Beast* make a secret appearance for Barbara's birthday, wheeling out a humongous cake to the tune of "Be Our Guest." On another day, Rosie featured a twelve-year-old girl with cystic fibrosis and asked her to mouth along to a song from *Rent,* her favorite musical. After the first lyric, Rosie had the cast magically appear behind the girl. The segment was such a feel-good tearjerker that ABC put it in their press kit to show to advertisers. "Rosie had a lot of heart," Frons said. "This is great TV. It's not *Game of Thrones,* but it's great."

Behind the scenes, the mood actually resembled that HBO saga. Two teams had emerged: those who were with Rosie, including her writer Janette Barber, who had come over from *The Rosie O'Donnell Show,* and those who were against Rosie. Producers brainstormed about how to get on her good side. Since she had a soft spot for single moms and gay men, those who qualified tried to play up their personal stories with her. One straight male producer even joked that he would pretend to convert so that he could keep his job. But the biggest mystery of all was how Rosie and Elisabeth had become such fast friends. Elisabeth attended her first Broadway show with Rosie and was invited to Rosie's house for playdates with their kids. They got so close that Joy speculated that Rosie must have a crush on Elisabeth.

"It was a completely different show," Joy said. "It became a lot about Rosie O'Donnell. She's a very dominant personality. She basically came in like Hurricane Katrina and she did change the show a lot. I wasn't crazy about it."

Joy pointed to all the tensions: "There was a lot of difficulty backstage. There was acrimony between her and the director. Her and the executive producer weren't getting along. Suddenly, she comes in and tells people, 'You have to do this.' And all of a sudden, I have to do something that I was not prepared to do—like sing and dance. That makes me anxious. I feel as though I'm being bullied."

Barbara, who came and went as her schedule permitted, saw her grip on the show loosening. The other cohosts no longer needed her to bail them out of tricky situations—since Rosie's star power arguably eclipsed Barbara's. At other times, Rosie was the rebellious daughter that couldn't be reined in. On mornings when Barbara did work at *The View*, she would shuffle in her robe from her dressing room to Rosie's across the hall, pounding on the door. Rosie liked to blast music on her laptop as she got her hair done. "Turn it down!" Barbara would mutter.

Geddie's influence also lessened. Rosie didn't trust his judgment on a number of things, starting with the selection of Hot Topics. "There would be a school shooting and he'd want to do lipsticks," she said. Rosie characterized those interactions by saying, "What the fuck do you know what women like? You don't know."

She refused to wear an earpiece, which the producers used to communicate with the talent during the live show. Rosie thought it destroyed their ability to spontaneously interact, and she urged the other cohosts to join her boycott. Rosie would tell most of the staff how frustrated she was with Gentile, for whom she'd falsely made up a diagnosis of autism. (She loved to play doctor, despite her lack of qualifications.) She knew that he stayed up all night to create sets for the musical acts, which were beautiful. But she was critical about most of his other decisions, especially his screen cuts. Gentile always thought Rosie held a grudge because he'd turned down her offer to join *The Rosie O'Donnell Show*. He once overheard Rosie complaining to Joy about that.

Rosie has a different reason for why they didn't get along. She recalled coming to a meeting and seeing a baby in a producer's arms. "Is this Mark's baby?" she asked the woman who had been having an affair with him. Suddenly, the room went silent, and the whole staff looked at Rosie with disgust. Although Barbara knew about the relationship, along with everyone else, the unspoken rule was to never mention it. "Listen, can my style be abrasive in a community where secrets are paramount and reality is distorted and you don't know the rules of the cult? And you would never join one?" Rosie asked rhetorically. She nodded. ("That's not the reason we hated Rosie," one producer said. "We hated Rosie because she's a terrible person.")

During her first three months, Rosie made a huge impact in the day-time-TV landscape. She ignited a series of controversies, which only fanned interest in *The View*. She upset conservatives by saying "radical Christianity is just as threatening as radical Islam in a country like America where we have separation of church and state." She attempted a tone-deaf imitation of Chinese people, which many viewers found offensive. And she objected to how Kelly Ripa had spoken to *American Idol* finalist Clay Aiken. He was filling in for Regis Philbin on *Live with Regis and Kelly* when, in the middle of an interview, he covered Ripa's mouth to quiet her down. "I don't know where that hand's been, honey," Ripa told him.

While the clip had generated some attention, Rosie made it go viral with her own interpretation. On November 21, she went on *The View* and called Ripa's remark homophobic. "If that was a straight man, if that was a cute man, if that was a guy that she didn't question his sexuality, she would have said a different thing," Rosie lectured. "I was offended by that." Making the situation even more complicated, Aiken hadn't publicly come out of the closet yet.

Rosie had her say. The episode had moved on, with Rosie offering all members of the audience signed programs from the opening night of *Mary Poppins*. But Ripa's stern voice came crackling into the studio over a speaker. Ripa had called producer Alexandra Cohen, whose phone number Ripa had from their years of taking cigarette breaks together. Without asking for Rosie's approval, Geddie decided to patch Ripa through.

"Listen, I'm watching the show," Ripa said. "Rosie, I love you dearly. I have to strongly disagree. I think what you said is downright outrageous."

"Well, Kel," Rosie said, looking annoyed, "I come from my perspective. You talk on your show. I talk on mine."

Ripa wasn't having it. "You know better. You should be more responsible."

"I'm just saying from where I sit as a gay person in the world, I have to tell you, that's how it came off to me," Rosie said with a frown.

Oddly enough, nobody had talked to Aiken about what he thought. "Let's ask him," Joy said sarcastically. "Call him tomorrow. Let's keep this thing going indefinitely."

Years later, for the first time, Rosie explained the backstory of why she had come to his defense. A few days before he went on *Live* he had been a guest on *The View*. "He had come into my dressing room, crying about whether or not to come out. And I sat down with him and I talked to him. There had been a scandal by this time of the army man, or whatever, website he was on," Rosie said, referencing a tabloid story about Aiken. "He was inching his way out in the way so many born-again Southern Christians have to. I hugged him. Not only do I feel the twenty-years-older mother thing, I feel the twenty-years-old younger-gay thing." When she saw Ripa on TV that day, Rosie couldn't bottle her anger.

"So I had just held a crying boy and then watched him be gay bashed by Kelly Ripa," Rosie said.

After the show, Rosie heard from Aiken. First, she said that he thanked her for defending him. And second: "I didn't know how to come out, so you just did it."

Aiken's recollection of these events is slightly different from Rosie's. "I have a horrible memory, but I know exactly how this shit went down," he told me. Aiken said he'd been worried about his interview on *The View*, because a prominent news anchor had warned him the cohosts might ask him about his sexuality on TV. But that didn't happen. Instead, Rosie invited Aiken to her dressing room to talk privately before the show, kicking out her makeup team and his bodyguard. "She said, 'You need to find yourself a boyfriend in North Carolina—not in New York or Los Angeles—and just live peacefully there.' I said, 'You're very presumptuous, Rosie.' She took my hand, looked me dead in the eye and with more warmth than I think people would imagine she has, she said, 'Listen, I'm your sister.' I teared up. It was the very first time a stranger had ever gotten me to come out to them."

As he left her dressing room, Rosie promised Aiken a shield of protection. "Nobody is going to ask you about this on the show," she said. "And if they do, just let this dyke take care of it."

But Aiken had no idea that Rosie would make his sexual orientation a talking point after the Ripa incident. "I didn't see it the same way that she did," he said. "The truth is she outed me in a way, because I had not been out yet. When she said the words, 'If that was a straight man,' she was confirming that she knew that I wasn't. That was the worst day of my life. I don't think I'd had a moment more devastating to me. I remember feeling like shit that day and totally deflated. But I definitely wasn't mad at her." Aiken said that Rosie later helped him officially come out on the cover of *People* in 2008, by introducing him to her publicist.

To me, Rosie didn't mince her words about Ripa: "I think Kelly Ripa is mean and she doesn't like me, and she has never wanted to discuss what happened. She wanted to have this weird feud." Rosie said that under normal circumstances, she would have bonded with Ripa through her *All My Children* lineage. "She's the girl from Pine Valley. She and her husband met on the show. That's my fucking sweet spot. I would have loved her my whole life." The two never mended fences after the *View* incident. "I see her at concerts sometimes," Rosie said. "She just looks away."

In the end, Rosie was most upset with *View* producers for connecting the call. The show hadn't done that before. "Bill Geddie thinks that makes good TV—two women fighting." Rosie confronted them about it. "I said, 'Excuse me, Dusty and Bill, that would be the first time that you sabotaged me live on the air. It will not happen again. If it does happen again, I will not be on the show." Rosie paused for dramatic effect. "When it happened again, I left."

13

Rosie vs. Donald

As a talk show host, Rosie O'Donnell was skilled in identifying trends early. Sure enough, she tried to warn us about Donald Trump's misogyny a decade before his presidency. She could never stomach his false swagger, braggadocio, and, later, endless gloating about his ratings for *The Apprentice*. After attending his 1993 wedding to Marla Maples at the Plaza Hotel (and hearing all the details about their divorce), she wouldn't book him as a guest on *The Rosie O'Donnell Show* because she thought he was a jerk. "He's the most absurdly transparent con man," Rosie told me. "He's dumb. His parents didn't like him; they sent him away to New York Military Academy. He punched his kid in the face at college," she said, referring to a 2016 Facebook post written by one of Donald Jr.'s former classmates. Rosie brought up stories about his neglecting his parental duties while he played a real estate mogul instead. "He never spoke to his children," she said. "I'm friendly with Marla, which is how I was at his wedding. I know the shit that he did."

When pressed for more details, Rosie hedged, for once. "I can't say it. You know why Marla doesn't say it? There are real reasons you don't say it. People are afraid of him." She leaned forward in her seat. "I am not."

That became abundantly clear on the morning of December 20, 2006. It was Christmas on *The View,* and the set was decked out like the North Pole with a giant tree and wreaths. The staff could use a bit of holiday cheer. After four months of walking on eggshells, there would be a hiatus, when the show could reset. Despite all the turmoil backstage, *The View*'s ratings were still riding high. Senator Hillary Clinton was in the studio that day, making her second appearance on the show. Her advisers had decided that she could use *The View* as a warm-up act, as she prepared to announce her bid as the first plausible female presidential candidate in US history. Clinton had agreed to sit through some chitchat, to gauge how she fared in the crossfire about what it was like to be a woman eyeing the nation's most powerful job. She'd be "revealing everything, from whether she wants to move back to the White House in '08 to what she really thinks of the war in Iraq," the show's announcer vowed.

Normally, nothing would have stopped Barbara from face time with a Clinton. But the senator's booking had materialized late, leaving Barbara adrift: she was on a Caribbean vacation, aboard a yacht with Judge Judy Sheindlin and Cindy Adams. Rosie was free to steer the show without any pushback. The guest cohost that day was entertainment lawyer Crystal McCrary Anthony, joining Joy Behar and Elisabeth Hasselbeck, who had fully adopted her new role as Rosie's work wife. It confounded most of the producers, including Bill Geddie, that they had become so close. "I remember Bill and I both shaking our heads when Rosie and Elisabeth decided to go together to buy the staff Christmas presents," said producer Alexandra Cohen. "They did it as a team, like, 'We're buddies.' Are you serious?"

In the Hot Topics meeting, Rosie was eager to pounce on a melodrama involving Donald Trump. For several days, tabloids had been following a story about how the winner of the Miss USA pageant, twenty-one-year-old Tara Conner, had been caught using cocaine and partying in Manhattan clubs, putting her crown in peril. Trump, as the owner of the contest, could have ceremoniously fired her. But why would he do that when he could bet on her sobriety in exchange for wall-to-wall publicity? On December 19, the day before Clinton's visit to *The View,* standing before a wooden podium with a white tarp from the Trump Organization in the background, he held a press conference during which he announced a lenient verdict. "Tara is going to be given a second chance," Trump said, botching the pronunciation of her name. "She's agreed to go into rehab." Trump hadn't notified Conner of his decision in advance, and she thought she was going to be flogged in public. She was so startled, she wept in front of the cameras, as she expressed her profound gratitude. It was, to Trump's delight, a clip that played all over cable news.

Rosie had no intention of following the other outlets, which had framed the saga as a happy ending. (Fox News's angle: "Still Miss USA.") "She said, 'We'll do something fun,'" Geddie remembered. Rosie gave him a taste of her Trump impersonation, flipping her hair to one side, to mimic his comb-over, and speaking in a thick New York accent that sounded like Barney Rubble on testosterone. "It made me laugh," Geddie admitted.

The show started. After a frenzied discussion in which Elisabeth confessed that she'd stayed up late the night before with her husband to re-upholster a bench, Rosie cut to a commercial.

"We'll talk about Trump when we come back," Joy said with a sneaky grin.

"Oh, jeez," Rosie sighed. "I'm getting nauseous. I don't enjoy him in any capacity. We'll be back talking about Donald and his hair loop."

That was enough of a tease to attract the attention of at least one captive viewer. Trump, who spent his mornings glued to the TV even before he resided at 1600 Pennsylvania Avenue, was watching from his lair at Trump Tower. Was he a regular fan? "In those days, it's not like it is now," Geddie said. "Everybody watched *The View,* particularly in the media world."

After the commercial, Rosie tried out her new material. "All right," she said. Her argument had a feminist slant. She was outraged that Trump was using this young woman's drug problem to promote himself. "So

Donald Trump is in the news again. Because his show *The Apprentice* is starting again in January, he held a big press conference to see if he was going to allow Miss USA—such a prestigious title . . ." Although Rosie had a clear take on the story, her commentary was improvised. She first mimicked Conner's voice as she cried. Then Rosie introduced her outrageous Trump caricature, complete with the bad hair and boorish voice. "Listen, this guy annoys me on a multitude of levels," Rosie riffed. "He's the moral authority? Left the first wife, had an affair. Left the second wife, had an affair. Had kids both times. But he's the moral compass for twenty-year-olds in America? Donald, sit and spin my friend! I don't enjoy him. No, no, no."

Anthony, the guest cohost, tried to cool things down by defending Trump's business record.

Rosie wasn't allowing it. "He inherited a lot of money, and he's been bankrupt so many times, where he didn't have to pay. Do you know what saved him the second time? After his father died, with that money, he paid off his bankruptcy." She knew this jab would get back to Trump because it had to do with his finances. "Here comes a lawsuit," Rosie said with a laugh. "Get ready. This could be good."

"He sues, you know?" Joy warned.

"I can imagine," Rosie scoffed. "He's going to sue me, but he'll be bankrupt by that time, so I won't have to worry."

By the end of the segment, Joy's head fell to the table in uncontrolled laughter. "My memory of it was she took over the stage and went crazy on him," Joy recalled. "She pulled her hair over and made comments about his infidelities and his money, which probably really freaked him out. As you can see from the fact that he never pays his taxes, that's something he never wants out there. But it was funny. I enjoyed sitting there and watching it. It was a fabulous show."

That would be a tough act for Clinton to follow. The senator's appearance was no longer the biggest headline on *The View* that day. Dressed in a stiff pink jacket, her right foot stumbled as she ascended a step to greet the cohosts. She had to catch herself from falling. "Hi, everybody," she said. The interview was controlled and scripted, a departure from her more relaxed demeanor on *The Rosie O'Donnell Show*. Clinton talked about how she'd navigate the presidency and her years in Arkansas, where she juggled motherhood with her career. Elisabeth asked her if she'd support Barack Obama, then a junior US senator from Illinois, if she didn't run.

"Well, you know I'm going to wait and see how all this develops," Clinton said calmly. "He's a terrific guy. We are going to have a lot of good people running in the Democratic primary. Everybody who wants to compete should compete. Let's throw open those doors." Nobody imagined that Clinton wouldn't be the nominee. A *Newsweek* poll released that week had her defeating Rudy Giuliani and John McCain in the general election.

"Maybe we'll be rewinding the tapes one day, and maybe we will have sat with the first woman president," Elisabeth said, concluding the exchange on a pleasant note. "You never know."

After the show wrapped and Geddie had returned to his office, a phone call was already waiting for him. Who could it be? In the ugly weeks that followed, "people thought it was about her doing an impression of him. I thought it would be that she made fun of him and his hair," Geddie said. "It wasn't."

Trump was outraged about the line related to his wealth. "I have never filed for bankruptcy," he barked on the line.

Geddie apologized. "I'm sorry, Mr. Trump. It was all done in good fun."

That technique didn't work. Trump threatened—as he's known to do—to sue *The View*, ABC, and Barbara Walters for spreading lies about him. "I'll be talking to my lawyers," he huffed.

Geddie attempted a different approach. He told Trump that he was going to call Barbara and they'd get back to him. Geddie knew that his boss would want to hear about this, even from a far-off seaside adventure. "Barbara happened to be on a boat somewhere with Judy Sheindlin. You can't make this shit up," Geddie said. Barbara hadn't seen the episode yet, but the prospect of getting embroiled in a public lawsuit with Trump worried her.

"This is terrible," Barbara said. "If we did something wrong, we have to say we did something wrong."

"It's more complicated than that," Geddie responded. "He's been part of businesses that have gone bankrupt, but he has not personally gone bankrupt before."

Barbara sprang into damage-control mode, thinking that she could clean up this mess by talking to Trump. "He was a good friend of Barbara's," Geddie said. Barbara, who had interviewed Trump many times over the years, asked Geddie to arrange a three-way call. When Trump answered (he always picked up his phone quickly back then), Barbara presented herself as a sympathetic ally. She told Trump that she would issue a statement clarifying his finances when she returned to TV in a few days. Rosie's name came up, and some harsh words may have been exchanged about her, depending on whom you believe.

Rather than wait for the next episode of *The View*, Trump went nuclear. He always subscribed to the adage that there is no such thing as bad publicity, and this was his chance to dominate the airwaves, serving as his own spokesperson. Trump appeared on more than twenty programs with one goal in mind: to viciously attack Rosie. His interviewers included Anderson Cooper, David Letterman, *People* magazine, *Access Hollywood*, *The Insider*, and *Good Day LA*. If he couldn't be in the studio, he'd call in, hurling offensive labels at her and threatening to steal Rosie's wife away from her. (As if he had the power to turn a gay woman straight.) In the days that followed, Trump called Rosie "fat little Rosie," "stupid," "a little clam," "unattractive," "that animal," and a "degenerate."

Rosie responded on December 27, through her blog, with a haiku: *a young girl in nyc / meets a pimp / he cons her into a life of illusion / she works for him.* That only provoked Trump. "I'm a pimp because, unlike her, I gave a girl a second chance," he told CNN's Cooper. "That's why I'm a pimp? You're not allowed to make statements like that, Anderson." In his press blitz, he detailed his private conversation with Barbara, revealing to anyone who would listen that she expressed profound regret at hiring Rosie. "Barbara fully understands what Barbara told me," Trump said to the Associated Press, after Barbara tried to deny it. "At the same time, she can't say that because she has to work with that woman. But she won't be working with her long. I mean, that thing will explode because Rosie's wacko."

Trump's claims were often left unchecked by professional journalists, who gave him all the free airtime he desired. "I'm not running for office," he said on CNN, when asked about his choice of words. "I don't have to be politically correct." The boisterous media tour offered a preview of the strategy he'd later adopt as a presidential candidate, one in which he lashed out against powerful women such as Hillary Clinton, Elizabeth Warren, Megyn Kelly, and Carly Fiorina with impunity.

"I knew that Donald Trump is particularly wounded by being made fun of by women," Joy said. "He doesn't like it. He turned on me, too, because I made a joke about his hair. She got him, and he could not control himself. He could not stop talking about Rosie O'Donnell, calling her every name in the book, going after her physicality. It was disgusting. He's a nasty man." Joy said that the feud revealed his true character. "I am not shocked by his behavior right now because I sat there and saw the whole thing."

For Rosie, who wore her heart on her sleeve, the Trump attacks disrupted her life and family. She felt as if she'd been left alone to deal with his vitriol. "That was the hardest thing to watch," said Janette Barber. "All she did was the same joke every comic in the country was doing. The only reason he did that, in my opinion, is because *The View* was so relevant and she was so visible and brilliant. If you were to mention Rosie, you were in the press."

Rosie said she was shocked that when Trump attempted to humiliate her, other powerful women didn't come to her defense: "I thought, 'Well, here comes Gloria Steinem and the new head of NOW and maybe Susan Sarandon and every fucking feminist—Robin Morgan, Lily Tomlin, and Jane Fonda.' Here comes the woman tribe that are going to stand up and go, 'Are you kidding me?' Let's take out some fact sheets. This man was slandering me with the help of Roger Ailes and Fox News. It was a full-on character assassination, the same way they try to do it with James Comey or anyone they don't like." She said that Steinem has since apologized to her for staying silent.

For years, Trump continued to wage his war with Rosie for his own benefit. He offered her $2 million to appear as a contestant on *The Celebrity Apprentice,* which of course Rosie didn't accept. He dragged her name into two presidential debates to avoid answering difficult questions about his own behavior toward women. During a lunch, Rosie revealed another way the Trump fight resurfaced in her life. "In 2015, my son and myself were targeted by trolls on my Twitter account. And I hired a forensic digital person and they found it was the Russians. I have this thick binder from the investigator of what they did. So Roger Ailes and Fox News, if they target you, they will not stop."

Rosie blamed the media for giving Trump a free pass. "If you're a kid who grew up in New York and you're my age, the ridiculousness of his essence is obvious. It's infuriating to me that when he started to run, the news media didn't do its due diligence. Everything I said about him in 2006 is factual and true and available on the internet. There's no reason for the world to be this fooled. And shame on us for not rectifying that."

Rosie blamed another person for this debacle. In Rosie's opinion, Barbara Walters didn't do enough to protect her. After her feud with Trump got nasty, Barbara and Bill issued an anodyne statement, not siding with either

Rosie or Trump. When Barbara returned to work, Rosie was on vacation. Barbara issued another statement, clarifying that Trump hadn't personally declared bankruptcy and insisting that she had never uttered a bad word about Rosie to Trump. It wasn't enough for Rosie, whose life had been turned inside out. The paparazzi were camping outside her house. She felt targeted.

On January 8, 2007, her rage exploded. That day will live in infamy at *The View*. Producers still talk about the dressing-room fight as if they were watching a volcano erupt. "Rosie wanted to be defended," Joy said.

That day in the Hot Topics meeting, Rosie came in looking deflated and sat down quietly, without talking to anyone. Barbara entered the room and made the mistake of walking up to Rosie, as if nothing had been wrong. That's when Rosie lost it. She leaped up, and started "to berate her," according to Geddie. He later called it "the moment she went at Barbara."

In a tirade, Rosie shouted insults at Walters. Rosie was furious that Barbara hadn't reached out to her in the last ten days. "I definitely yelled," Rosie recalled. "I said how disappointed I was and how shocked and hurt I was that she wouldn't stand up for me. I felt very betrayed about her going behind my back and speaking to Donald Trump in Trumpian language. I said something about her daughter, which I should not have said. But I did."

Rosie told the creator of *The View* that she was a bad mother. "No wonder Jackie can't stand you," Rosie yelled, referencing Barbara's strained relationship with her daughter.

"Do not speak about my daughter," Barbara said.

"Barbara is completely unprepared for this, and also not one of those people that likes a big confrontation," Geddie said. "And certainly not a confrontation in a room full of senior and junior staff—there were a lot of people in the room. I can't tell you everything she said, but it was nasty. And she does it for about forty seconds, maybe a minute. I finally said, 'Enough. You can't talk to her anymore like this.' And she turned on me, saying how much she hated me for a variety of reasons."

Geddie had given up trying to establish a functional relationship with Rosie. "We were the parents," he said. "One person said to me, 'You're the father that raped her, and Barbara Walters is the mother who let it happen.' Well, what can I do about that? If that's where we're starting from, I don't know how to rectify that."

What made the fight even more dramatic was the contrast in Rosie's and Barbara's physical statures. Geddie said that Rosie towered over Barbara, who was frail and much smaller than her. "I did not tower over anyone," Rosie told me. "I was sitting in my makeup chair, and she was sitting in her makeup chair. It wasn't my best moment." Rosie had initially decided that she wanted to be at *The View* to act as Barbara's shield. Now she was tearing her down. Trump had forced the two women to turn on each other.

"Barbara afterward said something to the effect of, 'It took you long enough to get in there and break that up,'" Geddie said. "I was shocked by it, too. Barbara, at that time, wasn't a kid. She was well into her seventies. She's not somebody you scream at. You don't scream at older ladies like that, regardless of who they are, and you certainly don't scream at Barbara Walters, the person who hired you."

Some staff, in retelling the story, said it looked as if Rosie wanted to physically harm Barbara. "I don't think that Rosie would ever hit Barbara," Geddie said. "I don't think that's what she does. I think she gets furious. I don't think she's going to slug you." But metaphorically, Rosie had taken the gloves off. "We knew we had an issue," Geddie said. "It was a terrible thing." Barbara looked shaken as she made her way up to the studio. As Geddie left the room, his shock turned to relief. He thought ABC would have no choice but to fire Rosie. But despite complaints from Barbara herself to top executives, the network didn't do anything. The message got back to Barbara that Rosie was at *The View* to stay.

"Well, he's at it again," Rosie said two days later, after another attack from Trump.

"That poor pathetic man," Barbara said, offering a public olive branch to Rosie. She'd finally disavowed Trump.

Yet privately the two women had entered the point of no return. It would be impossible to think that Barbara and Rosie could coexist on the show after that dressing-room fight. "When Rosie came on, she told me she wanted to be a passenger on the bus. She didn't want to drive it," Geddie said. "But she didn't like where the bus is going."

Barbara had to find a way to stealthily fight back—and somehow eject Rosie from her seat. "This was a power struggle for the heart of the show," Geddie said. *The View* wasn't big enough for the both of them.

14

Ladies Who Punch

It started to look as if Rosie O'Donnell might emerge as the winner of the tug-of-war for *The View*. Barbara Walters had created the show and could interview anybody about anything, but Rosie outshone her when it came to connecting with daytime viewers—she had the relatable gene. Barbara also didn't have the advantage of face time at the studio every day, since she kept a sporadic schedule. As the moderator, Rosie held the keys to the kingdom. She wasn't shy about dictating editorial decisions, inventing her own segments, suggesting guests, and overriding Bill Geddie. Many of the longtime staff members tripped over themselves to try to impress her.

"A lot of insecure people who were producers—and Elisabeth Hasselbeck—they thought Rosie would be their ticket," said Alexandra Cohen. "She was Rosie O'Donnell. If you didn't fall in line, what's going to happen?" Cohen told Geddie she couldn't believe how quickly Elisabeth had shifted her allegiances. "Bill always liked Elisabeth," Cohen said. "I just remember saying to him I was getting so enraged with her. I saw the way she tried to align herself. She was doing what my producers do, asking, 'Where does my future lie?'"

That strategizing was because of the real possibility that Rosie could inherit *The View*. Barbara, who was seventy-seven, would need to retire sometime. Even if she wanted to work forever, not many octogenarians were entrusted with the responsibilities of live TV. In conversations with the staff, Rosie reinforced the impression that Barbara's last day might come sooner rather than later. She compared her boss to an elderly relative who needed help in the kitchen to make a delicious meal because she couldn't do it on her own. Rosie shared that analogy with me on two occasions: "Just the same way your grandmother at Thanksgiving makes the turkey and stuffing. This year, she's ninety-two and she can't. So she stands by the stove and your mother helps her. You go, 'Nana, this is the greatest stuffing ever.' But everyone knows Nana didn't make the stuffing, because she can't anymore. But Nana still deserves respect at the table."

Rosie believed that by continuing to let Barbara appear on *The View,* Geddie was tarnishing her legacy. Rosie would frequently say that Barbara had lost her polish, as evidenced by occasional non sequiturs during Hot Topics and lapses in her memory. Barbara, never one to back down from a fight, engaged in her own smear campaign against Rosie. She'd call up Anne Sweeney or Disney's CEO, Bob Iger, to spread stories about how Rosie had alienated the staff and was driving everybody nuts. And Barbara would bad-mouth Rosie in front of other employees when Rosie wasn't there.

Since Rosie had signed only a one-year contract, she had to negotiate a new agreement that spring. Despite Barbara's attempts at sabotage, ABC wanted to keep Rosie, because of the ratings surge. ABC was considering two scenarios. Either Rosie would stay on *The View* for one or more seasons. Or the network would spin her off into her own daytime talk show. With rumors about Oprah Winfrey ending her daytime run in the near future (she left in 2011), ABC needed insurance and wanted *The Rosie O'Donnell Show* back on TV.

Regardless of what Rosie decided, Geddie believed his days on *The View* were numbered. "The reason he would have thought he was being fired is that Rosie was walking around going, 'I'm going to get you fired,'" said Brian Frons, the head of ABC Daytime. "She wanted everybody fired."

Rosie made it clear that Geddie was one of her targets. "She didn't like that she was working for someone," Geddie said. "And I have to say this, on behalf of Rosie, I understand that. She ran her own show the way she ran it, and it was successful. I think she thought she would be able to transform the show more into something like *The Rosie O'Donnell Show*. More Broadway. More giveaways. It was my job to stop that, to say, 'We have a successful show that I need you to fit into.'" Although he'd just bought a high-rise apartment for his family across the street from *The View*, he started exploring the idea of a new life in Los Angeles. When Geddie left town to produce Walter's annual Oscars special in February 2007—with guests Ellen DeGeneres, Eddie Murphy, Helen Mirren, and Jennifer Hudson—he stayed on the West Coast for a time, walking off his own show because his relationship with Rosie had turned so toxic. Cohen quietly stepped in as the interim executive producer, holding down the fort as the producers waited for a resolution.

"It was horrible," Cohen said. "I was running around putting out fires. She was attacking my staff. Everybody was living in fear." Rosie's impulsive management style created a chaotic, nervous mood, fueled by widespread panic of getting fired overnight. When Barbara was in charge, although she could be demanding, she never threatened to ruin producers. With Rosie, staffers were flung into last-minute scavenger hunts. One morning, Rosie announced that she wanted a *Power Rangers* outfit as a surprise present for a young child who was part of a human-interest segment. Several producers went running to the nearest drugstore. When one of them miraculously found the costume, Rosie wasn't impressed. It was in the wrong color. "Look, I would say that she had a great producing mind for some things," Cohen said. "But we were a very small staff. We did the best we could."

Rosie's personality loomed large over the set. Cohen recalled how Rosie diagnosed herself with so many conditions, it was hard to keep track. "She was bipolar," said Cohen (which Rosie no longer thinks she is). "She was manic-depressive. She was on the autism spectrum, and she had everything under the sun." One day, they were all watching TV in the makeup room. "There was an ad for restless leg syndrome, and we started joking about it," Cohen said. Rosie didn't laugh. She proclaimed, "I have that."

Her list of complaints about the show was long. "I'd come in every once in a while," said Frons, who lived in Los Angeles, "and I'd fucking have to have dinner in Nyack"—close to where Rosie lived—"at America's worst Mexican restaurant. We'd have two or three hours of her ranting about Bill or Barbara or what wasn't happening in America at that particular moment. Sometimes she was right. Sometimes she was wrong. Our job was to encourage what was right, and when it was wrong, to try to get it toned down."

On TV, Rosie had the first half of the show under her control because she could pick how she presented the Hot Topics. But she lost her temper frequently over how the camera operators handled her more creative segments. "She always had a problem when we were doing an arts-and-crafts demo," said Cohen, an area *The View* had not explored before. "That's when she would come down on the directing staff. Some shot wouldn't happen the way she wanted it. When Bill left, I was really running interference between the producers and Rosie, the other talent and Rosie, and the people coming in and crying. At the same time, people were kissing her ass."

As the director, Gentile got the brunt of Rosie's wrath. "She's clinically insane," he said. "Not like Bill O'Reilly, he's crazy. She's medically insane. The best talent she has is making you believe she's normal." He said that her reign over *The View* resembled a foreign nation under an oppressive regime. "She was like Pol Pot in Cambodia. She was going to go through the country and she was going to kill everybody and have it her way. From day one, she was here to teach these morons how to do a show. Everything we did was wrong, no matter what it was." If anyone doubted her judgment, Rosie referenced her shelf of Emmys at home as proof that she was right.

Gentile learned that Rosie was trying to get him fired. "She trashed me to the network," he said. "She convinced them I was the biggest bum on the planet. We were all paralyzed." He said that his anger reached a tipping point when she came down on him for something so trivial he doesn't remember what it was. "She started screaming, and some intern came down and said, 'Rosie wants to see you in her office.' I said to myself, 'I can go out with dignity or I can cower in fear like everybody else.'" He took the former route. "I faced the demon myself. I got up and walked down to her office and I had a screaming match, in which I told her, 'You don't have anybody here fooled. You're calling everyone out for their mistakes, but everybody's got your number. You make as many mistakes if not more. Everybody knows it. You don't have talent. You don't have all the skills you claim to have. You are denigrating people that are working under you.'"

The View was consumed by so much turmoil that Gentile's outburst got lost in all the noise. The network didn't even reprimand him for yelling at talent. "I went back to my office," recalled Gentile, "and I said to my stage manager, 'Here's what I want you to do. Your job for the rest of the time I'm here—whether they fire me or whether I live out my contract—is to make sure I never see her in person again.'" For the rest of the season, the show's director wouldn't walk into the studio unless it had been cleared of Rosie.

A little later, Rosie tried to make amends by telling one of the other stage supervisors to compliment Gentile about a musical performance. He didn't care. "You tell her no matter what she says to me, it doesn't matter," he responded. "She's dead to me."

Before their last confrontation, Gentile had enlisted two other employees to join him in a group complaint to human resources about Rosie's abusive behavior. They filed their grievance with Tanya L. Menton, vice president of litigation and employment practices at ABC. "It didn't do any good," Gentile said.

When I asked O'Donnell about it, she had no knowledge of Gentile's complaint: "I don't know what he went to HR for. What, that I told people he had a child with one of the other staff members while being married?"

⟳

ABC was determined to keep *The View* together, even if the show had splintered into dysfunctional tribes. In February, during her visit to Los Angeles for the Oscars, Barbara issued her ultimatum to Frons at Spago, telling him that she and Geddie refused to return to the show unless Rosie was gone.

"Really, Barbara and Bill were going to walk away from the show they created?" Frons said. "I don't think so. All this is negotiable. It's about power. Who controls the show? Ultimately, the people I want to control the show are the viewers. I want to give them what they want to see, which is Barbara and Rosie and Bill."

Rather than relying on a seasoned agent, Rosie was using her brother Ed, who had worked in ad sales at NBC, as her negotiator. "He did the ratings comp and the price of commercials, and he said, 'This is how much you made the company this year,'" she recalled. "So I said, I wanted five million dollars, which is a lot less than what I was making on my own show, by tens of millions of dollars." Frons didn't agree with the math. "If we had known the ratings were going to be that good at upfronts," he said, referring to the spring period in which networks sell advertising in advance, or "upfront," then "we would have sold it at a much higher price. But we didn't."

As these talks were going on, Geddie decided that he'd cooled off long enough from *The View*. But more—and different—trouble was brewing. When he returned a month later, Rosie and Elisabeth had finally turned against each other. Rosie kept producing Elisabeth, voicing concerns that she was too stiff and emotionally distant. Elisabeth was mad that Rosie wouldn't stop asking her questions during Hot Topics, trying to trip her up about George W. Bush's policies instead of simply debating her. When Elisabeth complained to Geddie about this, he offered her some advice. If Rosie tried to do that, Elisabeth should try the same technique on her—by rattling off questions that would make her stumble.

That led to an unwieldy exchange on the morning of March 29. The ladies were at it with guest cohost Marcia Gay Harden. The Hot Topics focused on how (or if) Bush used the September 11 attacks to go to war in Iraq. As if that weren't enough to chew on, Rosie was espousing conspiracy theories that secret explosives at 7 World Trade Center caused it to crumble, suggesting that the US government played a role in the nation's deadliest terrorist attack.

"I hope people across the world don't think what George Bush is doing represents the American people, because the last election shows it does not," Rosie said.

"But let me ask you this," responded Hasselbeck. "What concerns me is there's this environment now where we're more apt to trust our enemies than our allies."

She didn't quite get a question out before Rosie hurled one back to her. "Would you say, Elisabeth, that you trust the Bush administration as much as you did when he first took office?"

Elisabeth, sounding wobbly, answered that she did.

"Nearly everyone in this administration is under indictment or suspicious." Rosie listed off Karl Rove, Donald Rumsfeld, and Alberto Gonzales. "What do you have to do to get impeached in this country?"

Joy had reliable material teed up. "What you have to do is you have to have Monica Lewinsky come into your office."

Harden, the Oscar-winning star of *Pollock*, objected to the use of the phrase *war on terror*, dismissing it as propaganda.

"Exactly, Marcia Gay, thank you!" Rosie cheered. "It makes people into evil and good." Then she went one step too far. "What I'm saying is, in

America, we are fed propaganda. And if you want to know what's happening in the world, go outside of the US media, because it's owned by four corporations. One of them is this one." Rosie didn't mention Disney by name, but she was clearly calling out her employer. "And you know what? Go outside of the country to find out what's going on in our own country, because it's frightening."

"You think we're brainwashed as a whole country?" Elisabeth said. "I think not."

"I think our democracy is threatened in a way it hasn't been in two hundred years," Rosie preached. "If America doesn't stand up, we're in big trouble." She questioned how a tower from the World Trade Center collapsed because, she argued, such a fire couldn't melt steel. "We're going to take a break and we'll be right back in America, land of the free, home of the brave, peace out."

Just like that, even though she hadn't realized it, Rosie had talked herself off *The View*. And it wasn't, surprisingly, because she had just declared that 9/11 was an inside job.

In the first seven months of Rosie's tenure, Frons had made it his full-time job to defend her. After the Clay Aiken spat, he told colleagues he understood where she was coming from. "Obviously, as a gay woman, she was very concerned about gay rights," Frons said. "So even though Kelly Ripa felt insulted and she was on a sister show, I back my star. It was coming from a place that was real and caring." Frons also stood up for Rosie during the Trump implosion. "She felt strongly that women needed to be respected, and she felt that whole thing with Miss USA was disrespectful to women in general. Within the context of the show, that works for me. Not a problem.

"The hard one was when I was vacationing in Costa Rica with my family. And after a three-hour hike in the rain forest, I came back to my little hotel that didn't have a phone in the room and someone came up to me and said, 'Mr. Frons, Ms. Sweeney called for you.'"

He dialed her back immediately. "What did she say this time?" he asked with a sigh.

It was a quick moment that could have been lost to the average viewer. But not for ABC—the network's entire chain of executives were humiliated that Rosie had instructed the American public to not trust its news division. Frons frantically called Rosie from Central America to figure out how to fix this mess. She was adamant that the media couldn't be believed (a jarring argument a decade before Trump adopted it as part of his presidential platform). Although Frons convinced her to apologize, the damage had been done. "That was a passionate moment that cost her tens of millions of dollars," Frons said.

It had to do with the nature of the TV business. "People don't understand the economics of local TV," Frons said. "There are only two things that you give a shit about. Your money is coming from local news at six p.m. and local news at eleven p.m. So if somebody comes on your network and says, 'You can't trust the news on this channel,' you have a problem." For decades, ABC had cultivated a stalwart image as the trustworthy destination for news, through programs such as *World News Tonight, 20/20, GMA,* and Oprah's syndicated talk show, which many viewers lumped in that category. "That's basically like walking into a Wolfgang Puck restaurant and saying, 'This food is made of body parts,'" Frons said. "It's really crazy. She didn't think about corporations or local TV stations in a personal sense. There are people who run these things. The largest employee base at ABC is probably the news department."

The local affiliates revolted. They didn't want to shell out money to program Rosie as a lead-in to the evening news. "The phones lit up, particularly from the Southeast of the country, and they said, 'We're not buying that show,'" Frons said. The idea of a stand-alone Rosie talk show was no longer an option. As for *The View*, ABC decided Barbara was right, and that Rosie was too much trouble. They told her they couldn't meet her $5 million salary requirement, which was the easy way out.

Rosie was confused. She told someone at *The View* that she thought her negotiations had been going well. She never realized the true reason the network turned against her. "They didn't give me enough money," Rosie explained to me. "They said, 'No.' I said, 'I'm going to go.'"

Barbara was thrilled by the latest turn of events, since it meant that she'd finally regain the control over *The View*. It was also a relief for half the staff, including Geddie and Gentile, whose jobs would be saved. On April 25, Rosie officially announced that she'd soon be departing the show.

"Okay," she said, after reminding everyone that it was the day after Streisand's birthday. "Big news. Breaking news. Did you hear it's on CNN as breaking news?"

"I heard," said Barbara stoically, dressed in black, suppressing any trace of a smile. "I know a little bit about it."

"I've decided that we couldn't come to terms with my deal with ABC," Rosie blurted out. "So next year, I'm not going to be on *The View*. . . . That's showbiz. But it's not sad, because I've loved it here."

"My turn." Barbara dialed up her acting chops. "You keep saying don't be sad, we should all be happy. And I am sad. I induced you to come here. I knew you were only coming for one year. I hoped that it would be more than one year. We have had, to say the least, an interesting year."

As the other cohosts offered their farewells, Barbara had another addendum. "I would like to make one thing perfectly clear. I do not participate in the negotiations for Rosie. It is ABC Daytime." Barbara didn't want any blood on her hands.

"I'll tell you who's sad," Joy quipped. "Donald Trump. He's on a ledge right now. How am I going to resuscitate *The Apprentice* now?"

Rosie reminded viewers why she signed on to *The View* in the first place. "I was at home. I thought, 'A year with Barbara Walters. Who could resist that?' Honestly, you're a living legend."

"You know"—Barbara finally allowed herself to crack a smile—"it's better being a living legend than a dead legend."

Rosie's last day would be in late June, per her contract. The morning that she revealed she was leaving, sixty-five camera crews camped outside *The View*'s loading dock, trying to capture a glimpse of Rosie in her car. She was a media sensation, the Paris Hilton of daytime. Her departure dominated all the cable news programs, from CNN to late-night TV to Bill O'Reilly. The next day, Joy counted off some of the mentions, noting there wasn't an hour of TV that didn't include a shout-out to Rosie.

Guess who else weighed in? Donald Trump went on another media tour to declare victory against his nemesis. "It does say something that the guy is a businessman and this is what he does with his free time," Rosie cracked. "He's got an interesting, new hair color. Jell-O orange! I think it's kind of comical, all the men yelling at all the women—as usual."

A few days later, Frons ran into Iger at a screening room at ABC, where they were both watching shows for pilot season.

"You should fire her for what she said," the CEO of the Walt Disney Company hissed.

Frons knew he had to push back. "If we do that now, she's going to come after us about freedom of speech. What is *The View* about?" He suggested that Rosie would try to tear down the show and inflict damage on Barbara. "If we throw her out," he recalled saying, "it's going to be really bad for us. We will have cornered somebody. And she's not somebody you want to corner.

"But if one more thing happens, and it's her fault, that will be the end of it," Frons promised.

It was only a matter of time.

15

My Mouth Is a Weapon

n her final weeks on *The View*, Rosie O'Donnell's interactions with Elisabeth Hasselbeck grew more and more contentious, which is the narrative that most viewers remember about the two women. But Rosie genuinely cared about Elisabeth. She saw the show's Republican as a pet project, someone that needed mentoring. "I loved her," Rosie said. "Here's what I said, 'I'm the senior. She's the freshman. I got a really good player on the freshman team, but I have to teach her how to loosen up.'" One of Rosie's favorite instructions: "Nobody wants facts, Elisabeth. Everybody wants feelings.'"

Elisabeth tried to incorporate some of that advice, but she'd revert to her old ways. Rosie didn't like how Elisabeth would shift into Fox News mode to defend George W. Bush's policies as a pro-war, anti-abortion Republican. Rosie ran up against the same problem with Elisabeth some of her cohosts had. "Bill Geddie spent thirty minutes coaching her in her dressing room daily," Rosie said. As she offered this morsel of information, she picked up my tape recorder and moved it closer to her mouth. "I don't know if you got that part," Rosie said sarcastically, speaking louder. "She would sometimes take those notes to the table."

Rosie criticized Elisabeth for lacking a personal connection to her arguments. "I tried to get her to talk more about her own self and how she felt rather than being a robotic pundit. Our show is not a show like *Crossfire*. It's about four women expressing their feelings about their lives and what's going on in the world. You have to have access to your own feelings, not just reiterate lines you heard spoken somewhere else."

When it became clear that Elisabeth didn't want to be molded by Rosie, their friendship was irreparably damaged. It became a ticking time bomb for the show. Rosie and Elisabeth traded daily blows during the show's Hot Topics debates. On the surface, it was always about politics—and in spring 2007, there was plenty to argue about. But the subtext behind these clashes was that Rosie felt betrayed by Elisabeth, who'd cooled on Rosie. As Elisabeth had learned from *Survivor,* she saw that it was time to defect to her original alliance. After Rosie announced that she was leaving, the power dynamic tilted back to Barbara Walters, who was smart enough to keep a safe distance. She decided to skip out on many of Rosie's last shows, leaving Elisabeth alone to defend the turf.

Their exchanges felt increasingly awkward. For example, in the middle of April, Rosie posted on her blog a question from a fan, who asked if Elisabeth was pregnant. Rosie said she had no idea, which only stoked rumors on the internet. On April 30, 2007, Elisabeth relented and confirmed that she was three months pregnant with her second child. "I figured we're going to be lonely without you," she said on air, looking at Rosie. "So, Tim and I thought we should get busy and maybe make a little co-host."

Barbara was overjoyed that the baby was due in November, in time for sweeps. The show would need a boost after losing their buzz magnet. Even on her way out, Rosie was still a one-woman publicity machine. She censored herself even less than before, and she turned Hot Topics into a rage session about Bush, finding new and inventive ways to attack his motives for invading Iraq. (To Rosie, Bush's villainy was second only to one other man's. At a charity dinner at the Waldorf Astoria, she slammed

Trump: "Eat me! It was always my dream to give an old, bald billionaire a boner.")

"You have somebody who has senioritis," said Brian Frons about Rosie's behavior on the way out. "Remember being in high school? It's May. I'm done in mid-June. I'm ready to go." He noticed a change in the intensity of Rosie and Elisabeth's squabbles. "They'd had enough of each other."

There was another complication. Joy was right when she speculated that Rosie had romantic feelings for Elisabeth. "I think there was underlying lesbian overtones on both parts," Rosie claimed, as she described her chemistry with Elisabeth. Rosie backed up this idea with some dubious evidence: "I think this is something that will hurt her if you write it. She was the MVP of a Division One softball team"—at Boston College—"for two years that won the finals. There are not many, in my life, girls with such athletic talent on sports teams that are traditionally male that aren't at least a little bit gay."

Although she was attracted to Elisabeth, Rosie never wanted to act on it. "There was a little bit of a crush. But not that I wanted to kiss her. I wanted to support, raise, elevate her, like she was the freshman star shortstop and I was the captain of the team." Rosie changed sports metaphors from baseball to basketball. "I was going to Scottie Pippen her. If I was Jordan, I was going to give her the ball and let her shoot. But it was in no way sexualized."

Rosie explained that intimacy came hard for her given her difficult childhood. "I was sexually abused by my father. I am not a person who has sex for fun. I have to know you. I have to love you. I have to work through a meditation to get to a place where I'm able. I've had sex with eight people in my life."

She tried to fix their problematic relationship. On May 1, after a nasty fight about whether oil propelled us into Iraq, Rosie took to her blog: *u have seen my last hasselbeck spat. 2 day was it no more.* She didn't want to wage any more attacks on a pregnant mother. That wasn't a promise she could keep. On May 17, Rosie and Elisabeth circled back to the Middle East. Instead of actually debating, they took a combative route, firing off questions to trip each other up.

"I just want to say something—655,000 Iraqi civilians are dead," Rosie said. "Who are the terrorists?"

Elisabeth looked stunned, and she dug in the knife. "Wait, who are you calling terrorists now? Americans?"

"I'm saying that if you were in Iraq, and another country, the United States, the richest in the world, invaded your country and killed 655,000 of your citizens, what would you call us?"

Fox News reported that Rosie had branded US troops "terrorists," which stung because she had visited veteran hospitals and donated to them. Even blue-state MSNBC attacked her, with guests on a panel on Chris Matthews's *Hardball* blaming Rosie for making that claim.

Rather than tune out the coverage, Rosie let it get to her. She wanted Elisabeth, as her onetime ally and friend, to stand up against the right-wing media. But Elisabeth had no reason to do that. On May 21, she urged Rosie in the morning meeting to explain what she had meant. But Elisabeth wouldn't defend her on TV, which was the final straw in their friendship.

David Tutera, the wedding planner once banished from *The View* because of Star Jones, stopped by that week for a lifestyle piece. "I think it's the most uncomfortable segment I've ever done on television," Tutera said. "When the cameras were on, you can't tell. When they were off, you felt like something bad was going to happen, that horrible energy." He noticed the two cohosts weren't making eye contact. "Rosie is just a cannonball."

Rosie provided a similar description of herself: "It's almost like chaos kicks me into a gear. In a way, my mouth is a weapon. I, for a living, am a wordsmith. And so, I'm heavily armed. When I'm angry, I can . . ." She imitated the sound of pellets firing from an air rifle. "Most people can't do it that fast."

On May 23, that anger finally exploded, in what will forever be remembered as doomsday on *The View*. In its decade of existence, the show had been responsible for its share of feuds. But nothing in daytime TV history could have prepared viewers for this breaking point. Although Rosie had once sworn that she would never replicate *Jerry Springer*, she was about to give that show a run for its money. "They became very personal on air," Joy Behar told me. "That's the thing you try to avoid on television. I don't get personal. I never had a personal fight with Elisabeth Hasselbeck, and that's why we're fine."

Barbara was absent that morning. "I remember we were downstairs in the makeup room," said the comedian Sherri Shepherd, who was filling in as a guest cohost. As Elisabeth talked, Rosie made sarcastic asides to no one in particular—the tension was building. "I got makeup and hair," Sherri said. "I'm a Pentecostal girl. I said to them, 'Do you speak in tongues, because we need to start praying. I don't know what is going on here!' When we got to the table upstairs, nobody was talking. I could see Rosie is mad."

On TV, Rosie kept her feelings in check for a few minutes. After a commercial, Joy pulled out a page of complaints against Bush, whom she called "the worst president that we've ever had in the history of this country." Elisabeth frowned. "Let me get through the list," Joy said.

"It's very long, so we might be here for a while," Elisabeth huffed.

Rosie stayed on the sidelines at first. Joy objected to a number of infractions from Bush, including his reluctance to visit New Orleans right after Hurricane Katrina and his inability to pronounce the word *nuclear* correctly. Elisabeth tried to shut down the discussion. "We're a democratic society," she said. "You have the election in 2008 to change things."

"Do you know how much damage this guy can do in a year and a half?" Joy said, incredulous. "He can invade Iran for all we know." Elisabeth insisted that the Republicans in Congress backed Bush for not pulling out of Iraq because it would send the wrong signal to our "enemies."

That gave Rosie an entrance. "You just said our enemies in Iraq. Did Iraq attack us?"

"No, Iraq did not attack us, Rosie," Elisabeth said. "We've been there before. I'm saying our enemies, al-Qaeda, are you hearing that?"

"Please, let's have a conversation," Joy said.

"Do you know why I don't want to do this, Joy?" Rosie's voice was cold. "Let me tell you why. Here's how it gets spun in the media: big, fat, lesbian, loud Rosie attacks innocent, pure, Christian Elisabeth, and I'm not doing it."

"I haven't heard that line," Elisabeth said.

Suddenly, the debate had changed its direction. They were rehashing the details of their broken friendship in front of millions of viewers. "Every time when you've been hurt, did I reach out to you?" Rosie asked.

"I just don't understand why it's my fault if people spin words that you put out there or phrases that suggest things," Elisabeth said. "I gave you an opportunity two days ago to clarify the statement that got you in trouble. I did it as a friend."

That inflamed Rosie. She accused Elisabeth of not siding with her.

"Excuse me. Let me speak," Elisabeth said.

"You're going to doublespeak."

"I'm not a doublespeaker! I don't believe you believe that our troops are terrorists." Elisabeth told Rosie that she shouldn't have used the death toll in Iraq as part of their previous debate.

"It's true, you don't like the facts," Rosie said, contradicting the advice she often gave Elisabeth.

"I'm all about facts."

Sherri tried to cut to a commercial, but the show still had time left. "They wouldn't let it go," Sherri told me later. "It was the worst feeling in the world."

In the control room upstairs, director Mark Gentile kept cutting back and forth as in a Ping-Pong match. When Rosie's mother-in-law had visited the day before, he'd used a split screen so viewers could see her in the audience. Rene Butler, the show's technical director, quickly suggested following that template as the arguments ratcheted up. Gentile approved it. "I said, 'That makes sense, because the reaction is as important as the person delivering the information,'" Gentile recalled. "That's all it was."

From the corner of her eye, Rosie saw in the monitor what they had done and she was fuming. She thought the show was sabotaging her for ratings, since *The View* had never used a split screen in a Hot Topics discussion before. She'd get to the bottom of this, but she had to fend off Elisabeth first.

"They're your thoughts," Elisabeth said, wagging her finger at Rosie. "Defend your own insinuations."

"Every time I defend them, it's poor little Elisabeth that I'm picking on."

"You know what? Poor little Elisabeth is not poor little Elisabeth."

"That's right. That's why I'm not going to fight with you anymore, because it's absurd. So for three weeks, you can say all the Republican crap that you want."

Elisabeth struck another low blow. "It's much easier to fight someone like Donald Trump, isn't it? Because he's obnoxious."

Joy and Sherri stood up to leave the table, which drew some laughter in the studio.

"I think it's sad," Elisabeth said, not easing up. "Because I don't understand how there can be such hurt feelings when all I did was say, 'Look, why don't you tell everybody what you said?' I did that as a friend."

"What you did was not defend me," Rosie said, her voice quivering. "I asked you if you believed what the Republican pundits were saying. You said nothing. And that's cowardly."

"No, no, no," Elisabeth replied, furious. "Do *not* call me a coward. Because, number one, I sit here every single day, open my heart and tell people exactly what I believe. It was not cowardly. It was honest."

"Is there no commercial on this show?" Joy said. "What are we on—PBS?"

The feud lasted for ten minutes, but encapsulated an entire season of TV. "I didn't enjoy it," Joy told me. "I thought people were complicit in making it go on and on." She pointed to staff behind the scenes. "And then the director put up a split screen, which made Rosie very angry."

At the commercial, both Rosie and Elisabeth were so riled up, they had to physically back away from the table. Producers followed Elisabeth to make sure that she was okay. "After it ended, I said, 'Elisabeth, how's the baby? You've got to calm down,'" Sherri recalled. "Then I was with Rosie. She said, 'I can't take this. I'm so tired of this.'"

The tourists in the studio looked frightened. "It was like watching your parents fight," Sherri said. In the greenroom, the yelling echoed over the guests, who were waiting to join this act on live TV. "Alicia Silverstone was shaking," said Sherri, about the *Clueless* star, who was scheduled to chat about how veganism had made her a calmer person. "She was terrified."

Rosie returned to her seat and finished the show as if everything had gone back to normal. How did she manage to do that? "Well, I'm a professional," she said. "I'm an expert at what I do. You want to come to my apartment? There are a lot of awards and accolades."

Rosie's altercation with Elisabeth hit a deep nerve for her. "It felt like a lover breaking up," Rosie said. "The fight that we had, to me as a gay woman, it felt like this: 'You don't love me as much as I love you.' 'I've taken care of you.' 'You have not.' 'How could you do that to me?' 'I didn't do anything to you.'"

After the show ended, Rosie yelled at Alexandra ("Dusty") Cohen, who had been in the control room, about the split screen. "It was shocking to me," Rosie said. She accused the producer of plotting to take her down.

"Dusty called me and said, 'She's blaming me for your split screen,'" Gentile said. "Bill called me and said, 'I know what you did. I know why you did it—just don't do it again.' That shows you there was no conspiracy. He had nothing to do with it. It was me."

Rosie doesn't buy that explanation. "I think although Mark Gentile is a good enough director to possibly do a split screen without rehearsal, he didn't do anything without rehearsal. That man would rehearse like someone with OCD who can't stop washing his hands. He would rehearse and rehearse and rehearse. I don't believe that was an off-the-cuff shot that just happened to come up."

But she declined to provide an explanation for how they had conspired to get her. That day, Rosie grabbed some of her stuff and made her way for the exit.

As she was leaving, Joy stopped her in the hall. "Are you okay?"

"No, I'm not." Rosie was in tears. She called her publicist Cindi Berger and told her she never wanted to return to *The View* again. She was devastated at the way Elisabeth had acted. "Here's a person who had been in my home, swam in the pool with my kids, who I'd done everything I could to connect with, including taking her to her first Broadway show. I have photos of it. I took her kid to see *Sesame Street Live!* with my kids. I made an effort. It felt very backstabby."

Rosie blamed many other people for letting her down. "It was like a girl fight from high school. And it hurt my feelings. Not just what Elisabeth did. What Mark Gentile did. What Joy Behar did. She brought up the topic and stoked the fire, and they went right to the split screen. She was very good friends with Meredith. I think it was upsetting to Joy that I came in and got all this attention." But Rosie has no hard feelings about that. "I've always loved Joy."

After a year of wall-to-wall coverage about Rosie, the fight was the final cliff-hanger. It received more press attention than anything else that had ever happened on *The View*. "Rosie v. Elisabeth: The Gloves Are Off!"

read the *Los Angeles Times* headline. "The Breakup" is how *People* described it. Fox News, CNN, the *New York Post,* and every celebrity blog had their own take, with some outlets referring to it as a "catfight." "When I left, everybody in the world called me," Sherri said. "They wanted to know if they could fly me out to talk about it. I said, 'It's none of my business. And it would be a disservice, because I didn't know the behind the scenes.'"

Donald Trump couldn't resist another opportunity for free press. Surprisingly, he sided with Rosie. "I think anybody that's against the war in Iraq is the winner of the fight, because to justify the war in Iraq—only an imbecile could do that," he told *Extra*. But later, after he watched the clip, he reversed his verdict and crowned Elisabeth the winner.

Geddie went home that night exhausted. "I don't know why this is the first thing that comes to my mind," he said. "The thing that I remember was watching stories that evening on the local news. And people were talking about being in the audience like they'd witnessed a mass shooting. It was a horrible experience. I hope I never have to go through anything like that again. I mean, in retrospect, it's kind of funny. But at the time, I remember thinking we absolutely terrorized the audience that day. They didn't know where to look and where to turn and couldn't wait to get the hell out of there."

This battle had one last casualty. Following Rosie's exit, her writer and friend Janette Barber packed up her office because she knew that she wouldn't be returning. She spotted a magazine tear sheet of Elisabeth on an employee bulletin board. "I happened to have a Sharpie in my pocket," Barber said. "As I'm walking by, I drew a mustache on the picture. I figured the other writers who were on the same floor, they would know it was me, and this would be a funny goodbye."

The *View* publicist didn't appreciate the prank. Someone on the staff slipped a story to the *New York Post*'s Page Six that Barber had destroyed an entire floor's worth of artwork featuring pictures of Elisabeth. "Photographs at *The View*'s offices were defaced," read a network statement. "ABC Legal and Human Resources are investigating the matter." They eventually decided that Barber could never enter an ABC building for the rest of her life. "At most, I owe them two dollars and ninety-five cents for a *Ladies' Home Journal*," Barber said.

Rosie took the next day off to celebrate her wife Kelli's birthday, and she posted a series of comments on her blog that suggested she was done with *The View*. Rosie kept complaining about the split screen. Then came the official word. Barbara was all too happy to have Rosie permanently gone from the show. "It was a good enough reason for us to all agree to go our separate ways," Frons said. "That was the end of it."

The next new episode aired on May 29. Just as the show went live, Barbara started to involuntarily cackle from Rosie's moderator chair. "Why is this woman laughing?" Barbara asked herself, as she couldn't suppress her glee. "What a nice way to begin the week."

"What's new?" asked Whoopi Goldberg, who was filling in.

"It's been quite a week as all of you know," Barbara said. "It's a week that makes us in many ways"—she looked down to her notes—"very sad. There was a little contretemps on the air. I think the Iraq War brings out very hot feelings." She leaned forward. "As most of you know, Rosie O'Donnell is not coming back to finish the last three weeks on the show. Rosie and I have been emailing each other all weekend with the most affectionate notes, because we are very close friends." Barbara once again relieved herself of any responsibility. "I would like to make it very clear Rosie was never fired." Barbara offered a glorious forecast for her own longevity. "We've been a hot show for ten years. And we are going to be a hot show for many years to come."

One pundit had a different reading on the situation. "Rosie will be back," Trump had said immediately after the fight.

16

Rosie Detox

Rosie O'Donnell had a going-away present for Barbara Walters. In the summer of 2007, as *The View* tried to move on by hiring two new cohosts, Rosie was putting the final touches on a book. She'd received a $2 million advance for a memoir about her ruminations on fame, which she called *Celebrity Detox*. She would donate all the proceeds to her charity for Broadway kids.

Rosie saw this as a cleansing from *The View*. "They lie for a living," she told me. "From Lisa Ling to Debbie Matenopoulos, every person who has left that show has been fired—except for me! And it's like the Trump administration. They will just continually lie and present a false front. They would go on TV and pretend to be friends when bad things were happening. You have to talk about it."

The last person who should have seen her latest manifesto was Barbara, who didn't speak to Rosie anymore and was trying to escape from this messy divorce. Yet an early copy of *Celebrity Detox* arrived one day in the mail at her offices at ABC News, with a note from Rosie about how much she loved Barbara. Rosie had a funny way of showing it. After Barbara cracked open the pages, she was livid.

Rosie had kept the contents of *Celebrity Detox* a secret from most people, including her and Barbara's publicist, Cindi Berger. The book featured a series of vignettes about Rosie's time on *The View* along with passages from an unpublished manuscript, some poetry from her blog, and memories about her childhood. She didn't burn the house down by writing a juicy tell-all about her daytime cohosts. But one chapter—written as a letter to her brother Eddie—landed like a grenade.

"It's a difficult situation, because I got hired to do a job, I came, I did the job, I delivered, but I'm still not accepted here," Rosie wrote. "I'm never going to be accepted here." Without mentioning Mark Gentile's name, she called the show's director "inconsistent" because of his "murky shots." She found him to be "tense, tightly wound. Art has to come from some-place quiet."

But her sharpest arrows were aimed at Barbara. Rosie wrote that dur-ing commercial breaks at *The View,* fans would yell, "I love you, Rosie." Barbara, in a "school-teacher tone," would tell them, "It's impolite to say 'I love you' to one person when there are four of us up here."

Rosie had put in writing what nobody at ABC would even dare to whisper in the halls—that Barbara should probably retire. "At some point, a person gets tired," Rosie wrote. "It's inevitable, the aging process. I can feel it myself. Barbara Walters is almost twice my age and she's been doing this for nearly half a century; at some point it becomes necessary to step back." Rosie implicated Bill Geddie in keeping Barbara on TV. "I would like him to feel her fatigue, be in her bones; I'll bet it hurts there."

Then Rosie offered her own judgment on Barbara's career: "Maybe it's time for her to take a break. To go off the air, find the ground, sit down. Rest. She deserves that."

Barbara had no intention of going anywhere, and she certainly wasn't going to take career advice from Rosie. Barbara handed her copy of *Celebrity Detox* to a publicist at ABC News, with directions to contain the damage. The network's West Coast daytime management team got involved. ABC secretly leaked Barbara's edition of *Celebrity Detox* to the

New York Post. The paper could write an article about it under one condition: ABC wanted to cast Rosie as a villain by having psychologists evaluate her mental health after skimming the book.

On September 16, 2007, the *Post* ran its story, "In the Mind of Rosie O'Drama," three weeks ahead of the book's publication. The lead sentence said it all: "Ranting Rosie O'Donnell is full of rage, has a profound distrust of men, craves public adoration, shows signs of post-traumatic stress disorder and dishes out her anger mostly to women because of deep-seated abandonment issues over her mother's death, said a psychiatrist after reading her latest memoir, *Celebrity Detox.*"

The medical professionals quoted in the piece determined that Rosie was a control freak who couldn't get along with anybody. For gravy, the *Post* included a statement from Barbara: "Rosie has written a sad book, but I prefer to focus on the happier times we had and the happier times we hope to have in the future."

Rosie never knew that Barbara was behind the hit job.

The press tour for *Celebrity Detox* seemed to fall apart before it even began. Rosie created a ruckus in early September by ranting about an error on the cover that had the wrong year of her mother's cancer diagnosis. "This book has been more of a pain in the a** than it was worth," she blogged. That prompted *Access Hollywood* to report, "Rosie O'Donnell lashes out over her own book."

Other outlets quickly started picking up the controversial statements. "Rosie O'Donnell has some words of advice for Barbara Walters: Go already," read a *People* article from September 11, 2007. After the book finally hit shelves on October 9, critics were confused by its lack of cohesiveness. *Entertainment Weekly* (which complained that Rosie "nurses a lot of grudges") graded it D.

While doing press, Rosie let it slip that she was in negotiations to return to TV. Given her success tackling political subjects on *The View*, MSNBC wanted to give her a nightly talk show that would air at 9:00 p.m., the time slot after its biggest star, Keith Olbermann. At the time, I was at 30 Rockefeller Center taping a TV appearance, and I overheard Olbermann talking while in a makeup chair about how the Rosie contract was a done deal. A few days later, I approached Rosie, who was signing copies of *Celebrity Detox* at a Borders bookstore in Manhattan's Time Warner Center. She told me she was definitely going to MSNBC. "It's happening very soon," she promised. "I'm following Keith."

At the last minute, the network got cold feet and never took her on. By blabbing about it too early, she spooked them. (*View* producers had a theory that Barbara had a hand in sabotaging it, by dissing her to MSNBC executives.)

"I'm glad I didn't do it," Rosie told me a few years later, because she was a fan of the person who eventually took over the hour. "Watching Rachel Maddow to me is like taking a class at Harvard. She's so freaking smart that, half the time, I have to watch it twice to understand the totality of what she's saying."

With no offer for a daytime or nighttime show, Rosie's agent threw her hat in the ring for other opportunities. She had volunteered to replace Bob Barker on *The Price Is Right*, but talks stalled because CBS didn't want to move the show from Los Angeles to New York. In November 2008, she starred in a one-off variety show, *Rosie Live*, which aired on NBC on the night before Thanksgiving. She'd recruited her pals Alec Baldwin, Clay Aiken, Harry Connick Jr., and Alanis Morissette to perform skits and songs. But it was a ratings turkey, with only 5.25 million viewers.

"Two words: dancing food," wrote the *Los Angeles Times*'s Mary McNamara. "*Rosie Live* ended with dancing food. There's nothing else to say, really except perhaps, Liza Minnelli. *Rosie Live* opened with a little song and dance from Liza Minnelli, who rose to the stage, as if from the grave, to sing a duet with O'Donnell, in a luminous white suit, complete with fetching Broadway hat. Liza, we love you, we will always love you, but there is no shame in retirement."

While promoting *Rosie Live* in its lead-up, Rosie couldn't resist taking a few more jabs at *The View*. She told reporters that the ladies weren't friends in real life. Barbara had to respond cryptically on TV: "There are some people who have done this show and then for years feel they have to dump on it maybe for their own publicity. And that not only hurts me, but I resent it."

On her blog, Rosie posted a video of herself watching the clip. She let a webcam focus on her face. "I did not know what Star Jones and Debbie Matenopoulos did. But, lady, she is pissed off!"

Rosie continued to stir up trouble during an interview with Conan O'Brien. "Listen, I don't want to dump on the show in order to benefit my own career," she said, with a deadpan delivery. "Because, I didn't have a career before that show. So I'm very thankful to *The View* for the help that it's given me in my life. And I'm a big fan of the program and the producers."

"That's the scariest smile I've ever seen since Jack Nicholson in *The Shining*," O'Brien said.

She didn't reveal it, but Rosie was hurt that the show had moved on without her. "I felt like Lord Voldemort, whose name shall not be spoken," she told me. "Even when there were photos sometimes, they would crop me out."

Since she could work only when she wanted to, Rosie returned to semiretirement. She spent her time listening to TED Talks, painting in her crafts room, and taking long vacations to Miami. Her wife, Kelli, moved out in 2007 and they separated. Rosie also broke up with her blog. "At the beginning, no one knew what a blog was and I took that art form,"

she told me. "It was a discovery for myself. After a while, it sort of defeated the purpose. The media has changed a lot. I had to hear about myself on *Entertainment Tonight*."

Despite her having been a movie star in the nineties, the acting offers dried up after she'd become a famous talk show host. "People have a definite opinion of you either way," she explained. "It's hard to get lost in a character in a movie. You almost stick out." She had a drawer of scripts that she'd written in binge sessions. In 2009, she starred in a Lifetime Movie based on one of them, called *America,* in which she played the psychiatrist of a teenage boy in foster care.

In an interview around that time, she told me that she had tried her hand at directing—her son Parker's school play. She couldn't do another one because the next year they staged *A Midsummer Night's Dream.* "I'm Shakespeare illiterate," Rosie said. "I could not get it. And then I got the CliffsNotes. That didn't help."

Then, she also dreamed of starring as Miss Hannigan in a Broadway revival of *Annie.* "I would do it in five seconds. I already know the whole thing." She belted out a favorite line from "It's the Hard-Knock Life" to me over the phone: *You'll stay up till this dump shines like the top of the Chrysler Building!*

Rosie wanted another shot at a talk show. In 2011, she was negotiating with NBC (again), this time about the possibility of returning to daytime with her own show. That's when she got a visit from another member of TV's royal family: Oprah Winfrey. They may not have been able to share airtime before, but they were in different places now that made a collaboration possible. Oprah was leaving *The Oprah Winfrey Show* to launch the Oprah Winfrey Network. She needed strong, inspirational programming for women, and she wanted to bring Rosie on board as one of her stars.

Rosie decided to back away from the NBC offer because she loved Oprah so much. "I wanted to be on Oprah's team," Rosie told me. She signed a two-year, multimillion-dollar deal to host *The Rosie Show*. Oprah was hoping to transfer some of Rosie's *View* buzz and viewers to her new network.

Unlike the variety show, *The Rosie Show* premiered on October 10, 2011, to good reviews. She recycled some of her favorite tricks, including fun celebrity interviews with the likes of Russell Brand and Valerie Harper, along with more musical ditties and games with the audience. But the show's ratings quickly fizzled, averaging only 186,000 viewers.

It was one thing to be a successful talk show host. It was another to be putting on a show for almost nobody. The pressure got to Rosie. She started spinning in many directions. She wondered if she needed to be more political or focus more on serious guests.

Rosie picked fights with Oprah's longtime director Joe Terry, because he couldn't get the shots that she wanted. She made the job of her bandleader, Katreese Barnes, strenuous by calling out impromptu on live TV for songs to be played. "I'm not upset that I don't know 'Into the Woods' by heart," Barnes told me in an interview for *The Daily Beast*. "A little heads-up would have been nice."

The blame for *The Rosie Show* didn't fall solely on its host. She arrived at OWN shortly after the launch of the network. Rosie was slotted for 7:00 p.m. nightly, when most of her cultivated audience was sitting down for dinner with their families. Outside of that, it was hard to find the show on most TV dials. Oprah had asked Rosie to relocate to Chicago, to tape in the old studio from *The Oprah Winfrey Show* so they wouldn't have to fire stagehands and crew at Harpo. But that proved to be a bad fit. Rosie was a native New Yorker. In the Windy City, she looked homesick.

"She was surrounded by people she didn't know," said Janette Barber. "They were putting her in positions as producers that weren't working. Honestly, Rosie needs to sit. Did you ever notice that when she stands, her hands become an issue in a monologue? So don't float her out there. If you make her comfortable, the genius is going to come out."

After Christmas, Rosie moved to a smaller studio and got rid of her audience. But the writing was on the wall. *The Rosie Show* was canceled by Oprah in March 2012 after six months of dismal ratings. "I wish I could have done a little better for her," Rosie said. "It was a little disorganized."

By then, *The View* had totally moved on. "Rosie thought she was coming in to save us," Bill Geddie said. "You can't change this successful show. The person who got that was Whoopi. She always got that she worked for us. She was the custodian of a franchise that existed successfully long before her." Geddie shook his head. "Rosie never got that."

Part Three

Whoopi's View

17

Sister Act

Why would Whoopi Goldberg want to downgrade to television? Barbara Walters couldn't process this career U-turn. Here was the Oscar-winning star of *Ghost* and *Sister Act* taking up residence as the center square in a neon tic-tac-toe board for a reboot of *Hollywood Squares*. It was February 15, 1999, and Whoopi was a guest co-host on *The View* to promote her new game show. Most movie stars were still wary of spending a full hour at the Hot Topics table for fear of being seen as auditioning for Debbie Matenopoulos's seat, but Whoopi wasn't so precious about her image. Besides, she was proud to be producing *Hollywood Squares,* and she wanted to tell viewers about it.

Dressed in black from head to toe, with a pair of shades that dangled over her nose, like a true nineties celebrity, Whoopi rolled with the irreverent mix of news and girl talk. Since it was Presidents' Day, Meredith Vieira started with an obscene joke about Whoopi being a frequent visitor to the Oval Office, "but never on her knees."

That made Whoopi laugh. "I anticipated getting subpoenaed, but it never happened." She admitted that she refused to sleep over at the White House in case anything cataclysmic happened.

After a commercial break, the rest of the ladies cleared the stage so Barbara could conduct a one-on-one interview. Whoopi was prepping for her third lap as the host of the Academy Awards, and in a few weeks roughly 46 million viewers would tune in to watch her royal entrance as Queen Elizabeth I, decked out in a corset and a wig to the delight of everybody in the room (especially Meryl Streep). Whoopi only agreed to the notoriously difficult assignment after Oscars producer Gil Cates played up what it would mean to have a black woman emcee the last telecast of the twentieth century.

"Is there anything this woman can't do? She is our national treasure!" Barbara singled out some of Whoopi's recent accomplishments. "Why did you need *Hollywood Squares*? You're a big-time actress!"

"'Cause it was a good job, more than anything. A lot of good money. But also a little bit of control over what I was doing. You know, I've never had any control over movies. I've never produced any of my movies. I never got to that place where I could ask for those things."

"Why not?"

"I think because I didn't realize that was mine for the asking. Now I know. And I love television."

Barbara couldn't resist connecting the dots. Maybe Whoopi *could* apply to be a *View* cohost. As soon as Barbara blurted it out, she joked that Whoopi would be too hard to work with. "We feel she's a little overbearing, too strong."

"Everyone says that," Whoopi said. "Until they get to know me. And then they never come around."

Nobody took this exchange seriously because Whoopi was too big for *The View* in 1999, and the show couldn't afford her. Born as Caryn Elaine Johnson in 1955, Whoopi (as she renamed herself after the toy cushion) grew up in the New York City projects with a dream of becoming an actress. After a series of odd jobs, she joined an improv theater group in California, which helped her fine-tune her stage presence. In her late twenties, Whoopi traveled with her one-woman sketch show, called *The Spook Show*, to

Europe and then back to New York. Director Mike Nichols, who caught a performance, was so dazzled he took Whoopi under his wing, transporting her to Broadway in October 1984. The director of *The Graduate* was drawn to her unique talents. "One part Elaine May, one part Groucho, one part Ruth Draper, one part Richard Pryor, and five parts never seen before" is how Nichols described Goldberg to *The New York Times*. Her show became an HBO special, 1985's *Whoopi Goldberg: Direct from Broadway*, where she gained even more exposure.

That same year, Steven Spielberg cast her as Celie in *The Color Purple*, which earned her a Best Actress Oscar nomination. Whoopi became the first bankable black female movie star in Hollywood. Her two biggest hits were 1990's *Ghost* (where she won an Academy Award for playing a clairvoyant) and 1992's *Sister Act* (as a lounge singer who poses as a nun). By the time the 1993 sequel for *Sister Act* rolled out, the film's poster didn't need to spell out her last name. Whoopi had become a six-letter brand with international recognition.

Whoopi showed the world that female actresses of color could rule the box office, making room for Whitney Houston, Queen Latifah, Halle Berry, Tiffany Haddish, and others to follow. Keeping up with her multidimensional talents, Whoopi attempted a late-night talk show at the peak of her stardom in 1992. As the female counterpart to *The Arsenio Hall Show*, *The Whoopi Goldberg Show* lasted for a year, despite her A-list interviews with Joan Rivers, Carol Burnett, and a young Neil Patrick Harris. Compared to Barbara, Whoopi had a less confrontational—and more conversational—interview technique. In one episode, she lamented to Goldie Hawn about the double standard that women faced in Hollywood, where they weren't applauded for being strong and true to themselves.

"Unfortunately, it's confusing to men," Hawn said, about what happened when she tried to express her opinions to directors. "Suddenly, you're a bitch."

"It is possible to have it all." Whoopi tried to personify that. She once told me that her pal Elizabeth Taylor taught her an inventive trick. Every time one of her movies opened to big numbers, she'd call up the studio the next Monday and ask for a gift of a classic painting that she'd wanted. This allowed her to amass a fantastic art collection, with pieces by Andy Warhol and Cristina Vergano.

In Whoopi's forties, as is the case for most actresses, the starring roles in movies started to diminish. She still kept working, appearing in made-for-TV fairy tales such as ABC's *Cinderella* (as Prince Charming's mother) and NBC's *Alice in Wonderland* (the Cheshire Cat). Whoopi wasn't a prima donna by any stretch, but she had her quirks. When she traveled back and forth between New York and Los Angeles, she took a bus—called "the rolling house," with a bedroom and two alternating drivers—because she was scared of flying. She put on a lot of miles for *Hollywood Squares,* which she exited in 2002 when the production company tried to lower her salary.

In 2004 Whoopi's career hit another wall because of George W. Bush. Whoopi was performing at a fund-raiser for Democratic presidential nominee John Kerry when she made a cheeky joke: "I love bush. But someone is giving bush a bad name." Although it might seem tame by today's standards, the line created hysteria in the press. The next morning, the *New York Post* reported that she had delivered "an X-rated rant full of sexual innuendos against President Bush."

SlimFast dropped Whoopi as their national spokesperson. The Democratic National Convention didn't invite her to attend Kerry's speech in Boston. She stopped getting offered movie and TV roles, and she blamed the joke for that. "I never thought living in America, especially as a comic, you could be gotten economically like that," Whoopi told me later, sitting in the kitchen of her home in New Jersey. "I didn't work for years."

When Meredith left *The View,* Whoopi's team approached the show to see if they'd consider her as the new moderator, since she'd been a frequent guest. But Barbara, who was smitten by Rosie, didn't think she needed Whoopi.

In the summer of 2007, Barbara Walters found herself at a seemingly impossible fork in the road. Without Rosie O'Donnell, her earlier prophecy about *The View* might come true and the show might not survive with a new cast. To fight off a ratings drop, Barbara decided that she'd need to inject energy by hiring two new cohosts, bringing the number of ladies at the table back up to five. She'd have to leverage everything she and Bill Geddie knew about television to select the right women. But she also didn't want another loose cannon who'd spar with her endlessly on—and off—television.

The latest research conducted by the network pointed to trouble. Viewers polled by the strategy firm SmithGeiger responded that they saw Barbara and Elisabeth Hasselbeck in a more negative light as a result of their feuds with Rosie. "We believe Barbara and Elisabeth both remain assets of the show and will rebound quickly, assuming the fighting and controversy of the show are behind us," read the report, which I was able to look at. The document provided some guidance on hiring the new moderator: "In searching for a new cohost to fill the vacancy left by Rosie, *The View* should seek out a woman who can provide strength, humor, and a touch of the unexpected, without crossing the line into over-the-top outrageousness, arguing or name calling."

In her heart, Barbara wanted the moderator job for herself. There was no reason to worry about *The View* tarnishing her reputation anymore. And she was at a place in her career, at seventy-seven, when she had more time, because she wasn't chasing as many breaking news stories. She'd retired from *20/20* in 2004, as the program abandoned long-form journalism for trashier stories. Over the years, Barbara had gladly stepped in as the moderator when either Rosie or Meredith was out. But she had to face a hard truth: *The View* needed star power, and she couldn't justifiably take that job. "I thought it had to be a big name and so did Barbara," Geddie said.

Barbara once explained to me the conundrum that she had faced: "I felt funny, even though it was my show, saying, 'Why not me?' That's what happens when you wear two hats. When you're the producer, you say maybe there's someone better than I am. When you're me, you say, 'I'm as good as them!'"

Barbara and Bill had three names in the running to join *The View*. They were all black women, which wasn't a coincidence. The show wanted to speak to this important demographic that watched daytime TV. In time, this casting would be one of the smartest decisions that *The View* ever made, given the outcome of the 2008 election.

The first choice to replace Rosie was Whoopi. Not everybody was completely sold on her, though. "The only reservation I had was that Whoopi had done her own show and it had failed," recalled Brian Frons, who was privy to the decision making. "And there were two other things. One, was she going to bring the energy? Number two, was she going to dive in on the stuff"—such as pop culture and reality TV—"that was maybe less interesting to her given her sophistication and intelligence?"

The other option was Gayle King. Back then, before taking over as the coanchor of *CBS This Morning*, she was still known to America as Oprah's best friend. Some of the producers at *The View* favored King because they believed she was the most like Meredith. They thought, with her background in news, she could introduce the show's Hot Topics with the right touch, seamlessly moving from serious to silly stories. Everybody in daytime TV wanted to emulate Oprah. This would be as close as you could get.

Without making the show's intentions known to the public, Barbara asked King to audition. On June 20, Barbara introduced her. "We are very happy today to have our colleague and our friend Gayle King with us," Barbara said. "Gayle is a very busy lady. She is the editor-at-large of *O* magazine. I love that magazine."

Joy couldn't resist poking around, wondering what King's job entailed. "We need someone who's a liaison between Oprah in Chicago and me in New York," King said, not really explaining her duties. "And that's what

I do." She then talked about how she wished that O. J. Simpson, who had written a book called *If I Did It*, would go away, and she defended Hillary Clinton for picking a song by a Canadian—Celine Dion—for her campaign anthem. "If it's a good song, it doesn't matter to me," King said.

The following day, on June 21, King returned without Barbara, to give the moderator seat a test run. "I have to tell you I'm such a news junkie," King said, as she transitioned to a story about an engaged couple that planned on returning all their wedding gifts. "I'm so fascinated by things in the news."

The research indicated the audience preferred Whoopi. She was more popular than all the other cohosts on the show, too. When asked to rate Whoopi's favorability on a scale from 1 to 10, 64 percent of respondents gave her a score of an 8 or higher, according to internal documents. That was better than Barbara and Joy, who were both at 53 percent. King stood at 51 percent. Elisabeth came in dead last at only 36 percent, down from 42 percent before Rosie had joined the show.

Ultimately, it had to be a gut call since the research couldn't actually predict who would save *The View*. Barbara, Geddie, and producer Alexandra Cohen all decided to put the new moderator to a vote. Cohen picked Gayle. Geddie wanted Whoopi. "And I guess I had the deciding vote," Barbara told me. "Although I think Gayle would have been wonderful, I thought Whoopi hasn't been seen for a while, and she's funny. I voted for Whoopi."

Geddie was confident they had made the right decision. "I knew Whoopi better than I knew Gayle," Geddie said. "She would come on and make the show work and do the things we asked her to do. She had also been beaten up a little bit. She had a rough run with movies. I thought that we could rebuild her career together. I thought that was exciting. It was also an honor to be with somebody who was so talented, so lauded."

The thing that had made King famous—her connection to Oprah— also worked against her with *The View*. Barbara worried that Oprah might try to somehow hijack *The View*, leading to another ugly turf war.

"My feeling with Gayle was—how do I say this in the nicest possible way, because I love her?" Geddie said. "She came from Oprah's world. Having just been through Rosie, I didn't need someone else telling me how to run the show. And I thought Gayle would be telling me how to the run the show. That was my honest opinion."

King was disappointed when she found out she wasn't chosen. "I was very interested," she told me. "But that didn't work out. I thought it would be fun because, listen, you get to give your opinion, which I love. I love pop culture. I love politics. I thought you get to do the two." And she would also have been able to sleep in, a luxury she's not afforded with her current morning show. "It had better hours."

Whoopi wasn't the only new cohost. *The View* also wanted to hire Sherri Shepherd, which is ironic, because she had to fight to be a guest on the show. From 2002 to 2006, the comedic actress played a peon at a TV network on the ABC sitcom *Less Than Perfect* with Andy Dick and Zachary Levi. "Everyone on that show had gone on," she told me. "They wouldn't book me." Her publicist told her that Bill Geddie didn't know who she was. "One day"—in March 2005—"Johnnie Cochran died. Star Jones had to go to his funeral. I was pregnant and on bed rest. And my publicist called to say that Bill said, 'If she came out here on a plane, we're booking her.'" Sherri boarded the next flight for New York. "I came in on a wheelchair."

Geddie liked Sherri's timing, and they had her back for more episodes. As the show was getting ready to dump Star, Sherri got the feeling that *The View* was trying to woo her for that seat. They even had an African-American producer talk to her about the advantages of working there. "I'm, like, 'Okay, you guys are sending a black woman to try to get me on board.'" Sherri laughed.

Meet the *View* co-hosts: Debbie, Star, Joy, Meredith, and Barbara, from the show's 1997 press kit. Also pictured (from left) producers Roni Selig and Jessica Guff and executive producer Bill Geddie. Credit: ABC

The ladies with their first victim—and guest—actor Tom Selleck on the premiere on August 11, 1997. Credit: © American Broadcasting Companies, Inc.

After the show, Barbara always held a post-mortem meeting with the staff. Credit: Bernadette Piccolomini

On April Fool's Day 1998, the cohosts faced off against their *SNL* doppelgangers: Molly Shannon (as Meredith), Tracy Morgan (as Star), and Cheri Oteri (as Barbara). Credit: © American Broadcasting Companies, Inc.

Hillary Clinton made her first *View* visit on October 13, 2003.
Credit: © American Broadcasting Companies, Inc.

Elisabeth, Star, Joy, and Meredith at the Christmas party, before all the wedding freebies wrecked their friendship. Credit: Bernadette Piccolomini

"Rosie O'Donnell is a great talent," Barbara said. "She also has, shall we say, emotional problems." Credit: © American Broadcasting Companies, Inc.

The View from the elevator: the cohosts rode together each morning from their dressing rooms on the second floor to the studio on the third floor.

Credit: Bernadette Piccolomini

Michelle Obama fist bumps Elisabeth as a guest cohost on June 18, 2008, before her husband accepted the Democratic nomination.
Credit: © American Broadcasting Companies, Inc.

Barack Obama became the first sitting president to grant an interview to a daytime talk show on July 29, 2010. Credit: © American Broadcasting Companies, Inc.

Cramming during a commercial.
Credit: Bernadette Piccolomini

Whoopi sits in Joy's lap during a Hot Topics meeting.
Credit: Bernadette Piccolomini

Director Mark Gentile in the control room.
Credit: Bernadette Piccolomini

Barbara with her beloved
hairdresser, Bryant.
Credit: Bryant Renfroe

On May 15, 2014, the 11 *View* cohosts gathered for Barbara's retirement.
From left: Whoopi, Meredith, Star, Debbie, Joy, Barbara, Lisa, Elisabeth,
Rosie, Jenny, and Sherri. Credit: © American Broadcasting Companies, Inc.

Senator John McCain at *The View* for his daughter Meghan's birthday on October 23, 2017. Credit: © American Broadcasting Companies, Inc.

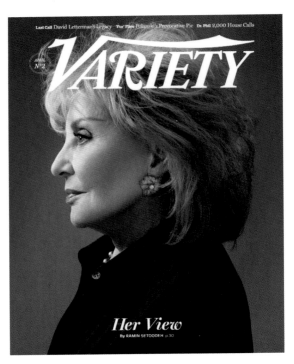

In April 2014, I wrote this *Variety* cover story on Barbara about her legacy and fifty-year career on TV.
Credit: *Variety*

Finally, Barbara Walters approached her in the hall one day. "We'd like you to come on the show, dear."

"I said, 'Barbara, I got a child with special needs,'" Sherri said about her son, Jeffrey, who was born in April 2005. "He's got all this stuff in LA. So I'm going to say no.'" Barbara wished her well. "I knew when she walked away that I maybe made a mistake. And they never called me after that," at least through the rest of the season. "I knew there were some things going on with Star, and I didn't like being part of it. I don't like drama."

That next year, Sherri was back as a fill-in. She was in the middle of a messy separation from her first husband, Jeff Tarpley, who had cheated on her. She laid it all out for the audience, and she killed it. Even Rosie started rooting for her, bonding with a hardworking single mom. Sherri appeared as the guest cohost on *The View* in May 2007 on the day of the infamous Rosie-versus-Elisabeth fight. Barbara was impressed that Sherri didn't sell out the show by doing interviews about what had transpired. Kathy Griffin, who was also vying for a seat on the show, was less discreet. "When Kathy came on the next day, she kept trying to go there and make jokes," Sherri recalled. "They were really uncomfortable. They knew I could keep my mouth shut."

Barbara decided to offer the fifth seat on *The View* to Sherri. It wasn't the most expected choice. Sherri had grown up as a Jehovah's Witness in Chicago, with a knack for comedy. Her stand-up routine was squeaky-clean, which worked in her favor for daytime TV. She'd spent the early part of her career as a recurring character on sitcoms such as *Suddenly Susan* and *Everybody Loves Raymond*. In 2007, she was cast as Tracy Morgan's no-nonsense wife on *30 Rock*.

"It was very interesting," Geddie said. "A lot of people said to me, 'Why do you want Sherri? You already got your black woman.'" This disgusting insinuation revealed how the tokenistic racism of network executives shaped the casting of a TV show. Geddie challenged the notion that Whoopi and Sherri were in any way similar. "I said, 'This is going to be a completely revolutionary thing.' A lot of white people think black people think the same about a lot of things—certainly ten years ago, they did. We were going to show they were completely different people with different points of view about almost everything except for they are black women."

Although that sounds like common sense now, it wasn't always the case on TV. For a long time, many panel shows thought they checked the diversity box if they had one woman (or man) of color as part of the cast. "Actually, it's one of my proudest moments, that we were able to hire two black women for *The View* at the same time," Geddie said. "I thought it spoke well of the show we were trying to create, and it spoke well of ABC for letting it happen."

The only problem: Sherri wasn't sure she wanted to do *The View*. She'd always thought of herself as an actress. If she moved to New York, she couldn't take her son with her until her legal disputes had been resolved with her husband, whom she divorced in 2010. "I was probably six hundred thousand dollars in the hole going through this custody battle," Sherri said. "I didn't have a lot of money." She was disappointed by how small *The View*'s offer was.

Sherri found a secret friend as she negotiated for more pay. Although Rosie had been banished from *The View*, she became Sherri's agent, texting her salary advice. "'This is what they are offering me, which is hugely, grossly low,'" Sherri recalled saying. "Rosie was amazing. She said to me, 'This is what I made. This is what Joy makes. This is what Elisabeth makes.' They had offered me a salary that was lower than Elisabeth. Rosie said, 'You're an established actress. Go back and counter with this amount!' They came up."

Rosie pushed her to ask for more perks. "They paid my rent"—worth $85,000—"for the first year," Sherri said. ABC had initially offered her one business-class plane ticket to New York. As part of her renegotiated deal, she got eight first-class tickets to Los Angeles to visit her son on the weekends.

The experience taught Sherri that women have to help each other out at the negotiating table. "To this day, if there's a woman who does a talk show, I'll let her know what I make," Shepherd said. In 2010, CBS launched their own knockoff version of *The View*, called *The Talk*.

"When Sheryl Underwood got *The Talk*, she had no idea what she was supposed to ask for," Sherri said. "She had no clue, and I told her. Of course they are going to offer you the lowest amount. I was very thankful to Rosie for what she did for me."

ABC had originally intended on revealing Whoopi and Sherri together as the new cohosts. But as the talks dragged on with Sherri, the press started reporting that the two women were joining *The View*. On August 1, 2007, Barbara promised viewers a surprise: "You may notice that we are only three. Well, we're almost four. Because today we have a very big announcement to make." But she didn't name Whoopi yet. Instead, she turned to a story in the tabloids about how Britney Spears was a bad mother and asked, "Are people picking on her or is this really out of control?"

After an interview with Jon Voight and a segment on "kids' summer gadgets," Barbara was ready to confirm what everybody knew. "You are about to meet the new moderator of *The View*, and we are thrilled," Barbara said in the show's last minutes. Whoopi entered the studio, as fans scrambled to give her a high five on the way to the stage.

"So, listen, did you ever watch *The View*?" Barbara asked.

"Once or twice," Whoopi said. "I remember seeing it. You look familiar." She said she had to unplug her home phone because her mother wanted to know if the stories about her new job were true.

Sherri officially joined the cast on September 10, 2007. "This is the worst-kept secret of the month," Barbara said as she introduced her to the Four Seasons' song "Sherry."

"Oh my gosh." Sherri sat in the middle of the table and let out a scream. "I'm actually one of the girls."

Nobody was sure if this new team would coalesce into a ratings victory. Whoopi's first day as moderator got off to a less-than-ideal start when she defended disgraced football player Michael Vick for his dogfighting ring that led to the death of innocent animals. "This is part of his cultural upbringing," Whoopi said, arguing that people in the South were accustomed to such things. She was swiftly denounced by animal rights groups.

Brian Frons called Whoopi that night at home. "There was a lot of bad press," he recalled.

"Hi, boss," she said. "Am I in trouble?"

"She was scared," Frons remembered. "You could hear it in her voice." Whoopi was worried that she'd already crossed a line. Frons assured her that the network still supported her. The next day, Whoopi issued a clarification that she didn't endorse animal fighting. She was just trying to point out that it was a long-standing tradition in parts of the country. It was her only early blip. In a few weeks, Whoopi had stabilized *The View* and created a new era of prosperity for the show.

Sherri had a more difficult time adjusting. When she'd come on for a day, it was easy to fire off a round of jokes and be done. But as a regular cohost, she suddenly found herself in the middle of lofty discussions leading up to the 2008 presidential election. She didn't know what to say. "It was the politics," Sherri told me. "I was a Jehovah's Witness. They don't vote. I never voted. Even though I'm not in the religion anymore, that's what I learned. I don't like conflict. I don't like debating and arguing. I was raised not to speak back to my elders. The lady who created the show was an elder. That was very hard for me. I was just a funny girl."

Sherri made an infamous mistake on her second week on the show. In the morning meeting that day, the ladies decided they wanted to talk about evolution vs. creationism. While getting her makeup done, Barbara looked at Sherri through the mirror and declared, "I want to debate my Christian friend."

Sherri had no idea what that meant. On TV, the discussion started off without much flare. Then Whoopi tried to make a point about rejecting something that we all know to be false: "Is the world flat?"

"I don't know," Sherri responded.

There was a second of devastating silence.

"What do you think?" Whoopi asked.

"I never thought about it, Whoopi."

"You never thought about whether the world was round?" Barbara asked.

"But I'll tell you what I've thought about," Sherri said, trying to recover. "How I'm going to feed my child. Is the world flat has not been an important thing to me."

"Didn't Columbus already work this question out?" Joy quipped.

This moment almost ended Sherri's career. "I was so nervous," Sherri told me. "I don't debate. I swear I blanked out in that moment. I literally had a brain fart." That clip suddenly became how people identified her. "I didn't realize until my phone was ringing off the hook how serious this was. People who had been rooting for me were completely ashamed. I think I lost my black card. Black people were, like, 'She has taken us back two hundred years.' Bill Maher said I should be fired with a stupid stick. Bill O'Reilly called me a pinhead. That's when it hit me: This is a huge show. I found out I was the second-most-googled person in the country."

The next morning, while she was preparing to go back on TV, she heard Wendy Williams say on the radio that Sherri could be replaced with a potato sack. Sherri lost it in her dressing room. "I broke down and cried. Someone went and told Whoopi, and she flew into the room."

"Sherri, Barbara picked you, which means she wants you," Whoopi comforted. "Look into my eyes."

"But she was wearing those colored glasses," Sherri recalled. "I said, 'Whoopi, I can't see your eyes!' And she flipped them up and said, 'Turn that off.' She really encouraged me."

Sherri realized she had to cram harder for this gig. She took the job seriously, studying the headlines of the day and coming up with personal takes on stories. "I started reading the newspaper. I never used to do that."

Whoopi helped her in another way to prepare for her new life in New York. One afternoon, Whoopi invited Sherri to the Time Warner Center for an interview Whoopi was conducting with Bill O'Reilly. Although Sherri had a wardrobe provided to her on TV, her own clothes were modest. "I wore what you normally wear in California, which is a Gap tank top, a denim skirt, and flip-flops," Sherri said. "I remember she introduced me to Bill, and he looked at me like roaches were crawling out of my head. Who is this person that represents *The View*?"

Like a great makeover scene from a romantic comedy, their next stop was a clothing store. Whoopi took Sherri to an Eileen Fisher boutique in downtown Manhattan. "She stood outside the dressing room," Sherri said. "I'm looking at the price tag, going, 'This is three hundred dollars!' The winter coat was eight hundred dollars. My credit card limit was two thousand dollars. I'm going, 'I'm not going to be able to afford this.' We go up to the counter and I don't know what to tell them when my card gets declined. I'm thinking, 'I'm going to embarrass Whoopi.'"

Sherri tried to gracefully leave the store. "As they're ringing it up, I said, 'I think I'm going to have to put some of these back.' They said, 'Oh, no. Ms. Goldberg already paid for everything.'"

Sherri couldn't believe Whoopi's generosity. "I hugged her and I was just bawling. She said, 'Pay it forward.' That's all she said. After that, I was chic."

18

Elisabeth's Last Stand

I f Bill Clinton helped put *The View* on the map, Barack Obama affirmed the show's place at the very center of the conversation. The 2008 presidential election was a nonstop marathon of debates related to gender and race, from Jeremiah Wright's inflammatory sermons to Hillary Clinton's razor-thin primary defeat and Sarah Palin's pro-life beliefs. *The View* was more than equipped to tackle all of that, thanks to the ingenious casting of its new panel.

"We never talk about race," Whoopi said on November 5, 2008, the day after Obama's historic victory. "This is the great thing about this show. We talk about things that no one else on television talks about."

Whoopi had spent the night of the election at home, watching on TV as the Obamas ascended the stage at Grant Park in Chicago. She called her mom to ask a question that hadn't occurred to her before: *Did she ever think she'd live to see this day?* Her answer gutted Whoopi: *No, I never thought this day would come in my lifetime.* "I always thought of myself as an American with all of the promise that America holds," Whoopi said on the show. "But suddenly, last night, I felt like I could put my suitcase down."

The other ladies tried to offer their own takes, with Elisabeth unravel-ing a saccharine story about how she told her daughter, Grace, there were no losers from the election. Barbara still couldn't get over how Hillary Clinton had fallen short despite her immense campaign funds. But none of these opinions on *The View* would have resonated without the two African-American women at the table.

Sherri Shepherd wept with happiness as she talked about voting for the first time, taking her son, Jeffrey, along with her to the polls to cast her ballot for Obama. As a young girl, she'd always been told she wouldn't have the same opportunities as other people because of the color of her skin. "To look at my son and say, 'No limitations on you,' it is an extraor-dinary day for me," Sherri said, her words cracking. *The View* had un-doubtedly reclaimed its voice.

In her first year as moderator, Whoopi had kept the show running without any major scandals, and, more important, she'd actually improved on Rosie's strong numbers. "We were in the catbird's seat," said Bill Ged-die. "We had two black women at the table for this historic event. That year, when Barack Obama became president, that whole political season leading up to John McCain and *Game Change* and Sarah Palin; that, to me, is the best *The View* ever was! I always figured after Meredith left it was going to be diminishing returns. It wasn't. We were on *Time*'s most influential list. We were flying high. The wind was in our hair, man."

Barbara naturally took credit for Whoopi's career comeback. "I do feel that we started a whole new chapter in Whoopi's career, and I must say she's always appreciative," Barbara told me in 2011. "Not everyone says thank you, but Whoopi always does. In this case, we offered her a new opportunity and a steady job. It just gave her a boost to every aspect of her life."

Whoopi viewed *The View* as a financial safety net. The show allowed her a multimillion-dollar paycheck (which Whoopi needed because she covered the living expenses of several of her family members), while it left her afternoons free to produce TV shows, documentaries, and plays.

Whoopi didn't try to control and litigate every aspect of *The View* as Rosie had. Whoopi was more laid-back, and she deferred to the other cohosts and the crew. She saw herself as an employee-for-hire, not the boss.

Sherri proved her own worth as she dialed up the humor at the table. Some producers initially questioned if the audience could forgive her for her flub about the earth's being flat, but she overcame that. Geddie pulled her aside early to tell her that she wasn't talking enough.

"If you don't speak up, Barbara will eat you alive," Geddie advised her.

"That's when I learned to speak up," Sherri said. "Barbara gave me more room and respect." If Sherri got cut off, she'd push back, telling the *View* creator that she needed to finish her point. "Some people on social media would say, 'How dare you speak to Barbara like that?' What are you talking about? Barbara taught me how to do that."

The daytime viewers didn't miss the toxic fighting. They stuck with the show, even as the iciness among the ladies thawed. It helped that the 2008 campaign provided more than enough drama for Hot Topics. Because *The View* was an established TV brand, the candidates saw it as a valuable platform for reaching women voters. The only political star of the season that the show couldn't snag was Sarah Palin, who stopped doing interviews after her disastrous sit-down with the *CBS Evening News*'s anchor, Katie Couric. But Elisabeth spent an October weekend in Florida campaigning with the vice-presidential hopeful, a reminder that the personalities on *The View* weren't journalists. On TV, Elisabeth wore a T-shirt that she designed herself with the words "Real AmeriCAIN Hero," over protests from ABC about it looking like a free ad.

In September, John McCain became the first Republican presidential nominee to brave the program. It was one of his toughest interviews (no offense to George Stephanopoulos), as the five cohosts jumped all over him. A headline from *The New York Times* said it all: "*The View* Couch Not So Cozy for McCain."

"No softballs coming from me, even though you have my vote!" Elisabeth said, teeing off a tense conversation about overturning *Roe v. Wade*.

Whoopi wanted to know if McCain believed in the separation of church and state, wondering what would happen if Palin replaced him in a tragedy. When he described himself as a strict constitutionalist, she asked, "Should I be worried about returning to slavery?"

But the most awkward moments arrived courtesy of the resident liberal. "I believe if he's elected, he will go back to the old John McCain that he used to be, unless the Republican base has him by the short hairs," Joy said, speaking about the senator from Arizona as if he weren't seated next to her.

"He's so polite," Barbara said as McCain winced.

"You used to be more of the maverick. Then you turned," Joy said a few minutes later. "You became more lockstep with your party, with George Bush's policies." She brought up a few smear-campaign ads, including one that said Obama wanted to teach sex education to kindergartners. "They are lies, and yet you at the end of it say, 'I approve this message!'"

McCain tried to duck. "I would be glad to come on this show with Senator Obama."

"You bring us Sarah Palin, we'll ask Barack Obama," Barbara said. That showdown never took place, but the Obamas were the first presidential couple that backed *The View* from the start, using the show to communicate to moms in America. Barack's first *View* appearance was as a rising star of the Democratic Party. He returned as a presidential candidate in March 2008. That interview got off to an easy start with Joy asking if he was related to Brad Pitt, which had been reported in the press. "I guess we're ninth cousins, something removed," he said. From there, he spent ten minutes answering difficult questions about Jeremiah Wright, as he made the case for why voters should choose him over Hillary Clinton, whom he was still fighting in the primary season.

Michelle Obama made a series of visits, too, filling in as a guest cohost in the summer of 2008. "I have to be greeted properly," she told the table. "Fist bump, please."

"When Michelle Obama came to cohost with us, Lizzie was going away for the weekend," Sherri told me. "She's so OCD, she made a long list for the babysitter. I remember taking the list and throwing it on the floor." The future first lady witnessed that exchange. After she left, Michelle called Elisabeth from the car to chat with her about being able to let go of the little things as a mom. "Elisabeth broke down in tears," Sherri told me. "I think she'd deny it to this day. I was, like, 'How the hell did you get a call from Michelle Obama? You don't even like the woman!'"

Even Bill Clinton forgave *The View*. In September 2008, he clocked his first visit, predicting that Obama would win the election. While he was there, he revealed his admiration for one of the show's cohosts. "Bill Clinton loves black movies," Sherri recalled. "I have an underground hit called *Who's Your Caddy?*" He leaned over during the commercial break. "He said, 'I watched *Who's Your Caddy?* five times!' He knew all my lines from a movie I did with Big Boi and all these comics."

The next time Clinton was on, Barbara was deep in a conversation with the former president backstage about world affairs. He stopped her for something more important. "Did you see Sherri in *One for the Money,* where she played a hooker and she was so good!?" he asked about a little-seen crime caper starring Katherine Heigl. To prove he wasn't bluffing, he brought up a scene where Sherri's character pulled a doughnut out of her purse. "He knew everything that I'd done in this movie," Sherri said. "I remember Barbara looking at me. She'd go somewhere with Hillary and Bill. She'd come back and say, 'I just want you to know Bill Clinton is such a big fan of yours. He won't stop talking about you.'"

The View coasted through Obama's first term. The high point was that Obama made another visit in July 2010, as the first sitting president to grant an interview on a daytime talk show. Obama, who wanted to talk directly to the America public about his policies before the midterms, was pop-culture savvy enough to know what he was doing. He'd made one of his inaugural TV pitches on Tyra Banks's talk show and later used Oprah's endorsement on the eve of the Iowa caucuses to knock down Clinton.

But nobody received a free pass on *The View,* not even the commander in chief. Sherri told the president that many black people felt that they weren't getting enough support from his administration. During the commercial, he wanted her to know that he'd heard her. "Sherri, I try to do as much as I can," he told her.

As *The View* approached its fifteenth birthday, the show was still a force. In 2011, I was backstage working on a profile of Whoopi for *Newsweek.* After quizzing me about why I wasn't writing about her, Barbara invited me to her dressing room. "It's very interesting to me because the audience loves Whoopi," Barbara said. "And she is not without controversy." Barbara offered me an example. "We were talking about some television show. Whoopi said, 'As for me, I'd rather stay home and smoke a joint.' Someone else does that, you would get letters. But Whoopi does it in such a good-natured and honest way, the audience applauded. That's Whoopi." Barbara sounded at once both complimentary and a little envious.

"Our ratings are very high," Barbara concluded. As I got up to leave, she stopped me. "I just want to say, whether it's on-the-record or off-the-record"—she strained for suspense in her voice—"this is a terrific lady." I was momentarily confused why she was acting as if she were sharing government secrets, before realizing that she was still a master at manipulating the press.

Whoopi had taken over Rosie's old dressing room, but it didn't have the same bad juju. She had lined a full wall with shelves to display more than a hundred colorful sneakers, from Alexander McQueen and other high-end designers. On the morning of my visit with Whoopi, she was less buoyant than usual. She'd just learned about her friend Elizabeth Taylor's death. After recounting some of her memories to me, Whoopi left to moderate the show. The show had an obnoxious guest that day.

"Why doesn't he show his birth certificate?" said Donald Trump, who had just started spreading his birther conspiracy theories about Obama.

Whoopi cringed. "I'm sorry, is Hawaii not part of the United States? Am I blind?" As Trump rambled on, Whoopi wouldn't let him off the hook. "I think that's the biggest pile of dog mess I've heard in ages. It's not because he's black—"

"It has nothing to do with it," Trump insisted.

Although nobody could imagine Trump as a future politician, the exchange made waves. The press noted that Whoopi had challenged Trump and came close to calling him a racist, and he didn't get mad at her as he did with Rosie. Trump knew that she was too popular. According to the Q Scores company, which tracks celebrity favorability, Whoopi was more liked than Oprah.

That year, *The View* managed to outlast the biggest star of daytime. In May, Oprah invited the five cohosts to her studio for a final interview before leaving daytime, as a way to pass the torch. Barbara sent Oprah's producers scrambling minutes before airtime, when she ordered them to find a clip from 1984—the first time she visited Oprah's set. The trip to Chicago was also stressful.

Barbara wanted someone to sit next to her on the plane. Joy, who'd been her traveling companion in the past, had no interest in making that sacrifice. She'd grown tired of hearing the same stories about how Jackie resented her mother, and Joy didn't want to be trapped with Barbara for two hours. Finally, to fix the situation, Barbara's hairdresser, Bryant Renfroe, upgraded to first class, using his own frequent-flier miles.

He owed his friend. Barbara had recently set him up—through an acquaintance of Jackie's—with Joseph Dwyer, the man who'd become his husband. "How often does that happen?" Renfroe said. Barbara had shown him a picture of the eligible bachelor on the day they were taping an interview with Jennifer Lopez for one of her specials. Barbara approached matchmaking with the same verve as she did chasing a scoop. "And the whole time at the interview, it was all about, 'Did you talk to him yet? Have you met him yet? When are you going to meet him?'"

"It's going to work," Renfroe recalled Barbara telling him. When it did, Renfroe asked Geddie to be the best man at his wedding in December 2011.

One reason the *View* staff was so insular was because the show didn't fire many of its producers. Barbara didn't think it was worth the trouble. She'd rather keep her inner circle close than risk them leaking horrible stories to the press. (That's not to say those stories didn't leak anyway.) But there were two notable exceptions. Despite landing many of the show's biggest stars, the booker Sue Solomon got caught by the network in a thorny ethics violation in 2013. The show's publicist Karl Nilsson had heard murmurs about Solomon engaging in activity that violated the company's standards. She'd store the free press copies of hardcover books mailed to the show by publishers, load them up in a rolling suitcase (called "the bookmobile" by the staff), and sell them to the Manhattan bookstore the Strand for pocket change.

Although Solomon was only making small sums of money, Nilsson tattled on her. When a human resources manager confronted Solomon, she admitted it, not realizing that it was a fireable offense. Barbara tried to save her by mounting a defense, but it didn't do any good. ABC wanted to make an example out of her, to demonstrate that they had a zero-tolerance policy for freebies in a post–Star Jones workplace. After *The View* axed Solomon, they were down one less booker to wrangle the celebrity guests.

The next casualty was even stranger. Joy increasingly found herself at odds with her comedy writer Andrew Smith, who had been on the staff since the beginning of *The View.* They had been squabbling because Smith claimed that Joy used some of the jokes that he wrote for her on *The View* for a new prime-time show she was hosting on HLN. Smith wouldn't let it go, complaining that she owed him a second paycheck. Joy was over it, and she asked Geddie to get rid of him.

When Geddie tried, Smith clutched his chest in horror, like he was having a heart attack. "He didn't have a heart attack," said Joy, who heard about it later. "I wasn't in the room. The word is that he collapsed." An ambulance pulled up at the *View* studio and wheeled him away to the hospital, where he told friends that he was diagnosed with a broken heart. Smith plotted for revenge by spending years on a manuscript for a *Devil Wears Prada*–like roman à clef about working for a daytime talk show, titled *In the Ladies' Room.* He featured savage lampoons of everyone on *The View,* from an executive producer ("Bad Bob") who was only concerned about being on camera himself to a transgender cohost with rage issues to Beverly Frost, an iconic yet superficial journalist who milked her interactions with celebrities to advance her own fame.

When the narrator of the story is about to get fired, he fakes a heart attack to save his job. The character plots against his boss, an over-the-hill comedian reminiscent of Joy Behar who cares more about her hair than her zingers. However, no publisher would touch this twisted diatribe, which he quietly self-published to no acclaim or notice.

"I never read it," Joy said. "Was it any good?"

The View had fought through its share of adversaries, but none compared to Mitt Romney. The next Republican presidential nominee was such a bore that the cohosts couldn't build up much interest arguing about him in 2012. "We thought the next election would be just as big for us," Geddie recalled. "It turns out that Barack Obama versus Mitt Romney was not interesting to anybody. We went all-in and you never saw the dial budge."

The View faced competition from *The Talk,* the CBS panel show started in 2010 by actress Sara Gilbert with gushy conversations with celebrities but no politics. Although the show got off to a soft start, CBS kept tweaking it until it started to pick up steam. It had one advantage that *The View* didn't. One of its cohosts, Julie Chen, was the wife of former CBS chairman Leslie Moonves. "We're not at all affected by *The Talk*," Barbara once told me. "I don't think the success of her show diminishes us. Nor do I think the success or failure of *The View* affects them." Barbara was aware that they had promotional leverage. "The only thing I'll say is, if you're married to the president of the network, you get more promos." (Chen left *The Talk* in September 2018, after CBS fired her husband for sexual assault allegations.)

But *The Talk* was hurting *The View* by closing the gap in the ratings. In 2011, as part of a series of management shake-ups, ABC pushed out Brian Frons as the head of daytime, with a less experienced network executive, Vicki Dummer, taking over his duties. "That led the network to come to us after the election and say, 'This whole political stuff isn't working,'" Geddie said. "It's kind of funny now when you think about it."

ABC wanted to get rid of Elisabeth, who was never popular with the liberal executives to begin with. Research showed that her likability numbers were low. They'd never rebounded after the Rosie feud, and ABC blamed her polarizing personality for keeping ratings on *The View* stagnant. Geddie argued that the numbers didn't tell the whole story because viewers loved to loathe Elisabeth. "Here's what would happen," Geddie said. "The focus group is full of people who are willing to spend an entire day for fifty dollars and a free sandwich. Are they Republicans? No. You're listening to liberals talk about Elisabeth Hasselbeck."

As all these discussions were going on, Barbara was suffering from a series of health setbacks. She'd managed to stay on TV through her early eighties, an extraordinary feat. She had no interest in signing off, even though she'd dangle it as something that would hypothetically happen one day. "I never believed she would retire," Anne Sweeney told me. In May 2010, Barbara had open-heart surgery to replace an aortic valve, as doctors stopped her heart for thirty minutes. She was ordered to rest.

But she sneaked out of bed for the Obama interview. "I remember looking at her, going, 'This woman has nine lives,'" Sherri said. "She's not in heaven because she knew Obama was coming."

The next time she needed serious medical help, her recovery wouldn't be so quick. In January 2013, at eighty-three, Barbara fell and cut her head at an inauguration party in Washington, DC. Ten days after that, she came down with a rare case of chicken pox, which she told colleagues she contracted from an acquaintance, the actor Frank Langella, who had been Whoopi's boyfriend. When Whoopi announced Barbara's diagnosis on *The View*, the audience got quiet. "Apparently, she'd never had it as a child," Whoopi said. "She's not allowed any visitors. We are telling you, Barbara, no scratching. We love you, we miss you. We just don't want to hug you."

"This is what you get for interviewing Honey Boo Boo," Joy Behar said, laughing.

Producers say that when Barbara returned to work in March, she wasn't the same. Her memory was foggy, and although she could still fire off tough questions, she would get tripped up about the chronology of events. It was time for her to think about slowing down. Around that time, she had lunch with Sweeney and asked her to write down the year 2014 on a scrap of paper.

"A couple months later, she said, 'Do you have that piece of paper?'" Sweeney recalled. "She picked her date."

In the meantime, the network was getting anxious about *The View* as the vultures started circling. Dummer wanted to move quickly to do something for the next season, so that the ratings could improve in Barbara's last year. "We need to change things up and get rid of your far left and far right—Joy and Elisabeth—and make the show more daytime friendly," Dummer told Geddie.

"Which, of course," he added, "was the kiss of death."

There may have been a reason to fire Elisabeth. But dumping Joy was a kamikaze move. Viewers consistently ranked her as one of their favorite cohosts on the show. For whatever reason, ABC thought they had to scrub clean any trace of politics from *The View*.

It's not exactly clear who pulled the trigger. Some of the network executives blame Barbara, claiming that she had grown tired of Elisabeth and her backstage temper tantrums. They say that she helped expedite Elisabeth's demise by arguing that she needed to be replaced. When asked about that, Barbara dodged any of the blame. "These are not Barbara and Bill's decisions," she said, about what happened to Elisabeth and Joy. "The network is also involved. I think the feeling was, if one went, both had to leave. We needed to shake things up."

Geddie tried to save them. "My whole argument was, 'You can't tell what the show is going to be until Barbara leaves. Why not let her leave and we can regroup and see how the show feels?'" He reminded the network that what made *The View* special in the first place was its emphasis on politics.

"No, the show is hemorrhaging now," Dummer decided. "We need to change now."

"Television is not a very patient business," Geddie recalled.

They broke the bad news to both ladies at the same time. One day after the show, Geddie and the network's vice president of daytime programming, Randall Barone, called a meeting with Elisabeth. They told her that ABC wasn't renewing her contract for Season 17 of *The View*, and she'd have until the summer to find a new job. "Did she know it was coming? I don't think so," Geddie said, confirming for the first time that Elisabeth was fired from *The View*. She started crying.

"She was emotional," Geddie recalled. "I was emotional. When you do a show like *The View*, these people are forced to give themselves every day. They walk out relatively unprotected and have to say something that may get them in trouble. So our job as producers is to know they have a soft place to land. We were in the papers almost every day. They were coming after us every day. We got really close."

Then Geddie and Barone went to Joy's dressing room. "I had no clue really," Joy told me. "I was, like, 'Hi, guys.' They were very sheepish because they knew they were making a mistake. They said, 'We're not renewing.' I said, 'Thank God! I've been waiting for this.'" She volunteered to leave that week, but Geddie told her they needed her for a few more months. After sixteen years, Joy was ready to move on.

"I had been planning to get out of there," Joy said. "It's very hard to give up a high-paying job. It's like leaving a marriage. No one is getting hurt. You're just bored."

Geddie was torn up about it. "I was trying not to cry like a baby. To me, Joy—as much as Barbara and Meredith—was a very important part of the show. It was hard for me to let her go. It was hard for me to let Elisabeth go. It would have been easier for me to go with them."

On March 7, 2013, Joy Behar announced that she was fleeing *The View* that August to focus on unspecified projects. As was the case with almost all the fired cohosts that preceded her, she framed it as a decision that she made on her own. No sooner had she bid her farewell than press reports surfaced that Elisabeth would also be getting the boot.

Yet the show wasn't ready to reveal that yet. On March 11, Barbara delivered a stern lecture, assuring viewers that Elisabeth had a place at the table for as long as she'd like to stay. "We have no plans for Elisabeth to leave this show," she lied. Behind the scenes, Barbara was working to help Elisabeth land on her feet. Barbara turned to her friend Roger Ailes at Fox News. It was the least she could do for a colleague. Barbara didn't want Elisabeth to attack the show on her way out in the same way as Rosie and Star had. Ailes agreed to sign Elisabeth, although he let it be known at Fox News that he only hired her as a favor to Barbara.

Two months later, in May, Barbara had her own announcement. "So let me say that I have been on television continuously for over fifty years," she said, as old glamorous head shots popped up on the screen. "But in the summer of 2014, a year from now, I plan to retire from appearing on television at all." She made it clear that no one was forcing her off her show. "I'm perfectly healthy. This is my decision. I've been thinking about it for a long time. And this is what I want to do."

If anyone was ready to write her off, she issued this warning: "Remember I have another whole year to go. I look forward to the next year, to my last season."

She didn't want to go. But she could at least take comfort in dragging out her farewell tour for as long as humanly possible. For the next twelve months, ABC would be throwing her a never-ending retirement bash.

And there would be one more change. On July 10, Elisabeth made her final headline on *The View* by dropping the bombshell that it was her last day. There was no reason to worry—she had another job lined up, although she didn't tell viewers how she got it or why she had to leave. In the fall, she'd begin as the coanchor of the morning show *Fox & Friends*.

Elisabeth, who never talked about getting fired from *The View*, thanked everyone who worked on the show, heaping praise on Barbara for teaching her everything about journalism. Elisabeth told producers she didn't want a party on her way out. She made a hurried exit as soon she stepped off the set.

"Bye, Elisabeth," the director Mark Gentile said to her backstage. She wouldn't respond. "I was a little hurt," he said. "I understood the emotions."

But she'd get the last laugh. After Elisabeth and Joy were gone, the ratings for *The View* fell off a cliff.

19

Mommie Dearest

As the eleventh cohost on *The View*, Jenny McCarthy found herself in a horror movie. She took the job expecting to bring some humor to Hot Topics, but that wasn't possible given the atmosphere on the set. Barbara Walters was in despair that she was retiring, and she made it clear that she didn't want to go quietly. Whoopi Goldberg had no patience for Barbara's clinging to whatever power she had left. And ABC bosses soon realized that they had accidentally dumped what had made *The View* successful—the panel's fire and ice.

Jenny, who had been a guest on *The View* in the past, had already survived a traumatic encounter backstage. "You know the movie *Mommie Dearest*?" Jenny asked me one afternoon over lunch. "I remember as a child watching that movie and going, 'Holy cow!'" She paused for effect. "I've never seen a woman yell like that before until I worked with Barbara Walters."

In 2007, Jenny was promoting her book *Louder Than Words: A Mother's Journey in Healing Autism,* in which she argued that vaccines weakened her son's immune system and triggered his autism. She claimed that she had improved Evan's health through a gluten-free diet of cod-liver oil and vitamins along with behavioral therapy. Even though this treatment wasn't supported by any medical research, her fame as a former *Playboy* model, MTV host, and actress provided her with a big megaphone. "I was on *Oprah*," Jenny recalled. "Everyone was coming out of the woodwork. I was mainly getting, 'Thank you for speaking up.'"

Her publicity tour took her all the way to *The View*. Before the interview, a producer told Jenny that Barbara wanted to speak to her.

"I walked into her dressing room and she blew up at me," Jenny said. "She was screaming, 'How dare you say this! That autism can be cured?' My knees were shaking. I remember my whole body was shaking."

Jenny responded that she never used the word *cured* to describe Evan's condition. That didn't matter. "You're such a liar!" Barbara screamed.

"This lasted for about seven minutes," Jenny said. "Finally, someone pulled me out of the room. I went back to my dressing room, not knowing what the fuck to do. One of my heroes just chewed me a new asshole, and I'm going on live TV. I'm freaking the fuck out." The producer told her that Barbara didn't want Jenny to walk onto the set as a guest because that would prompt the audience to clap. Instead, the interview began with Jenny on the couch, wedged between the ladies, with the camera on Barbara for an introduction.

"As they pull out from her face, I'm sitting there, terrified." Jenny wasn't worried about what she had to say; she thought Barbara wouldn't let her speak. "It was not like I was trying to prove a scientific fact. It's my story. I knew she couldn't outsmart me in this interview, because she can't tell me what happened with my child. I was able to calm myself down."

The conversation played out more peacefully than it had in the dressing room. Barbara challenged Jenny—as any journalist would—about the idea that autism could be cured. Only later did Jenny wonder if Barbara had lost her temper because of her sister, Jackie, who had died in 1985. Barbara often said that she thought Jackie might have been autistic. "Back then, there really wasn't anything you could do about it," Jenny said. "She didn't want to hear that there was maybe a possibility that her sister could have gotten better."

When Jenny finished the interview, she made a promise to herself. "I said, 'I'm never going on the fucking *View* again. Ever.' Cut to a few years later, I have more books to sell."

On her next appearance—in 2012—Barbara couldn't have been more welcoming to Jenny, who was promoting a memoir titled *Bad Habits: Confessions of a Recovering Catholic*. "She fully read my book cover to cover," Jenny said. "She came to my dressing room and quoted dirty stories from it, asked me to autograph it for her, and she had no recollection that I had been there before. She was hugging me, loving on me. I was, like, 'This is the craziest fucking shit I've ever experienced in my life.'"

Jenny saw an opening for herself. After two decades as a goofball on TV—she'd channeled a bawdier Vanna White on the 1995 MTV dating series *Singled Out*—Jenny wanted to graduate to more substance. "I remember thinking to myself, 'I want to do something that has a little more class to it. And spread my wings a little bit.'" In 2013, she hosted a cable talk show on Friday nights, where C-list stars guzzled down martinis. "My VH1 show was a little too raunchy. I wanted something in the middle."

Then she heard about Joy Behar's departure. "I thought to myself, 'That's where I'm going next.'" Bill Geddie invited her to audition for Season 17. "I went on and it went great, and I went on again. They said, 'You're in the top consideration to be a cohost.'"

As she waited for an offer, she pursued an opportunity with CBS for her own daytime show. It would be filmed in Chicago, where she lived with Evan, but Jenny didn't want to become another celebrity with a flop in the afternoon. She believed, perhaps naïvely, that there would be more job security on *The View*. "I would rather be on a show that's established," she told herself.

That summer, in 2013, CBS tried to get her to sign with them. Jenny called Geddie on the July 4 weekend to let him know that she was about to accept the deal.

"Shit," he said. "Give me an hour."

Geddie had been trying to find the perfect cohost to replace Joy and Elisabeth Hasselbeck, to bring more pop culture expertise to *The View*. Since the network wanted the show to steer clear of politics, the new hire would need to be fluent in celebrity gossip and reality TV, such as *The Bachelor* and *Dancing with the Stars*. That was the winning formula on *The Talk*, which still trailed *The View* in the ratings. Geddie had tested Brooke Shields for the new seat, but market research revealed that viewers found her too stiff. "I liked her," Geddie said. "For some reason, our audience never warmed to her." Another option: the comedian Ali Wentworth, from *In Living Color*, who was married to *GMA* coanchor George Stephanopoulos.

Since Barbara didn't feel strongly about any of the options, she let Geddie choose his favorite. "I always thought early on, if we could have gotten Jenny McCarthy, we would have," he told me. "She was too big of a name then." He made the case to ABC, and they drafted a contract. "I thought that for the show they wanted to do, she was a good choice."

One red flag that no one seemed to worry about was Jenny's views about autism. It hadn't come up as a problem in any of the trial shows, and Geddie didn't think it would define her on *The View*. He'd told her they wanted her to riff on movie stars. "How Bill sold it to me is that they actually let go of Joy and Elisabeth because they wanted to get rid of politics," Jenny said. "It was polarizing. That's the word he kept using: it was very *polarizing* to the audience."

He told her, "We want pop culture, irreverent, fun, sassy."

"I checked all those boxes for him."

On July 15, Barbara cheerfully introduced Jenny as the latest cohost on *The View*, an announcement that was met with an avalanche of negative press. Many critics thought that by hiring Jenny the show was giving her a platform to spread wrong information to parents about not vaccinating their children. Media outlets that didn't normally cover daytime

TV, such as the *Columbia Journalism Review* and *The Nation,* voiced their disapproval.

Time's TV critic, James Poniewozik, wrote a post with the headline "Why ABC Shouldn't Have Hired Jenny McCarthy." He expressed concerns about Jenny's becoming the new Elisabeth, with quackery instead of political controversy. "Discussing the news, even at 11 in the morning, comes with responsibility," he wrote. "And for a show even remotely about news—and a career newswoman like Walters—to legitimize McCarthy's dangerous anti-science because she will probably get crazy attention and ratings is irresponsible and shameful."

Jenny believed that the hostility toward her originated from a lobbying group that wanted to silence her. "I had to deal with a hurricane, a tornado. I consider myself to be pro-vaccine, but pro–safe vaccine. There's another group, they go out and try to get me fired from every job I've ever done. They are invisible but powerful."

Geddie tried to assure her that it didn't matter, that there was no such thing as bad publicity. Jenny wasn't so sure: "I knew way up on the totem pole, it would bother somebody, because big pharma is pretty powerful. If they told ABC they were going to pull some of their advertising, I could very well lose my job. I was a nervous wreck. I just let go of my own talk show in Chicago. I had signed a one-year contract with *The View.* Now I'm dealing with all this bad publicity and I have to feed my baby."

When Jenny started at *The View,* she wondered which version of Barbara she'd see every day at the studio. "Hopefully, I get the Barbara Walters who is nice," she told herself. The timing of her arrival made that unlikely. For Barbara, Jenny represented that the end was near. At eighty-three, Barbara still had plenty of energy, but she found herself facing a mixture of complicated emotions, from aggravation to fear about being forgotten. Her memory was cloudy, and she'd been known to make odd outbursts in private conversations. "Imagine a woman like Barbara Walters," Jenny explained. "It's her last year and she doesn't want to leave. Think about that. And I'm the new bitch there."

One day in Hot Topics, Jenny sounded off about Katy Perry dating the bad-boy musician John Mayer. "I saw Barbara's face with her big saucer eyes look at me," Jenny said. "Then we went to a commercial. She said, 'Who is it that you're talking about and why are you bringing her up?'"

"I'm, like, 'That's Katy Perry. You interviewed her last week!'"

Jenny recalled, "That wasn't the right thing to say. I felt everyone kicking me under the table." The other cohosts had devised a method to send signals to one another about how to deal with Barbara. "You either had the knee hold or the kick under the table."

During another show, Jenny referred to herself in the third person, telling a story about meeting a fan. "Who is Jenny McCarthy?" Barbara asked on TV.

Jenny played it off as a joke. "I totally brushed it off. That's where Barbara's head was. She was spacing out. She was checking out."

Within days, *The View* had new instructions for Jenny. "I was told, 'We cannot do pop culture anymore because she doesn't know who the people are.'" *The View* instructed Jenny to tackle politics. "I panicked, because I don't consider myself a political person. My controversy is in vaccines. I know I'm not talking about that every day. Now I had to figure out, 'Am I coming out as a Republican or a Democrat? Where do I stand on all the social issues and political issues?'"

At the start of the season, Jenny had visited Whoopi's house, thinking they could maybe be friends. "I loved her in *Ghost,*" Jenny said. "I'm a fan. I thought I was going to work with the Whoopi that people thought they might know—fun and funny." But Whoopi didn't warm to Jenny. "The table is an interesting dynamic because it reminds me a little bit of *Survivor.* There were allies, and there weren't many people to choose from. Do I side with Barbara, who is royalty, but she's leaving? Or do I take

Whoopi, who is a force to be reckoned with?" Jenny aligned with Sherri, knowing that they had similar personalities as moms with young boys. Jenny didn't want to build a friendship out of a power grab.

That left Barbara and Whoopi to face off, each with a grip on her own corner of *The View*. "There was a war between Barbara and Whoopi about Barbara wanting to moderate," Jenny said. "This is one of the reasons I decided not to ally with Whoopi. It broke my heart when Barbara would shuffle to Whoopi and say, 'Can I moderate, please?' And Whoopi would say no. How can you do this to a woman who paved the way for so many female journalists? The reason we're doing this job is because of Barbara Walters."

Barbara's fixation on the moderator's chair turned into an unhealthy obsession. In conversations with the staff, Barbara loved to complain about all the different ways Whoopi had botched an introduction or mixed up facts. Whoopi resented that Barbara was trying to run her over. "Whoopi was very angry," said Jenny. "She was angry that she wasn't being paid what she was worth, rightfully so." Whoopi had always tried to be a team player, but she felt that ABC wasn't treating her like a valued employee. One idea she had, to do a live version of *Sister Act* as a prime-time musical (like NBC's *Sound of Music Live!*, starring Carrie Underwood), was turned down by Paul Lee, the president of ABC Entertainment Group. The network hadn't even offered Whoopi a raise for keeping *The View* afloat.

As the friction grew, Whoopi frequently cut off her cohosts during Hot Topics to remind everyone who was in charge. "People don't understand," Jenny said. "Whoopi can knock over anyone in a debate. Her voice is strong not only in meaning but also in sound. I was able to get a point out in three words—like 'I don't agree'—and that's all I would be able to say. I would be stepped on or interrupted." Jenny thought that Whoopi didn't like that Jenny hadn't deferred to her enough. "I wasn't going to play a kiss ass. To me, Whoopi had an addiction to controlling people's thoughts, their words, the room, the table, your feeling, your mood. She had an addiction to controlling all of it and everybody."

The cohosts on *The View* always had a relaxed dress code, but Jenny felt that her wardrobe was under constant scrutiny. When she wore glasses on the show, viewers attacked her on Twitter for trying to look smart. "Really?" she thought. "I just couldn't fucking see. The teleprompter was so far."

In the past, Barbara hadn't paid much attention to the other cohosts' wardrobes, but this became a new tic for her. "We would all show up in the makeup room," Jenny said. "Barbara would check out what I was wearing. If she didn't agree with it, or it didn't complement her outfit, I had to change." Jenny estimated that over the next seven months she switched fifty outfits as a result of Barbara's withering gaze, as if they were doing a photoshoot at *Vogue* instead of a daytime talk show.

Barbara would object to Jenny's choosing a summer dress on a cold day. "What the hell are you wearing?" Barbara asked her about a sleeveless outfit by designer Victoria Beckham.

"Mind you, she doesn't look at anyone's clothes but mine," Jenny said. "I'd go, 'Barbara, you're wearing your own clothes.'" Jenny's outfits were pulled by a stylist. She'd try to remind Barbara, "Stores right now have the spring collection. There's nothing I can do.'"

"Change!" Barbara would demand.

"I always had to go put on a sweater." And then there was this: "She wanted to start dressing like me. There were times when she'd say change, and she'd make people run out and get that dress in her size. I was a human Barbie doll."

To protect herself, Jenny tried to avoid Barbara. "When I'd hear the shuffle of her feet, I knew that Barbara was after me. It would get faster. Oh my God—she's coming! Based on the speed of the shuffle, I would hide or get on the phone."

One morning that autumn, Jenny answered the door to her dressing room. Barbara was very upset about something she'd seen in the communal bathroom. She wasn't trying to be mean to Jenny. But she needed to express her disapproval—and she'd lost her bearings.

"Jenny, there's a tampon floating in the toilet and it's disgusting."

"I don't have my period. It's not mine."

"Do something about it!"

"I don't know what to do," Jenny said, flabbergasted. "She's standing in the hallway where the guests are, yelling at me about a tampon. I don't know. Maybe in her brain, she went, 'I'm going to the youngest, newest person here, because obviously she has her period and left a tampon floating.' This is Barbara Walters. I'm not going to yell at her. So finally I said, 'I'll take care of it. I'll take one for the team and I'll flush it.'"

⁓

As *The View* went back to a disaster zone, the network rang the alarm bells. At least under Rosie, the show was a ratings phenomenon. With Jenny at the table, people were turning it off. "We didn't bring the numbers up that year," Geddie said. "They blamed everyone but themselves. The idea that a show has legacies to maintain, this was lost on them." Without politics, *The View* had lost its edge and felt like every other copycat talk show.

Lisa Hackner, the new executive vice president of ABC Daytime, called a meeting with the cohosts to tell them that 30 percent of the viewers had left with Elisabeth Hasselbeck. All the jaws in the room dropped. "They felt we needed more conflict," Sherri told me. "I remember Whoopi making faces and saying, 'We're not going to fight at the table.'"

As *The View* tried to swivel back to politics, Jenny found herself in an awkward situation. "They did try to change me. They wanted Elisabeth back, and I wasn't Elisabeth. I would literally have meetings before the show of them trying to input opinions in me to go against Whoopi." Jenny wanted to quit. "I was going to work crying. I couldn't be myself. My fans were telling me, 'Where's Jenny? They aren't letting you be you.'"

If all this weren't hard enough, Barbara's health continued to deteriorate. One day, just as the show ended, she collapsed into the arms of a stage manager. She had to be taken to the greenroom, where they laid her down on a sofa. The staff called the paramedics. But Barbara, concerned that the sight of her on a stretcher would make it into the papers, instructed them to take her to her dressing room. Once inside, she locked the door and wouldn't let anyone in. "Barbara, are you okay?" they pleaded. She finally came out to be taken to the doctor. The next day, Barbara acted like it was business as usual.

Barbara, who had let her career define every facet of her life, couldn't fathom a future without the cameras. "She kept saying backstage, 'I don't want to go. I don't want to leave,'" recalled Jenny, who felt bad for her. "Look at what Barbara did to me. I had zero hard feelings. I loved her like a grandma. She didn't know any better." But Jenny was less forgiving of her other cohost. "Whoopi knew better."

That spring, Barbara pleaded with Whoopi one more time to allow her to moderate *The View* for her final days on TV. Whoopi wouldn't budge—she wasn't forfeiting her ground. When Barbara tried to go over her head by complaining to the ABC brass, Whoopi referred them to a clause in her contract that afforded her the show's sole moderator duties.

"Every day I went home and I was miserable," Jenny told me. "It really was the most miserable I've been on a job in my twenty-five years of show business. I kicked myself for not taking the CBS job, of course. But I felt there was a little bit of hope. I thought, maybe when Barbara leaves, the ratings will go up, because they kept saying the focus groups hated Barbara and that's why they were forcing her into retirement."

The viewers who grew up with Barbara could tell that it was time for her to let go.

20

Barbara's Long Goodbye

This was the end of the road for Barbara Walters. There would be no more day trips to the White House for strolls with the president or the first lady, no more traipsing through the halls of celebrity mansions, no more overseas excursions to dine in palaces with world leaders, no more scuffles with the publicists of ungrateful pop stars, no more phone calls to the mayor of New York City to break news, no more power lunches at Michael's to discuss the terms of her next exclusive. The American public was about to lose a voice that had defined contemporary news. "I've been on television for fifty years," Barbara told me in the winter of 2014, as her retirement clock ticked down. "Mickey Mouse is the only one who has been on longer than I have."

Barbara braced for retirement as if she were running for office. Her farewell resembled *The Never Ending Story,* with months of programming and special segments on *The View.* She participated in a two-hour prime-time retrospective about her career that aired in May 2014. And she'd agreed to a sit-down interview with *herself.* Yes, that's right—the final episode of *The View* featured Barbara vs. Barbara. The woman who faced off against her wasn't a CGI-created clone (although Mark Gentile had pitched that idea in a meeting), but the next closest thing: Cheri Oteri, reprising her impersonation from *Saturday Night Live*.

The comedic skit featured Oteri as Babs, gleefully envisioning her impending unemployment with trips to Costco and Six Flags with her dog, Cha-Cha. It needed to be pretaped because the producers were juggling a lot of A-list guests for that show.

"They were setting up, and we were sitting across from each other, dressed alike and everything," said Oteri, who wore a fuchsia jacket with pearls to match Barbara's. As they were ready to begin, Barbara looked into the monitor and squealed, "Oh my God! My hair is a mess!"

That caused an army of beauticians to storm the stage. "They lean in to Barbara, and they say, 'You're looking at Cheri's monitor!'" Oteri recalled. "And she started laughing so hard, I swear that endorphins were released in my body." Oteri waited for somebody to turn their attention to her. "The funniest thing was all the hairdressers just walked away. Nobody would even touch my hair."

In this uncharacteristic moment of levity, Barbara followed the advice from the show's closing line: She took a little time to enjoy *The View*. But more often than not, she embarked on her farewell tour with clenched fists and chattering teeth. When Whoopi tried to soothe Barbara's nerves backstage one morning by asking about the last time she'd taken a vacation, she went blank. Barbara was most terrified about all the free time that would loom over her. "I don't know how I'm going to fill the days," she confessed to me in her dressing room, after a *View* taping. "I've never had to in my whole life." She didn't count too many girlfriends as part of her social life, or hobbies outside of her demanding job. Her only family was Jackie, who lived in a different state. Did she go on dates? "I'm not going to discuss that part of my life," she protested. "I think it's unseemly."

During a Hot Topics debate after Valentine's Day, she accidentally caused a media uproar when she blurted out on *The View* that she owned a vibrator nicknamed Selfie. The flub arose from some teasing by Whoopi and Jenny McCarthy, which made Barbara go into a tailspin of confusion.

"We were all embarrassed," recalled one producer. As she left her apartment the next day, a camera crew from *TMZ* tried to catch her with some follow-up questions about the sex toy, which didn't exist. She had to issue a correction to viewers. "I don't have a vibrator!" she said on TV. "I don't even put my cell phone on vibrate."

To prove that there was life outside television, Barbara had enrolled in an art-history class at New York University. She arrived promptly at 1:00 p.m. from ABC. "I went for the first time on Monday to class," she told me a few days later. "There were seven of us, and the professor never showed up. We left at a quarter of two! I'm going to find another professor. That'll teach me."

She wasn't sure whether she could adapt to a more mellow lifestyle. "I don't know how I'm going to feel," she said, trying to downplay her fears. She insisted that she wouldn't cry, as Jay Leno had after he was pushed out of *The Tonight Show* that year. She had a sense about what she'd miss the most about TV: "When there are days I want to express an opinion, and I have no outlet."

For all the barriers that she'd shattered for women in the news business, Barbara's retirement would be most profoundly felt at *The View*. As her profile had diminished at ABC News, she still trudged through the doors of her morning talk show, with an unstoppable appetite for juicy stories and interviews. *The View* had given her a platform that she never thought she'd needed when she launched the show in 1997 as a side project.

"I remember a couple executives saying to me, 'Don't get too excited— she's sixty-seven years old,'" Geddie said about his early days on the show. "'Nobody wants to see a woman after the age of sixty.' You know what? They were right. That was the way it was back then. I didn't even think that was sexist."

The View managed to give Barbara longevity. It's not likely that she would have been a regular presence in homes in 2014 without the show. "Barbara went on through her mideighties," Geddie said. "I consider that a wonderful thing for her and a wonderful accomplishment. She proved somebody could do this for that long, on live TV."

When they'd launched the show, they thought her legacy was already sewn up. "How about this?" Geddie chuckled. "How ironic is it that whenever somebody talks about Barbara Walters in articles, it's never the Barbara Walters as the first lady of journalism, or the Barbara Walters specials, or Barbara Walters of ABC News, or Barbara Walters the first female anchor. It's always Barbara Walters creator of *The View*. You hear it all the time. It just makes me laugh. It's not that I don't think it was important. I just didn't think it would be as important given everything else she's done."

Although *The View* had served as a petri dish for vicious feuds, Barbara wanted to look past the bad times as she approached the end. "I never hold grudges," she said in our dressing-room conversation that winter. "This is such a crazy and tough business that you might as well make your peace." For evidence, she told me that she had just had lunch with Star Jones. "I don't like the way she left. I can barely remember the way she left! What good does it do for me to feel bitterness toward her?"

They had reconnected, after they both had heart surgery, and Barbara let Star take her on a shopping excursion. "I said, 'That's a great coat.' She said, 'I can get it wholesale. Let's go!'"

Barbara even forgave her most difficult cohost, and Cindi Berger helped orchestrate the reconciliation. In February 2014, Rosie O'Donnell set foot back on *The View* for the first time in almost seven years.

Even by Rosie's standards, she delivered a tour-de-force performance. "Is Hasselbeck here?" she asked on TV. "Just checking." She tore into recent headlines, including Philip Seymour Hoffman's death from a drug overdose and the toxic side effects of fame for Justin Bieber. She defended Dylan Farrow's allegations that her father, Woody Allen, had sexually assaulted her at seven. "I totally believe her," Rosie said. "I'm very good friends with Mia Farrow. She's the best mother I've ever seen."

"I know Woody as a parent, and I disagree," said Barbara, taking the side of an alleged child molester.

"But you can never really know what goes on in a house," Rosie said. These weren't the kinds of discussions that *The View* was having with Jenny

McCarthy at the table. "How did I do on that one?" Rosie asked her co-hosts about the Farrow story. "It's my first time back. I'm afraid I'll be exiled!"

"You'll never be exiled from this show," Barbara said meekly.

"I had seen her before that," Barbara said later, as she described prior interactions with Rosie at social events. Barbara indicated that not everyone on the show was as forgiving as she was. "There were some people behind the scenes here who were not happy. They had difficulties with Rosie."

Anne Sweeney, who still oversaw *The View*, was in the studio audience that day, and she didn't care about that. She was dazzled by how quickly Rosie had breathed new life into a stale talk show. Nobody had dared to suggest any names to replace Barbara with her still on TV, but Sweeney had an idea. It would be a long shot—and not necessarily a move sanctioned by HR—but if she could get Rosie back on *The View*, the show would crush *The Talk*.

As she finished her career, Barbara kept her calendar packed through the grand finale. On May 12, ABC News renamed its skyscraper headquarters on the Upper West Side the Barbara Walters Building. The rechristening took place with a ribbon-cutting ceremony with Bob Iger, Diane Sawyer, Robin Roberts, and dozens of news minions. "If I have a legacy, I hope that I played a small role in paving the way for so many of you fabulous women," Barbara said, dropping her voice to convey the bleakness of a world without Barbara Walters.

She was secretly demoralized that the plaque in the lobby with the building's new name was so small. "You have to really search to find it," she told me later. Then she started to interrogate me. "Tell me where it is. You don't even know. I'm not being humble. I do not know where it is."

More than one producer thought that retirement wouldn't actually be in the cards for Barbara, that she'd drop a surprise that she was staying on *The View* for all of eternity. In staff interactions, she sounded remorseful and anxious. But when the cameras rolled, she wiped away any smear of doubt that she'd made the right decision.

Barbara kicked off her final week on TV by staying up past her curfew to be a guest on *Saturday Night Live*'s Weekend Update, dishing out her greatest reporting tips to Cecily Strong. "Do not be afraid to ask the tough questions. Like, if you were a tree, what kind of a tree would you be?" Barbara said, referencing an often-ridiculed line she used on Katharine Hepburn. "Or, your place or mine, Brokaw?" (That joke has not aged well, given that the NBC News veteran was accused of sexual harassment in April 2018 by former colleagues.)

On *The View,* she pulled off an impressive trick when she lured all the original cohosts to sit on the sofa with her for one last dish session, including Meredith Vieira, Star Jones, Debbie Matenopoulos, Joy Behar, Lisa Ling, Elisabeth Hasselbeck, Rosie O'Donnell, Whoopi Goldberg, Sherri Shepherd, and Jenny McCarthy. But not everybody was on speaking terms. That morning led to an awkward face-off between Rosie and Elisabeth, who hadn't seen each other since their televised screaming match.

"Where is Elisabeth?" Rosie asked as she roamed the studio halls.

"Some of the people who worked on the show said, 'She hasn't left her dressing room and the door is closed,'" Rosie recalled. "I said, 'Let's change that.' I knocked on her door. I opened her door and said, 'How are you doing? What's going on?'" Elisabeth agreed to take a selfie with Rosie. Then Rosie let it slip to Elisabeth that the reunion had all been Rosie's—not Barbara's—doing. "I casually leaned over to her and said, 'Do you know this was my idea?'" Rosie told me the story that she had told Elisabeth. "While eating dinner with Anne Sweeney, I said, 'Do you know what would be great? To get all the cohosts back!' Anne said, 'Do you think everybody would come back?' I said, 'Everybody would say yes because it's Barbara Walters.'"

Rosie had once again proved her chops as a savvy producer: the stunt was a hit. But what was she doing having dinner with Sweeney? That would become clear later.

Barbara had hoped to sit down again with Monica Lewinsky for her last interview. "Of course I considered it, because of not only the personal relationship, but because Barbara is so well respected," Lewinsky told me. "I think really for me, ultimately, the interview we had done in 1999 had been such a seminal moment for me and in some ways for her too. Ultimately, I wanted to move forward and that might have felt like moving backwards. But it had nothing to do with Barbara. I let my first public words in ten years in my 2014 *Vanity Fair* essay speak for themselves."

Even without Barbara's dream get, it was time for her to take the plunge. Barbara's final show, which aired on May 16, had ABC executives from both coasts at *The View*. Sweeney and Ben Sherwood, the president of the news division, surrounded Barbara in her dressing room. Some big guests were lurking in the building, but producers kept them a secret by putting them on the other side of the floor—in the *All My Children* area.

As Barbara boarded the elevator for her last trip, she put her hand on Sherri's face and said, "You're the one that's the most improved. I'm proud of you, dear."

"And then of course I started bawling," Sherri recalled.

On TV, Barbara was eager to get the party started. "And I don't know who's on!" Barbara said.

The first guest, Hillary Clinton, snuck out and hugged Barbara.

"You know what?" Barbara said. "You look terrific here. Why don't you just take my place on the show?" Barbara, who hadn't been prepped with questions, criticized Sherri in the middle of the interview for calling the former secretary of state by her first name. "I don't call her by her first name," Barbara said, embarrassing everyone.

Clinton rushed to Sherri's defense. "Hillary is fine! I can't believe this day has come and I can't believe it's for real."

"Neither can I," Barbara said.

Surprise guest number two was Michael Douglas, who shared a birthday with Barbara. "If Hillary runs, I think you'd be a great vice president," Douglas told Barbara.

Then Oprah invaded the retirement party. She'd initially turned down the request, thinking that Barbara wasn't really leaving TV.

"I want to thank you for being a pioneer," Oprah said, clutching Barbara's hand. "And everything that word means. It means being the first in the room to knock down the door, to break down the barriers, to pave the road that we all walk on."

"She used to imitate me when she tried out for jobs," Barbara said gleefully. "I'm responsible for her whole career!"

Oprah once again told Barbara's favorite story—the one in which Oprah, growing up as a cub reporter, studied the way Barbara crossed her legs and asked questions. Oprah wasn't the only student of the Barbara Walters journalism school. As Oprah waved her hands, a parade of women anchors entered the studio one by one to pay their respects, including Diane Sawyer, Savannah Guthrie, Katie Couric, Maria Shriver, Jane Pauley, Deborah Norville, Tamron Hall, Gayle King, Kathie Lee Gifford, Gretchen Carlson, and Connie Chung. There was one terrible oversight. Carole Simpson, the former ABC News anchor who became the first black woman to moderate a presidential debate, later complained that she wasn't invited. "She was not happy, and she was right," said producer Alexandra Cohen.

Barbara beamed like a proud grandmother surrounded by a gaggle of offspring who didn't call or write. But that hardly mattered. She loved the attention. It almost made her forget how much she was going to hate retirement. "Starting soon, I may be available for supermarket openings and charity auctions," Barbara joked.

She read a farewell of career highlights that had been scripted for her on the teleprompter. The bullet points included rising at 4:00 a.m. for *Today,* navigating talks between the heads of Israel and Egypt in 1977, and flirting with Clint Eastwood. "Maybe it's time for him," she offered, on the chance he was watching. She looked at the camera wistfully, forced herself to smile, and bid adieu to five decades of broadcasting—but not before propping the window open a crack, in case she decided to crawl back through.

"Who knows what the future brings!?" she said with a maniacal smirk.

⟵∾⟶

The next surprise associated with Barbara's farewell wouldn't be met with as many cheers. Before she'd decided to retire, Barbara's lawyer had convinced her to sell her 50 percent ownership of *The View* back to ABC. He told her it would be foolish to hold on to a talk show for nostalgic reasons, and if it got canceled, her share would be worth nothing. Barbara agreed, collecting tens of millions ("that she didn't need," one producer observed), but she quickly regretted the decision. Even though she was still listed as an executive producer in the show's credits, ABC could sideline her from all their decision making. The sale was the reason she couldn't insist on staying on TV after she got cold feet about retiring.

"She sold her stake," Geddie said. "By the way, none of us knew this. The moment she no longer had a say, the show, as it was, was essentially over. I don't think any of us realized that. I think we found out too late that she wasn't one of the bosses anymore."

Throughout the summer, Geddie and his team had brainstormed ideas to jump-start a new era of *The View*, meeting periodically with the network to solicit feedback. They toyed with hiring a man (or two) as permanent cohost. *The View* started testing C-list celebrities, to see how Bill Rancic or Mario Cantone would do in the mix. "It had a fun energy," Jenny said. "It was a little bit more my temperature."

Lisa Hackner, ABC's head of daytime, was in a hurry to push the ratings back up. She told Geddie that they had to fire Mark Gentile to bring in a new director. "She did something in her ignorance," Gentile said. "That's the old Telepictures way—you fire the director. She didn't realize what a favor she had done for me. I would have stayed there until they fucking carried me out."

On June 26, *The View* staff was supposed to have a meeting with Hackner to discuss the new season. She mysteriously canceled at the last minute. "All of a sudden, everyone"—minus Whoopi—"gets a phone call that says, 'Go to this address,'" recalled Jenny. "Bill is, like, 'I'm getting fired.'"

"No way you're getting fired," Jenny told him. "We've been having meetings with them."

Geddie left to see what they wanted. The network told Geddie that they were going to bring in another executive producer to share the job with him, and he instructed his agent to get him out of there. "Bill came back, walked into his office, shut the door, spent thirty minutes in there, and never came back," Jenny said. "And then Sherri called her agent and said, 'I'm not going to that fucking building.'"

Cohen, Bill's second-in-command, was the next to get the ax. Then, through their agents, both Jenny and Sherri learned that they'd been dumped, too. "I was with Jenny when she got the phone call," Sherri said. "She was really upset. She had specifically asked Lisa Hackner, 'If you are not renewing my contract, let me know.'" According to Sherri, Hackner assured her that they were, and Jenny had moved Evan from Chicago to join her in New York.

"I'm comforting her and my phone is blowing up," Sherri said. "My manager called me and said, 'They aren't renewing your contract.'" As part of her renegotiation, Sherri had signaled to ABC that she wanted a significant raise. But she was stunned that they had dropped her without even engaging in talks. She'd seen the way the show dragged Elisabeth's name in the mud after they fired her, so she drew up a statement that she was leaving. Jenny followed with her own statement on Twitter ("If Sherri goes . . . I go too"). They all headed to Geddie's apartment to get drunk.

The lone remaining cohost was Whoopi, who had a year left on her contract.

Rumors started to swirl that *The View* was in talks with a certain former moderator for the ultimate comeback. The next day, on June 27, I wrote a column for *Variety* called "Why *The View* Should Bring Back Rosie

O'Donnell." That night, Rosie direct messaged me on Twitter: *Thank u*. Was it true that she was interested in *The View* again? Rosie confirmed that she was. Over a series of messages to me, she explained how she'd vetoed the plan to hire a male cohost and had gotten rid of Geddie because she hated him. Rosie's takeover had begun.

21

She's Back

Every time Rosie O'Donnell took a new job, she vowed she was a changed woman. In 2014, she had a legitimate case to make. Two years prior, she'd suffered a near-fatal cardiac arrest. "When you have a heart attack and almost die, it kind of puts things in perspective instantly," she told me over a lunch at Sarabeth's. "And it did for me." As part of her rehabilitation, her doctor told her that she had to lose some weight. "Although I'd thought about having a gastric bypass, which is what Al Roker and Star Jones had, a side effect is you have very poor control of pooping. If you eat sugar, your body will empty what's in it. I have such anxiety over the concept of going to the bathroom in public. I don't ever pee in public. I don't ever poo in public." She didn't care that she was oversharing. "That's the reason I would never do that surgery."

Instead, she had a vertical sleeve gastrectomy, where a surgeon removed the side of her stomach without cutting her intestines. "I was probably 241 pounds when I had it," she told me in 2014. "Now I'm 190. You're not really hungry because it affects the hunger hormones, which has a weird name like a *gremlin*." (It's called ghrelin.) "And you can't eat as much because you're full. I never knew what the feeling of full or hungry was. If it was there, I'd eat it."

She said that she used to feast on burgers at McDonald's or Johnny Rockets and she'd stop at 7-Eleven for junk food. "I'd get three packs of Yodels, some bubble gum, chocolate-covered pretzels." The new Rosie walked into the convenience store one day to cheer herself up. "I looked all around," she said, but she couldn't find anything. "It's like your mind shifts. If I have a burger, it's without the bun and it's at a restaurant that has real meat, like sirloin."

In her family life, Rosie had remarried to Michelle Rounds, a woman that she'd met at a Starbucks. Together, they had a two-year-old daughter named Dakota, a welcome addition to Rosie's growing brood. She would spend her days watching *Frozen* on a continuous loop with the baby. To stay Zen, she'd committed to a daily ritual of meditation, during which she'd sit in the reclining chair of her bedroom for twenty minutes with her feet up, not speaking to anybody. "They give you an actual mantra, and you're not allowed to tell anyone," she said, about her two secret words that she'd repeat in her head. "For me, that's been the hardest part of meditating because I want to tell everyone. I want to go, 'Is yours the same as mine?'"

Before she signed another one-year contract with *The View*, Rosie visited Whoopi Goldberg. Rosie wanted to make sure that they could get along and that the show wouldn't interrupt her new serenity. "We talked it over," Rosie said. "We thought about what we would want to do for the show and what would work creatively. We were both totally on the same page." It wouldn't stay that way for long.

In July 2014, Rosie announced that she was officially replacing Barbara Walters on Season 18 of *The View*, starting in September. But in a few weeks, after more meetings with ABC, Rosie told everyone that she'd made a huge mistake—if she could have quit before she started, she would have.

Rosie and Whoopi had gone to see Lisa Hackner, who tried to tell them that they weren't running the show: they were *talent*, not the bosses. This didn't sit well with either woman. When Barbara and Bill Geddie were in charge of *The View*, the network didn't dare interfere. Now, a lot of cooks were in the kitchen, and they were all contradicting one another in passive-aggressive ways. ABC News executives were trying to wrangle control of *The View* away from the daytime team since Anne Sweeney was supposed to leave her post that fall. Her soon-to-be replacement, Ben Sherwood, wanted the news division to swallow *The View*, putting the executives behind *Good Morning America* in charge.

Everyone agreed on one thing: *The View* needed to be political again in the lead-up to the 2016 presidential election. After firing nearly all the cohosts, ABC had the summer to hire two more replacements to fill out the table. Rosie and Whoopi both strongly advocated for Meghan Mc-Cain, the millennial daughter of Arizona senator John McCain, as the show's next Republican. She'd been a regular guest, and they thought she was more grounded than Elisabeth Hasselbeck. Hackner balked, saying that McCain wasn't good TV. "It's fine," Meghan remembered thinking. "I'm going to move on with my life."

Who was going to actually make the call on the new hires wasn't clear. Sherwood had brought over his friend Bill Wolff, from MSNBC's *Rachel Maddow Show*, as the new executive producer of *The View*. But as soon as he got there, the stuffy Harvard man looked as if he were lost in a foreign country without a map. Wolff confessed to his staff that he'd never seen a full episode of *The View* and that he had been surprised when offered the job.

Rosie thought that none of these executives had any idea how to res-cue a daytime talk show. She started watching *The View* that summer, taking notes in her head on what needed to change. Rosie complained that Whoopi sounded "too angry" on TV, especially when she cut off the other cohosts after they disagreed with her. On Rosie's last outing on *The View*, she'd been the moderator. This time around, she'd need to defer to Whoopi on the direction of Hot Topics, which wasn't Rosie's style. The more veteran members of the staff, many of whom couldn't believe that ABC was letting Rosie back into the building, were already bracing for the worst.

In August, with no clear answers about whom to hire, ABC decided to hold an audition for the remaining chairs. The network invited Republicans S. E. Cupp, Ana Navarro, and Nicolle Wallace to a studio to practice with Whoopi and Rosie in front of an audience. Sunny Hostin, a legal pundit on CNN who had frequently filled in on *The View*, was another contender. (Rosie had already told everyone that Sunny was getting hired.) The network also threw in two ESPN personalities, Jemele Hill and Sage Steele. Stephanie Ruhle from Bloomberg TV made the cut. So did Lauren Sánchez, the former *Extra* host whose last application for *The View* had been sabotaged by Star. Sánchez wasn't aware that her ex-boyfriend's wife, October Gonzalez (married to former NFL player Tony Gonzalez), had been invited to try out, too. Even weirder, October hadn't done much TV, but ABC was desperate for a Latina cohost.

"It was like *The Hunger Games*," Rosie told me a few days after. "I think Whoopi and I were a little bit shocked at having to do a chemistry test, because I don't know if those things really work." Rosie thought bringing in an audience to watch them debate made it awkward. "It felt negative and competitive. I think maybe they should have taken us to dinner with the top candidates to see how we got along."

The auditioning women entered the studio in pairs, after they had gone through a packet of sample Hot Topics, choosing the ones that they wanted to discuss. Cupp was teamed with Hostin, and they picked a story with an abortion angle. "I thought, 'Great!'" said Cupp, who was pregnant at the time and hosting a revamped *Crossfire* for CNN. "I'm really passionate about that."

As soon as Cupp tried to offer her anti-abortion beliefs, "Rosie goes kind of ballistic," she recalled.

"Have you ever had an abortion?" Rosie asked Cupp.

"I don't know why that's relevant."

"That's lazy!" Rosie yelled. "If you want to do this show, you have to be able to tell your stories." Then she started to vent angrily, to no one in particular, "I can't have another Elisabeth."

"It got so personal," Cupp recalled. "It went from zero to one hundred in two seconds. It's just not my style to run into a crazy argument. She was simultaneously having a debate with me, which was live to tape, but also talking to producers who were not there. I'm, like, 'Is this part of the debate? Should I start debating whether you should have another Elisabeth?'"

Cupp was not prepared for Rosie's hostility. "I remember selective things. I remember a woman in the audience yelled, 'S.E. is right!' I blacked out after that. There's no recovering. Rosie was on a crusade against pro-life people like me. She didn't know who I was, but she knew she didn't like me." Cupp lost track of how long she sat there. "That's like asking how long was the car crash. All she saw was a cartoon conservative." Cupp isn't religious and supports LGBTQ rights. "Whatever conception she had about Elisabeth, she projected onto me."

After she left the stage, Cupp was so confused that she had no idea if she had succeeded or failed. "Was that good or bad?" she thought. "Do they want this kind of craziness or not? If not, she's the problem, not me." Wolff apologized to Cupp backstage, which she took as his way of telling her she was out of the running.

Cupp went to collect her stuff in another area of the building, not re-alizing that she was being followed. "So I'm picking up my things, and all of a sudden there's this woman right here next to me. It's Rosie. She's, like, 'Look, I'm going to be brutally honest. If you want to do this job, you're going to have to tell your secrets.'"

After chewing Cupp out, Rosie was now trying to be her career coach. "What do you do for a living, for example?"

"I talk about politics on CNN."

"Oh, really! So you don't need this?"

"I don't."

With that, Rosie walked away, to turn her attention on the other women.

"It was fucking crazy," Cupp said. "It was bananas. She's not a stable person."

With all the various factions vying for control of *The View,* nobody wanted to get his or her hands on the show more than Ben Sherwood. It wasn't just about exerting his power as he prepared to take over one of the biggest jobs in entertainment: overseeing ABC and the other Disney-owned networks. Sherwood had resented ABC's daytime programming because of, as one colleague put it, "NBC envy." Throughout Sherwood's career, working on *GMA,* he had wanted to add a third hour to his morning show to better compete with the four hours of *Today.* But he had an obstacle that he couldn't get around. Once *GMA* ended at 9:00 a.m., ABC stations aired *Live,* and Kelly Ripa had inserted a clause in her contract that guaranteed her that time slot. There was always a chance, though, that if Sherwood controlled *The View,* he could slowly morph the 11:00 a.m. hour into another, later edition of *GMA,* using the same crew and lesser-known ABC News correspondents such as Paula Faris and Sara Haines.

Sweeney's hire of Rosie had been the best defense to prevent the *GMA*-ification of *The View.* Even as a lame-duck executive, she refused to surrender the talk show. Besides, no love was lost between Sherwood and Sweeney, since he had pushed her out.

Sherwood had a dubious reputation at ABC. Growing up in a wealthy family in Beverly Hills, he was the subject of mockery as a graduate student in a 1988 *Spy* magazine article by Andrew Sullivan. The piece painted Sherwood as an insufferable Rhodes Scholar who had stuffed his résumé with summer internships, while annoying the hell out of his classmates at Harvard. "Machiavelli, who is widely misunderstood, said that in the long run it's not very important to be popular, because popularity is fleeting, but respect is permanent," Sherwood told the *Los Angeles Times* in an interview after winning the Rhodes.

When Sherwood returned from Oxford, he worked his way up the ladder as a producer at ABC, getting in the good graces of Diane Sawyer. In 2003, after leaving another job at *NBC Nightly News*, he intensely lobbied Sawyer to let him take over *GMA*, convincing her to let him replace her trusted executive producer, Shelley Ross. "Ben had been emailing Diane and sort of in a veiled way, leading her to believe that he was consulting for *Today*," Ross recalled. In the fall of 2003, Sawyer set up a lunch with Sherwood, which Ross attended. "Diane was asking him what's important now. And I remember Ben saying, 'Cruise ships!'" That year, stories about the outbreak of the norovirus virus had led to a viewership jump, but Ross didn't think it was practical—or possible—to send her anchors out to sea.

"There was a conga line of people who wanted my job," Ross said. "I didn't give much thought to any of them. I knew the job I was doing. I was increasing ratings and revenue." But *GMA* was still losing to *Today*, and Sherwood's pitch to Sawyer was that he would move them to number one. In the spring of 2004, he was appointed the next executive producer of *GMA*. Ross was moved, against her wishes, to oversee *Primetime Live*.

But it soon became clear Sherwood couldn't deliver, despite some elaborate plans. For example, in May 2006, Sherwood went to great lengths to prevent the cast of the hot summer movie *The Da Vinci Code* from appearing on *Today*. He thought he had an edge because his wife, Karen Kehela, the co-chairwoman of Imagine Entertainment, had shepherded the blockbuster. But *Today* bookers still snatched up director Ron Howard and the cast for a week of interviews in Europe with Matt Lauer. With millions of dollars at stake, Columbia Pictures didn't want to settle for a program with fewer viewers.

ABC News veterans told me that Sherwood never deciphered *GMA*'s secret formula of hard and soft stories. "I really think he was ill equipped,"

Ross said. "On morning shows, you're rated every single minute. And I don't think he's a real producer. Or a leader. People who work for Ben often will tell you that you're not working on the show, but you're working to advance Ben Sherwood's career."

Sawyer eventually lost patience with Sherwood, and they stopped talking. After she made it clear that she wanted to get rid of him, he moved to Los Angeles to "be closer to his family." He researched a 2009 book called *The Survivors Club: The Secrets and Science That Could Save Your Life.* Yet, after a few years away from the news business, he was able to sweet-talk Sweeney into allowing him to return to ABC. This time, he was rewarded with a bigger office as the president of the news division.

"I fancy myself a writer," Sherwood once told me. He often recited this line to his staff, which made his colleagues roll their eyes. When one of his employees made a crack to a friend of Sherwood's at the company that Sherwood wasn't actually a writer, word got back to him. "Ben made it his mission to make the employee's life as miserable as possible, forcing him to leave," recalled a former executive.

Back at ABC in 2010, he was determined to grow *GMA*'s audience. He started telling staff how unimpressed he was with coanchors Robin Roberts and George Stephanopoulos. "They are so boring together," Sherwood griped, as he plotted to replace one of them. He brought in Josh Elliott, a sports anchor from ESPN, and celebrity correspondent Lara Spencer to pad the *GMA* team. But Sherwood soon got on Elliott's nerves by starting to dress like him, asking for the brands of his suits. (Elliott left the show in 2014.) It's still up for debate if Sherwood and his team actually improved *GMA* or if they were the beneficiaries of luck. During his tenure, *Today* made the stupid decision to fire Ann Curry, and *GMA* galloped ahead because of the backlash. Suddenly, Sherwood stopped complaining about George and Robin.

Sherwood had his sights set on Sweeney's job. Even though he didn't program daytime, he helped broker a deal with Katie Couric to host a talk show following her poorly received five years at the *CBS Evening News.* It required some heavy lifting. After Oprah retired, some speculated that *The View* might take over her time slot in the afternoon. But that idea was quickly shot down because the owned and operated stations didn't want to replace Oprah with another talk show. They would rather program that slot with an hour of local news, which would be cheaper for them than a pricey syndication deal.

Sherwood spoke to Iger, and they made a backroom deal. They agreed to give up an hour by promising to cancel something soon (they later axed 2012's *The Revolution,* a lifestyle show with fashion expert Tim Gunn). As a result, the stations would still get their extra hour for news, and ABC would now have *Katie,* a daytime talk show that they billed as the next *Oprah.*

When Couric pitched her show to ABC in 2011, Sweeney asked her for her vision.

"Oh, Anne," said Couric with a whiff of condescension. "Don't you worry about that, dear. We'll take care of it."

Sweeney's blood went cold. Either Couric had been having side conversations, or she had a strange way of trying to sell a talk show. In the end, Sherwood took credit for bringing Couric to ABC. He was working overtime to undermine Sweeney, urging some of his powerful producing friends to sing his praises to Iger while taking a knock at his boss. Eventually, his campaign succeeded. Iger offered Sherwood Sweeney's job, and in March 2014 she announced she was leaving to pursue a new career—she decided at the last minute—as a TV director.

It didn't matter for Sherwood that *Katie* turned out to be a disaster, the *Gigli* of daytime TV. Since Couric was collecting a $16 million paycheck, she had to deliver a monster hit. Couric had the chops to handle hard and soft news on *Today,* but she was no Oprah. Her tenure at CBS had turned her into a news snob. According to staffers, she saw herself as such a serious journalist that she needed to intellectualize every story they pitched to her. That was fine for an evening broadcast. But in daytime, she had to steer softball conversations with Jessica Simpson (Couric's first interview in the fall of 2012) while plugging gift card giveaways from TJ Maxx. When she interviewed Joan Rivers, Couric insulted her by asking about her plastic surgery. Rivers ripped Couric in half, and the show had to cut out some of those exchanges from the final broadcast because they got so ugly. "What the hell is she doing?" muttered a producer backstage, taking Rivers's side.

Since *Katie* wasn't broadcast live, Couric had some room for error, since things could be reshot. But she went overboard, routinely filming ninety minutes of content for a single hour of TV. This wasn't just a nightmare for her editors, but also for her guests. Rachel Maddow was particularly annoyed to be kept waiting backstage as Couric kept slowly taping her segments.

Couric had enlisted an old NBC friend, *Today*'s Jeff Zucker, to be her executive producer. She also relied on a familiar hand from CBS, an executive named Abra Potkin, who came to ABC Daytime to help with some of the staffing. That led to two competing teams, as Potkin had Sherwood's ear as part of his circle. According to the producers I talked to, Zucker didn't have any faith in the daytime hands, who were inexperienced in news interviews. That made sense because Couric wanted her show to be newsier. The network was worried about that approach, but Zucker didn't want their input. When an ABC executive came to observe the show, Zucker locked her out of the control room.

All hopes that *Katie* could succeed were dashed after Zucker bolted from the show after four months to run CNN in January 2013. One staffer recalled a meeting where Potkin, as the boss, lay with her back on the floor. "If we can't get the ratings up, we're all going to be out of jobs!" she wailed. Couric didn't seem to care. She was ready to ditch daytime.

When *Katie* was canceled after two miserable seasons, *The View* inherited her fancier studio in time for Season 18. The show was now officially part of ABC News, in both location and management. Even though Potkin had been part of Couric's failed outing, she was able to position herself to consult on *The View,* along with everybody else. Rosie was happy that ABC was moving the *View* set because she had so many bad memories from the other building. And she couldn't go back there because of her anxiety over using the communal toilets.

As the president of Disney/ABC Television Group, Sherwood would soon alienate some of his most valuable talent. He tried to give notes to Shonda Rhimes, telling her that the pilot for her series *How to Get Away with Murder* didn't make sense. When she left for a lucrative Netflix deal in 2017, many ABC staffers thought that it was Ben's fault for acting as if he were her creative equal. Sherwood was responsible for not telling Kelly Ripa that he was stealing her *Live* cohost Michael Strahan for *GMA* in April 2016, which prompted her to stop coming to work for a few days and to deliver a stunning soliloquy on TV about respect in the workplace. But before all this happened, Sherwood was determined to make *The View* his first fix-it project.

By bringing on Wolff to head *The View,* Sherwood thought that he had hired a useful ally. But Sherwood hadn't anticipated the difficulties in managing all the strong women on *The View,* which Geddie had done without a lot of noise. At MSNBC, Wolff had worked with one host, Maddow, who ran a tight ship and produced her own scripts. "On his first day, in he walks in a suit and tie, and he was a sweaty, hot mess," recalled one staffer. "He was a nice guy, but every other word out of his mouth was *fuck*. He sounded like the coach of a Little League team: 'This is going to be fucking great. We are going to be fucking awesome again.'"

Wolff told his employees that he was going to have an open-door policy. "His door was never open after that," said one staffer. Wolff was overwhelmed by the constant flurry of questions. He never had the answers and he'd always say that he'd need to consult with someone else. When one of his employees brought up Elisabeth and Rosie's fight, Wolff confessed that he had no idea what she was talking about—that's how little he knew about *The View*. "The news people wanted a puppet," said an insider. "They wanted someone they could control. Here's Bill Wolff."

Regardless of who was in charge, ABC still had a dilemma: Who had won the *View* audition? The executives were underwhelmed by everyone. Hostin, who had been the favorite, fell out of the running because of her association with the Cupp fight, where she couldn't get a word in. Hackner was grasping at straws for names to brainstorm that weren't even viable choices. She wanted to know if they could hire Carrie Underwood at a moment's notice, even though the country star lived in Nashville, didn't talk politics, and would have been ridiculously expensive. Sherwood liked Wallace, who had been the White House communications director for George W. Bush, and he eventually made her an offer.

His only instruction to her was to dye her hair blond from brown. "Ben Sherwood called me and said, 'You're going to be my modern blond mom,'" Nicolle recalled. "He had told me to learn faster than George Stephanopoulos did—that you need to share your personal life with viewers. George had learned pretty quickly, and George wasn't on *The View*. So I thought that was a weird thing to say to me."

For the last seat, Wolff suggested someone who wasn't part of the test group. Two weeks before *The View* began, he called Rosie Perez, the star of such films as 1989's *Do the Right Thing* and 1992's *White Men Can't Jump*, who had been a guest on *Maddow* to talk about politics. Wolff asked her to come to ABC for a meeting. "We talked boxing for the first ten minutes of the interview," Perez told me about their conversation. They were both avid sports fans, although boxing hadn't traditionally been a topic that drove *The View*. ABC made Perez an offer on the spot because it had no backup plan. Two warning signs that this wouldn't be a good fit were that Perez wasn't a morning person, and she had already committed to a Broadway play that winter, Larry David's *Fish in the Dark*.

Rosie O'Donnell was a fan of Perez's life and work but was surprised to hear she was becoming her colleague. "I love Rosie Perez," she told me. "I didn't even know she was being considered."

Because everything for the new season of *The View* had been a discombobulated mess, Wolff was at the studio around the clock before the show went live, trying to cobble together the new set. The four cohosts practiced together only once. When Rosie saw the reconfigured Hot Topics table, Wolff had already lost her confidence. It was too small to hold all of them.

A familiar face returned to *The View* on September 15, 2014. No, not just Rosie O'Donnell. On top of everything else, Barbara Walters had decided that she'd had enough of retirement after only four months. She demanded that she come back on TV to bless the new cast of *The View*. ABC executives, wary of what might unfold if they let Barbara loose in front of an audience, wouldn't allow her a spot on the live show.

But out of respect, they cooked up a skit, since she loved doing those so much, in which she'd dress up like a queen. Once Barbara had arrived at the Barbara Walters Building, where *The View* now taped, it was as if she'd entered a bad dream. She noticed that the new set resembled an IKEA store. The green sofa where the ladies used to huddle had been changed to beige lounge chairs, which kept them all apart. Barbara didn't get one of those comfortable cushions. Instead, she was directed to the corner of the stage, where producers had set up a stiff red throne with golden armrests.

Barbara had dressed up for the occasion in a white blouse and a ruby-red belt, as if Margaret Thatcher had been given a cameo in *The Wizard of Oz*. Barbara took her seat, ready to remind viewers that she had invented the show. Unlike Bill Geddie, who always kept close tabs on the cohosts, Wolff kept a distance backstage. He walked into the greenroom (actually painted a lime green, thanks to a designer with a sense of humor) and spotted some of his friends who had played hooky to root him on. "Jesus Christ," Wolff whispered under his breath. "I feel like it's my bar mitzvah."

Before the audience was let in, the cameras rolled on a scene that was out of *King Lear*. Barbara was ready to parcel out her empire. She blessed all the new cohosts, who kneeled before her throne.

"And by the way, I was told I would have a crown," Barbara said. That was the cue for the prop guy to hand over a sparkling tiara. "Fits perfectly!" she said as she placed it over her head. Then Barbara had to vacate the set with thirty minutes left before airtime. She took a seat backstage, crossing paths with a group of journalists who had been invited to cover the new season of *The View*.

"Who are these people?" she muttered.

The studio, packed with VIPs, looked like a homecoming game, with two teams divided up. The ABC Daytime executives—Lisa Hackner and Randy Barone—were there, to keep up appearances that the show was still officially part of their portfolio. With them sat Abra Potkin. Closer to the stage were the real MVPs. Sherwood had brought along his team, a trio of ABC News veterans that operated like a three-headed cyclops, with their loyalty pledged to Sherwood. They were James Goldston, who would run ABC News after Sherwood got promoted, and his lieutenants, Tom Cibrowski and Barbara Fedida.

At 11:00 a.m., the new *View* was ready to roll. As the cohosts wandered out to Taylor Swift's "Shake It Off," they didn't exactly embody the song's carefree attitude. "Are we even on?" Rosie mouthed to Whoopi, who shook her head. Wolff had changed their entrance to a different door at the last minute, without realizing that he'd thrown off all their cues. Luckily, on TV, you couldn't see their confusion.

"Welcome to the newer *View*," Whoopi said. "Hey, this is a lot of brand-new stuff." She introduced the rest of the cast. Rosie O'Donnell charmed her way through her introduction, but both Nicolle and the other Rosie struggled to keep the conversation breezy. "Oh," stuttered Perez, when asked to talk about herself. "I'm sitting here with three fabulous women. I'm loving life. Wow."

The show felt disjointed. To settle her nerves, Rosie O'Donnell got up at every commercial break, armed with an impromptu stand-up set. Whoopi looked annoyed that Rosie was putting on her own show within the real show. This had never happened under Barbara, as she made the cohosts use the commercial breaks to look over their notes. When one member of the audience asked Rosie if they were adding a fifth cohost, she scoffed in mock outrage, "Get the fuck out. The show is thirty-eight minutes. Four is enough."

At least one other person was fantasizing about a fifth seat. As soon as the episode wrapped, Barbara came out of hiding. She took the stage and waved at the crowd and gave each of the cohosts a congratulatory peck, assembling them for a class photo with her.

With a pack of journalists waiting to interview the new cast, Sherwood rushed over to Barbara, looping his arm around hers. Her smile disappeared, and she winced at the sight of her new companion. "Come on, Ms. Walters," he said, pulling her away from the flashing lights.

Maybe she should have stayed. This next season of *The View* came close to being its last because Rosie and Whoopi would almost kill each other.

22

"Worse Than Fox News"

The first clue that Rosie and Whoopi wouldn't be compatible as co-workers dated back to 2009. Whoopi had made the controversial argument on *The View* that Roman Polanski hadn't committed "*rape* rape," about the 1977 criminal case involving the film director's sex acts with a thirteen-year-old girl. Rosie, who wasn't on TV at the time, couldn't let such an egregious claim go unchecked. During a radio interview on *Howard Stern*—she'd made peace with the shock jock through a mutual friend, the actress Mia Farrow—Rosie unleashed on Whoopi. "I said, 'That's ridiculous!'" Rosie recalled. "'I'm very anti–Roman Polanksi and anti–Woody Allen. I'm not for people who rape children. It's a pretty clear line for me.'"

Whoopi, who was stung by the criticism, sent Rosie a note. "It was a very angry letter," Rosie said. "And I wrote back to her and I said, 'You can't change your idols, and you will always be one to me. I'm sorry if that hurt your feelings. I have different feelings about it than you. And I stand up for what I believe, but I'll never be against you, Whoopi Goldberg.'" Rosie meant that, theoretically. But all bets were off once she returned to *The View*.

On her original tour of duty, Rosie had at least pretended that she was going to be everybody's friend. This time, she had her guard up. When Rosie reintroduced herself to the staff that summer, she looked detached, speaking slowly and deliberately, like the headmaster of a boarding school. It was a defense mechanism because she hadn't been given control over Barbara Walters's kingdom yet. As she pontificated about Season 18, Rosie made it sound as if she were the new executive producer, right in front of the man who actually held that role (not that Bill Wolff had the chutzpah to tell her to back down). That day, Rosie sputtered off a jumble of ideas about how the show would be smarter, focus more on news, and educate viewers. One part of her speech revealed just how much control she desired. "It's our jobs," Rosie said, "to make Whoopi better."

The room went silent. In the seven years that Whoopi had been on *The View,* nobody had needed to—or, frankly, had the courage to—give her notes.

"We're not going to do to Whoopi what we did to Barbara," Rosie continued. That made it worse. Rosie was suggesting that Whoopi (at only fifty-eight) was approaching her expiration date, and that it was their responsibility to cover for her until she left, which wouldn't be too far off in the future.

Rosie's words baffled the staff. They couldn't tell if she was speculating about what she'd like to have happen, or if she was working off actual information from the network. One of the producers texted Whoopi, telling her that she needed to get to the office quickly. When she arrived a little bit later, she and Rosie had an awkward exchange. "What's going on here?" Whoopi asked. Rosie realized that someone had tipped off Whoopi, which led Rosie to believe that the producers were out to get her. She stayed withdrawn in her interactions.

Rosie saw Whoopi as part of her restoration project because Rosie blamed her for the stodginess associated with *The View* in its later seasons. Rosie tried to get Whoopi to not wear an earpiece, which was a strange direction—Whoopi needed one to communicate with the control room.

"I never wanted to take the show away from her," Rosie told me. "For years, she sat there and said nothing. She was nearly not even present. She would hold the cards and never ask a question to a guest. It was quite obvious she was getting a paycheck and nothing else. I wanted to raise the level of the show, and therefore her as well."

Whoopi wasn't a control freak or a perfectionist, but she didn't take orders. She wondered why she wasn't getting any respect. When Lisa Hackner told Whoopi that Rosie was getting rehired on *The View,* Hackner mishandled the way she presented it.

"Rosie is coming back to save the show," Hackner had said.

Oh, really? Whoopi thought. *What have I been doing here?*

As a result, Whoopi never warmed to Rosie as a colleague.

Most of the veteran producers knew that Rosie and Whoopi would never survive at the same table. The staff didn't understand why Anne Sweeney and her daytime team thought this pairing would last, especially given Rosie's history on the show. But as bad as Rosie's eruptions had been with Barbara or Elisabeth Hasselbeck, this turned out to be much worse. It would soon come to be known as a fact among even ABC loyalists that working at *The View* was total hell.

The Season 18 premiere episode earned 3.9 million viewers, its highest ratings in eight years, as a result of the curiosity about Rosie's return to daytime TV. In a few days, those numbers swiftly dropped, after it became obvious that the show without Barbara had become a shadow of itself in its glory days. It felt as if the four cohosts were on different planets. Nicolle Wallace, who still kept her other job as a pundit on MSNBC's *Morning Joe,* relished wonky policy discussions. Rosie Perez wanted to talk about sports, making *The View* seem more like a product from ESPN. And Rosie O'Donnell looked defeated. With Whoopi as the moderator, she felt censored and restrained. Instead of entertaining America with her quick takes on news stories and her biting jokes, she kept flashing a death stare at Whoopi for interrupting her. "Some people would say, 'What's going on with you and Whoopi?'" Rosie recalled. "I was, like, 'Are you watching the show! It's pretty much right there.' I have no desire for a public feud."

One of Rosie's many mandates was to start the morning meeting a half hour earlier, at 8:30 a.m., to allow a jump start on preparing for the show. Whoopi, who took a car from her home in New Jersey, insisted that the meeting stay at the regular time of 9:00 a.m., since two hours had always been sufficient time to figure things out. ("There was no chance that Whoopi was getting there at eight thirty," said one producer, laughing.) Rosie, who also commuted from New Jersey, took Whoopi's objection as proof that she wasn't invested in fixing the show. As a compromise, Wolff tried to start the meeting at 8:45 a.m. "She was late the first time," recalled Rosie, who made a sarcastic aside to the staff about Whoopi's tardiness.

"I don't think she was interested at all," Rosie said about how Whoopi responded to Rosie's ideas. "We have different ways of treating our employment."

Rosie was furious at Whoopi for shutting down discussions about one major news story in particular. In 2014, dozens of women came forward to accuse Bill Cosby of rape. Whoopi didn't want to give those stories any airtime. "Because he's a black legend and she's a black legend," Rosie said, offering an explanation. "Black people have been oppressed for two hundred or more years. There are probably fifty famous black people in the nation, depending on how you define fame. It would be hard to rip one of your legends down." Rosie paused, to think about it some more. "Although, I will tell you this. If Barbra Streisand was accused of raping or doping young boys who were her fans, I would stand up against her. And I love her more than I love any human on the earth."

A few weeks into the show, Whoopi cut off Rosie during a Hot Topics debate to go to a break. Rosie whipped herself into a frenzy. She rushed into the audience, with a microphone in her hand, berating Whoopi about the way Rosie was being treated.

"This is going to be all over Twitter!" Rosie Perez gasped.

O'Donnell calmed down only after her assistant handed her an anti-anxiety pill. Staffers noticed that this new version of Rosie was more on edge than she'd ever been. In the shiny refurbished studio, she'd largely keep to herself, looking miserable. She'd quickly lose her temper whenever something wasn't going right, which happened all the time. If producers were slow to respond, she'd get in their faces, yelling about what needed to happen. She was so distressed about the show that she started complaining to celebrity guests waiting to go on about how terrible Whoopi was to her.

"Whoopi Goldberg was as mean as anyone has ever been on television to me, personally—while I was sitting there," Rosie told me. "Worse than Fox News. The worst experience I've ever had on live television was interacting with her."

Rosie had idolized Whoopi as an actress, but the reality of working with her didn't line up to what Rosie had thought it would be. She'd put Whoopi on a pedestal, like Barbara, and once Rosie got to know the real Whoopi, it all came crashing down. "I revered her," Rosie said. "She's a minority, feminist, smart, funny, groundbreaking legend who is black in America. I'm never going to not have respect for Whoopi Goldberg. But that was a painful experience, personally and professionally. With Elisabeth Hasselbeck, I didn't see her in a one-woman show that changed my life as an artist. But I did with Whoopi Goldberg, and I watched her make her way through a world, which is racist and sexist and homophobic, and succeed like only four women of color have in our age range. I didn't understand how she played on a team was different than the way I played on a team."

As the show unraveled into a modern-day set visit to *Whatever Happened to Baby Jane?* with Rosie and Whoopi channeling Bette Davis and Joan Crawford, Bill Wolff was swallowed alive by his two strong leads. Backstage, nobody was making any decisions. Wolff couldn't answer even simple questions, approving—for example—that the show's bookers reach out to A-list stars who were so big, they probably wouldn't do *The View*. "Hmmm," he'd reply. "Let me get back to you." Wolff started to have anxiety attacks and popped Rolaids in the office, as he tried to please everybody, while never putting his foot down. "He was a sweet man, but useless," recalled one producer.

"It was a crazy amount of change all at once," said Barbara Fedida, the senior vice president for talent at ABC News. "It was a table of women who had never worked together before. It was a new executive producer who had never worked in this genre—cable talk is very different than broadcast talk. It was unclear what promises were made to each person sitting at the table."

Under Walters, the morning meetings had always been run efficiently. Now these gatherings, regardless of the start time, had become bureaucratic ordeals. The room kept getting bigger. Those in attendance included Wolff and his new coexecutive producer, Brian Balthazar, who'd worked with Kathie Lee and Hoda on *Today*. In October, Ben Sherwood struck a fatal blow to the daytime side, when he officially put his news executives in charge. (Since Whoopi didn't trust Hackner, it made it easier to move her away from *The View*.)

Coming from *Good Morning America*, James Goldston, Tom Cibrowski, and Fedida would sit in to observe *The View*, as they filtered through the news stories or introduced cheesy segments such as View Your Deal, which had the cohosts peddling discounted merchandise such as luggage or sunglasses on TV. This was a recycled shtick from *GMA*, where it had been called Deals and Steals. Rosie refused to participate, and she vented out loud (and on Twitter) that it cheapened the show to hold a weekly garage sale.

The four cohosts would all receive a packet of potential stories for the Hot Topics meeting. Nicolle was game for anything, even pop culture stories that she didn't know much about. She'd offer to study *The Bachelor* or watch clips of the *Kardashians*. "Nicolle was the only one who tried to make it less awkward, so Bill wouldn't look like an asshole," recalled one producer. "She tried so hard."

The other cohosts never bothered to crack open the list. Rosie would sit quietly in the meeting, wearing sweats, Crocs, and a look of disdain.

"What do you think of Topic Number Thirty-Eight?" Wolff would gently ask.

"It doesn't interest me," Rosie would say.

Perez would sometimes chime in about something she'd heard on NPR that morning that wasn't included in the lineup. Her favorite stories, in addition to sports, were about AIDS, world peace, and immigration. But these complicated issues couldn't be quickly debated on morning TV.

The ABC executives knew they had to do something about the chemistry of the panel because the cohosts made for strange bedfellows. As Wolff had assembled a cast under the gun, he'd forgotten a golden rule of TV: stay young. Nicolle was forty-one, and the Rosies were in their fifties. *The View* was missing a millennial to make it multigenerational, which was Barbara's founding principle.

The ABC executives realized that they had also gotten the Republican component wrong. With Elisabeth, the show had used its conservative as a foil against all the other voices. Nicolle wasn't confrontational, and she spent most of her time on TV nodding at her peers. In one of her early episodes, the Hot Topics dealt with Donald Trump wanting to close the borders to Americans who had been infected with the Ebola virus overseas. "I think when Rosie O'Donnell and I were screaming at each other in agreement was when the first alarm bells went off about me," Nicolle said. "They thought, 'Oh, no! She's not going to fight with Rosie.' They'd been trying to capture lightning in the bottle again from the Rosie-and-Elisabeth years." When Nicolle wasn't on camera, she was joined at the hip with Whoopi, traveling with her to the hair-and-makeup room for camaraderie—and protection.

"Things boiled over," Nicolle said. "Rosie jumped on me one day about torture. She'd seen me on *Morning Joe* defending what George Bush had done on enhanced interrogations. She was really upset and got really mad about it."

When Rosie got heated in another meeting, Nicolle marched to human resources and reported her. "I can get . . ." Rosie trailed off. "I said, 'Are you kidding me? Are we not talking about Bill Cosby? Are we not talking about the number one story?' I raised my voice. I was in my dressing room, getting my makeup done, and somebody comes and goes, 'Nicolle Wallace just went to HR.'" Rosie couldn't believe it. "I didn't know what HR was, first of all."

Nicolle had brought her husband to work that day, as her own security guard. "I get out of my chair, walk in her dressing room," Rosie said. "I'm, like, 'What the hell happened, Nicolle? You went where?!'"

"I just felt you were threatening me."

Rosie, who later became friends with Nicolle, offered an explanation for why they weren't close on *The View:* "She was an ally to Whoopi Goldberg, who seemed to have an anti-Rosie agenda for all the world to see."

After Thanksgiving, Rosie told the staff that she had separated from her wife (they divorced the next year), after they'd been fighting at home. Her entire life seemed to be coming undone. Late on some nights, she'd call up a producer, saying that she couldn't possibly go to work the next day, sitting on TV next to "a rape defender" (meaning Whoopi) and "the woman who supported George W. Bush's torture techniques" (Nicolle). "I never took it personally," Nicolle said. "If she was upset that I worked for George W. Bush, it was never like I hid the cucumber."

For Nicolle, daytime TV was a roller coaster that was different from politics: "It was really dramatic. We all kind of had to ride Rosie O'Donnell's highs and lows, because she was going through a lot and pulled everyone in. She's so intense. If she's upset, we all kind of absorbed that. I think in some ways, Whoopi absorbed the brunt of it. They had some famous fights."

The network was simply trying to prevent another civil war on TV. "Once it was clear it wasn't going to work," Fedida said, "the only thing we wanted to do is not have it be a blowup disaster. We didn't want them to start fighting on the air to the point where the audience would be uncomfortable watching them. That was the mandate: get them on the air and off the air every day, and to make sure nothing crazy goes on."

On December 18, a discussion in Hot Topics about racism and President Obama turned into a bitter shouting match.

"Do you all think we live in a racist country?" Nicolle had asked.

"Without a doubt," Rosie said.

"Listen, you are a white lady telling me what is racist to you," Whoopi said.

"I'm a gay American who has been called a dyke," Rosie protested. "I know what homophobia and hatred looks like."

"That is not the same," Whoopi said.

"I have a black kid I raised, Whoopi."

"That is not the same."

The show's guest cohost that day, Laverne Cox, had to intervene to stop them from attacking each other.

"I thought my head was going to explode," Rosie told me. Her cardiologist, who was watching *The View* that morning, saw Rosie's carotid artery pop in her neck. "My doctor called me and said, 'Come in right now. Your heart rate during that is dangerous for you. I don't want you doing that show anymore.'" Rosie feigned ignorance. "But I could feel it. I felt it in the midst of fight or flight or freeze."

After the show went on hiatus for Christmas, Rosie didn't show up to Whoopi's annual holiday party at her house. Whoopi had hired the Santa Claus from 30 Rockefeller Center to mingle with her coworkers and famous friends. But as Rosie's comeback to *The View* was crumbling, she wasn't feeling any cheer.

❧

Was this how *The View* would die? Only so many scenarios could unfold. Either Rosie would let go or Whoopi would, to let the other one try to salvage the show. Or the two of them would hold on indefinitely, squabbling as *The View* sank into the black hole of cancellation. Already, rumors were going around ABC that the show might not make it another season—that's how catastrophic the last few months had been. If it went, Sherwood would get his extra hour for more sales on *Good Morning America*.

Just the thought of that made Whoopi cringe, but what could she do? After the holidays, Rosie received a late present—a back injury for Whoopi. The moderator was bedridden and called in sick for two weeks. And another cohost needed a leave of absence. Just barely into her *View* debut, Rosie Perez took off time in January to rehearse for her Broadway play because she said she couldn't juggle both. O'Donnell was finally getting a break. She had a clean runway to mount the relevant and edgy talk show she'd imagined *The View* could be.

But she didn't have it in her. Maybe if Rosie had started with more time at the beginning of the season, with a staff devoted to her, there could have been one more act as Rosie the talk show host. As the fill-in moderator of *The View*, with a revolving panel of cohosts that included men such as Mario Cantone and Billy Eichner, the numbers didn't rebound for Rosie. They actually dipped slightly because the show's fans missed Whoopi. Not even the show's creator could put *The View* back together again. With so many vacancies at the table, Barbara charged back through the door as a happy substitute on a few days. She was less polished than she used to be—stammering instead of crisply attacking stories—but it hardly mattered. The show had gone so far off the rails that Rosie was relieved to have Barbara's help.

One morning, in the Hot Topics meeting, Rosie addressed the staff. She wanted to know why a reporter from Page Six had called her publicist, asking about Barbara's memory lapses backstage. Despite so many paranoid discussions about press leaks that year, no one could figure out where they were coming from.

Rosie looked at a senior producer, Jennifer Shepard-Brookman, who was close to Whoopi.

"The leaks are out of control this year," Shepard-Brookman said, according to documents filed in court.

"Really, you don't think the leak is here?" Rosie countered. "Maybe one of you told your teenage sons and he leaked it."

Shepard-Brookman pushed back, denying that she (or anyone in her family) would do such a thing. She thought Rosie was picking on her because Whoopi wasn't there and started crying. A few weeks later, Shepard-Brookman sent an email to Rosie about the confrontation, listing some secrets about Rosie that she could have leaked if she'd wanted to. Rosie showed the letter to the network, which fired Shepard-Brookman.

"One of them tried to sue me," Rosie said, about a slander lawsuit that Shepard-Brookman filed that was eventually dismissed by a New York judge.

With all that Sherwood went through to get *The View* in the hands of ABC News, none of the top executives wanted it. They didn't think they could improve the show. When James Goldston, the head of the news division, asked Robin Roberts or George Stephanopoulos to do something, they listened because they understood that a newsroom had to have a hierarchy. But at *The View*, the cohosts couldn't be bothered with anything as conventional as a boss. The show turned out to be a huge time suck, with constant drama and never any resolution.

Nevertheless, the ABC News team had to at least try to attract some viewers back. They decided they would fire the cohost who had already taken herself off the show. They started testing other women to fill in for Perez. They weren't sure if they would just let her disappear into the fog of Broadway, or if they'd bring her back for one last goodbye. I wrote a story in *Variety* about their plan to fire Perez, citing internal complaints about her performance on TV. Pandemonium ensued. An organization of Latina leaders started a petition to save her job and demanded an apology from ABC.

O'Donnell and Whoopi, back from her own hiatus, had been kept in the dark. They called the network, demanding answers. On TV, O'Donnell assured viewers that Perez would return. The news team was terrified of creating an "Ann Curry situation," referring to NBC's disastrous firing of their beloved coanchor on *Today*. They backtracked and allowed Perez back on, even if the show wasn't working with her on it. (Their spinelessness became a subject of ridicule among the old daytime executives. Curry, they pointed out, had been on *Today* for fifteen years. Perez on *The View* had barely made a dent.)

This was all too much for O'Donnell. At home, in addition to her marital problems, her teenage daughter Chelsea had run away with her boyfriend, leaving Rosie panicked at what to do. (They were estranged for the next three years.) Rosie desperately wanted out of *The View*, and she begged her agent to get her out of her contract. This would never have been possible if the show were a hit, but given the low ratings and the across-the-board exhaustion from all the fighting, Sherwood approved it. When Brian Balthazar told Rosie that he planned on taking another job, Rosie wasn't fazed. "I'm leaving, too," she told him. She'd only lasted on the show for five months.

Rosie hastily announced her second exit from TV, citing her family and her health as the reasons she needed to go. She departed *The View* for the second time on February 12, 2015, looking to be relieved to finally be done with the producers and Whoopi. "I never wanted to take the show away from her," Rosie told me in 2018. "All I wanted to do is make that show be as good as it could be. Now it's unwatchable."

23

Enjoy the View, While You Can

The irony was that Whoopi Goldberg never wanted to be the guardian of *The View*. She'd inherited this prize, but she hadn't tried to outlast her opponents, nor had she hatched any schemes to be the last woman standing. It would have mattered more to Rosie O'Donnell if she had kept the show, or to Barbara Walters if she had figured out a way to freeze time and postpone her retirement. Whoopi never pictured *The View* as something that came close to matching her other career accomplishments. She considered following Rosie out the door, telling several producers on the show that she was ready to quit and let the show rot in the hands of the news team.

Whoopi's relationship with *The View* remains complicated. In early 2015, she told me that there were a lot of executives in charge who didn't know what they were doing, without naming them. She'd initially said that she'd talk to me for my book, when it looked like she'd be leaving the show. But she changed her mind, and she stopped doing any press for *The View*. Whoopi vented to an executive about how much she hated my book cover, which she discovered online, because it featured an illustration of her sitting at the same table as Rosie.

When ABC renewed Whoopi's contract for Season 19, she took a pay cut, from $5 million to $4 million a year, as a result of the ratings decline. The network decided that the show would go live on Fridays, to handle breaking news, in case the next election cycle got crazy (it did). Whoopi accepted a one-year deal on the condition that she only worked four days a week, meaning someone else would need to moderate on Fridays. She thought with the ABC News executives in charge, *The View* might not last much longer. If it did, she'd give herself a lifeboat to make a quick escape.

As the show trudged onward that spring without Rosie, the network prepared to pull the trigger on yet another reboot. Ben Sherwood had placed all the blame on the worst season of *The View* on the daytime team for foisting Rosie on them, even while his executives made the decisions that led to her demise. Now they were busy testing out other cohosts. Rosie Perez and Nicolle Wallace sat tight, unsure of what their futures would be. Bill Wolff vocally complained that the news team didn't communicate with him, and he couldn't get any directions.

Over the July 4 weekend of 2015, I broke the news that ABC executives were thinking about cutting both Nicolle and Rosie Perez. This time, there would be no reversing their decision. "Rosie Perez rang me and said, 'We got fired in fucking *Variety*,'" Nicolle recalled. "I was, like, 'What?' So I called Barbara Fedida, and I'm, like, 'Did we just get fired?'"

Fedida, who served as Sherwood's eyes on the East Coast, wouldn't tell Nicolle what was going on. "Shouldn't you have called me?" Nicolle wanted to know. "She was really mealy-mouthed about everything, and that was the only conversation I had with anyone in management. My agent couldn't get an answer."

ABC News later offered Nicolle a smaller role on the show, to appear one day a week. Nicolle declined the demotion, and she left with Perez. She never looked at *The View* as a news program. "The devastation of leaving probably had nothing to do with entertainment television," Nicolle said. "That, probably, wasn't a good fit for me. But the idea of not seeing Whoopi every day was crushing."

Nicolle didn't have any regrets about doing the show: "Spending a year there was like when I was in high school and went abroad. It enriched me in every way; it expanded my horizons. Doing television in front of a live audience retrains you." She saw her stock rise at NBC while covering the election, and she eventually got her own afternoon show on MSNBC.

Whoopi was furious that the network had dumped her friend without asking her what she thought about it. For a few weeks, as retribution for Nicolle's firing, Whoopi refused to speak to any of the ABC News executives. When Sherwood came to New York, he tried to get in a word with her, as he reminded her that he'd taken Lisa Hackner off *The View*. That line of reasoning didn't cut it for Whoopi. She blew up at him, telling him that his managers had permanently destroyed the show.

Then Wolff announced he was exiting to be the executive producer of *Chelsea,* Netflix's streaming talk show from comedian Chelsea Handler. He didn't last through the end of the show's first season. "He wasn't the right fit," Handler told me.

Since ABC was starting from scratch again on *The View,* they decided to throw everything at the wall for Season 19 to see what would stick. They unveiled a cluster of new cohosts: Raven-Symoné, the former Disney Channel star; Michelle Collins, a comedian; and Candace Cameron Bure, the conservative former child actress who played D. J. Tanner on *Full House.* But her schedule made her a part-time host, as she lived in Los Angeles, where she'd committed to shooting Netflix's revival of her sitcom, *Fuller House.*

To round out the panel, James Goldston asked *GMA Weekend* coanchor Paula Faris to take a seat at the table. Faris, who'd been a staple at ABC News, worried that *The View* would hurt her career. It did: Whoopi thought she was boring at the table. "She's not a journalist," Whoopi would say. "Barbara Walters was a journalist." Other than that, Goldston didn't want much to do with *The View.* He let Fedida, who had previously worked at CBS News, run point on it.

Sherwood, not knowing who could manage the day-to-day operations, needed some executives with daytime experience. The show took on Hilary Estey McLoughlin as a consultant. McLoughlin, who had been the second executive producer of *The Rosie O'Donnell Show*, had hit a rut in her career. She'd been at CBS, trying to launch a *View*-like knockoff that never made it past a pilot, with a panel that included Jerry O'Connell and his wife, Rebecca Romijn. The new executive producer would be Candi Carter, who had worked on *Oprah*, but she'd never been the one in charge.

As all these pieces were being assembled, McLoughlin decided that the show needed to re-sign Joy Behar, as the sixth cohost of this rotating panel. "It was a mistake to get rid of me," Behar told me. "They begged me to come back. First, I wasn't interested. I was in Provincetown with my husband, minding my own beeswax." McLoughlin sweetened the gig: she offered Behar the role of moderator on Fridays.

Drama had a way of finding *The View*, regardless of who was in the cast. No sooner had the season started than Michelle became the subject of an unpleasant controversy when she made fun of Republican presidential candidate Carly Fiorina's face. It became a scandal in conservative America. A network executive had to visit Michelle's dressing room to ask her to apologize. She blamed Joy for setting up the joke that Michelle bungled. Joy and Michelle came to dislike each other as the two comics on *The View*. Michelle had barely started as a regular cohost when the network decided that she'd been a bad hire. A few months later, they reduced her appearances. Then they fired her in June 2016.

As the show got into the swing of the 2016 presidential election, Candi Carter bad-mouthed Raven for not keeping up. Candace was a conservative, but she wasn't informed about politics in a way that made her useful for interviewing senators or presidential candidates. Having her on the show was a pain because she was never in New York. When she visited, it was like an aunt who dropped in for a few days, before she had to leave again to tape *Fuller House*.

The show was still suffering. With so much paranoia about leaks,

McLoughlin and Carter wouldn't talk about their plans in staff meetings out of fear it would end up in the papers. At the *Daily Mail*, a writer who went by a pseudonym was penning a series of articles that detailed verbatim some of the backstage fights. ABC thought that this was an inside job—that one of the shows dissatisfied producers was secretly writing these stories.

In the post-Barbara-and-Rosie era, *The View* could no longer convince big celebrities to be interviewed. The show found itself in an embarrassing situation when the cast of *Star Wars: The Force Awakens*, a film distributed by Disney, committed to the dark side—by agreeing to appear on CBS's *The Talk*. Producers flailed and placed a call to Disney CEO Bob Iger, who agreed to personally torpedo the booking. But Harrison Ford never made it on *The View* either.

One viewer still kept close tabs on the show. Sometimes Barbara would call the control room to offer a few words of constructive criticism. Despite telling me that she wouldn't watch the show because it would make her sad to not be part of it, she couldn't help herself. She had to know about all the comings and goings. In October 2016, *The View* cut ties with Raven, more than a year after her arrival, and the revolving door continued, as the search for the perfect cohosts seemed to be as elusive as finding everlasting love on *The Bachelor*. "It's too many," Barbara Walters said of all the cohosts that had been tried out. "I think you should tune in and know who they are. There are days when I tune in and I don't recognize anybody."

In the summer of 2016, Barbara thought it was time for another visit with her TV daughters. That August, ABC had cleared an hour of its schedule for a prime-time special starring the ladies of *The View*, timed to its twentieth season. Like Bravo's *Real Housewives*, another TV staple on which frenemies acted like girlfriends, the network envisioned a juicy reunion show with confessions about rivalries and shattered friendships.

The only missing ingredient to ratings gold were the cohosts, who hadn't signed on.

Carter wasn't managing the reunion show, but she still tossed off ideas. She kept telling the staff that the key to viewers would be getting Rosie and Elisabeth to face off one more time. Barbara believed she could get Rosie there. But Elisabeth wasn't responding to calls or emails. She had abruptly exited *Fox & Friends,* leaving in December 2015 after Roger Ailes decided that she wasn't enough of a team player. She'd only work mornings, refusing to engage with staff requests for the rest of the day, instead of living and breathing the Fox News brand.

As the pink slips at *The View* had piled up, the former cohosts got some revenge. When ABC came asking for one last interview, Rosie Perez, Nicolle Wallace, and Jenny McCarthy all turned down their invitations. Even Whoopi, who was employed by ABC, told producers that she wasn't sure if she would participate. Barbara offered to help save the day. She herself tried to reach Elisabeth, whom Barbara had made into a star. But Elisabeth wouldn't do this one last favor for her mentor. The hounding resulted in a terse email from Elisabeth's agent to ABC:

Hi. We have told a few people already that Elisabeth isn't interested or available for this, but thank you.

As the story of Elisabeth spurning Barbara spread throughout ABC, the reunion show fell apart. The ladies would never be getting back together again. "She told Barbara no," Star said. "That just wasn't right. There's nobody who had a more contentious exit than me—I walked out on the show in a pink suit. Why are you mad? It's not that deep."

On August 23, 2016, ABC aired their twentieth-anniversary special on *The View,* produced by David Sloan. An old hand at *20/20,* he had never worked on *The View.* It played less like Bravo and more like a bad infomercial. The cohosts who had agreed to talk—including Meredith, Star, Debbie, Lisa, Joy, and Sherri—never met. Instead, they were brought in to speak to the camera directly, ticking off some of their happier memories. Whoopi declined to be part of it. Barbara gamely reminisced about how her conceit for *The View* was challenged in its early days.

Despite a sound track of pop songs such as "Something to Talk About," a lot was left unsaid. The special didn't generate any headlines, nor did it offer insights into Rosie vs. Trump with only a few months before the election. ABC might prize itself for hiring some of the country's best journalists, but it failed to dig up any news related to one of its biggest franchises.

Over time, Barbara's trips to ABC ceased. She stopped doing live TV. She interviewed Trump before the election—he was still a friend—but she never visited him in the White House. Cha-Cha passed away. Her circle of visitors got smaller and smaller.

As for her other surrogate daughters, the last time they all gathered in the same room was right before her retirement. They all still cherished the memory. Debbie Matenopoulos, the youngest child, remembered waiting with Barbara backstage as she prepared to take the stage for her last bow.

"I'm really sad," Debbie told her. "My mom wants me to tell you, you can't do this! Nobody is going to watch the show after you leave."

"Oh, baby," Barbara responded loudly. "How long can the show go on? It's going to be canceled in a few years."

The other cohosts, some of whom were still employed by ABC, were all within earshot. They didn't know how to react to this depressing prediction.

"The whole cast was right there!" Debbie recalled. "They could hear us. But what are you going to do?"

As the creator of *The View*, Barbara Walters had made it acceptable for women in the news business to express their true opinions. Debbie laughed and said, "That's the beauty of Barbara Walters. She can say what she wants because she's earned it."

Epilogue

Ladies Who Punch Harder

As it turned out, *The View* wouldn't talk about my book on TV—it was perhaps the show's first forbidden topic—but that didn't mean the cohosts hadn't read it. After *Ladies Who Punch* arrived, Joy Behar sat in a communal kitchen at ABC News as a producer read aloud tidbits to her. They kept going as James Goldston approached their table, looking baffled that they were so absorbed by an exposé about their own show. "My husband read the whole book," Joy told me several months later. "He said, 'Everything is true!'" She laughed. "He said, 'The guy knew a lot! He must have had some good moles.'"

Weeks before the hardcover edition landed in bookstores, entertainment shows such as *Access Hollywood, The Insider,* and *Entertainment Tonight* started airing the stories from chapters that were excerpted in *BuzzFeed News, New York, Vanity Fair,* and *Time.* And the leaked recording of Elisabeth screaming at Barbara, which I'd acquired and published in *Variety,* went viral. "This book is SO DELICIOUS," tweeted the actress and talk show host Busy Philipps. "I highly recommend it. And now the audio."

Andy Cohen invited me to be the bartender on *Watch What Happens*

Live with Andy Cohen, as he tried to extract more gossip from me. Wendy Williams referenced the book so many times (mostly on her own talk show, but even once as a guest on *The View*), I lost count. Jenny McCarthy welcomed me on her SiriusXM series, where she vouched for the accuracy of my reporting. Rosie O'Donnell disavowed the book, and said—many times—that her participation was her "biggest regret."

For now, ABC has banned me from visiting *The View* set. The few interviews for this updated epilogue had to be done over the phone.

Elisabeth, who declined my numerous interview requests, decided that instead of talking to me, she'd write her own book. Coincidentally, her memoir, titled *Point of View: A Fresh Look at Work, Faith, and Freedom,* debuted a week before *Ladies Who Punch.* On March 26, 2019, Elisabeth reclaimed her old seat at the Hot Topics table for the first time since she'd been fired.

Her publisher had to force her to do the show. She probably would have canceled if she'd known, all these years later, that the cohosts would have new questions about her relationship with Rosie.

"Let me ask you this," Sunny Hostin said, reading a quote from my book—without saying where it came from—about Rosie's supposed mutual crush on Elisabeth.

Elisabeth took a deep breath. "This is how I believe this needs to be addressed," she said, as she spiraled into a convoluted answer. "I think what she said was reckless, untrue, and not only insulting, disturbing, when it comes to how she felt about somebody in the workplace." Elisabeth described Rosie's feelings for her as "the objectification of a woman in the workplace."

"She didn't say anything about the way you looked or anything," Joy noted. "She just said she had a crush on you."

"Number one, the feeling was not mutual," Elisabeth said. "Secondly, I think what she said about female athletes, it's a lie." As the cohosts tried to wrap the interview, Elisabeth kept going. "I forgive Rosie," Elisabeth said. "She has my forgiveness and I really pray she can have the peace that she deserves. That's my ultimate prayer."

"She's gotten much more religious," Joy recalled, looking back on that day. "Hasn't she?" The show's publicist, Lauri Hogan, who was also on the phone call, agreed. "My goodness," Joy said with a sigh. "I think that has kept her happy."

Asked about Rosie's comments, Joy didn't miss a beat. "Rosie is a force of nature," she said. "And nature never goes away."

During the Trump years, *The View* has adapted again, as it has under every president since Bill Clinton. Although Trump spent most of the 2000s positioning himself as a foe of the cohosts of *The View,* he managed to help save the show as it was fading into obscurity. With Barbara Walters gone, *The View* had lost any relevance it once had. Yet with Trump in the White House, along with a parade of dysfunctional appointees and daily scandals, Hot Topics has become appointment TV again.

On the morning after Trump defeated Hillary Clinton, producers noticed a jump in ratings, as Americans tuned in to see how the cohosts of *The View* were reacting to the surprise outcome of the election. "For a moment, we were framed as the face of the resistance," said Brian Teta, one of three producers who now manages the show. But he doesn't agree with the notion that the show's mission statement is to oppose Trump. "This is a place where people want to learn what the other side is thinking from our hosts."

After the election, a few cohosts were thrown overboard as the show fully swerved back to politics. The network lost Candace Cameron Bure in December 2016, because she couldn't keep up. Jedediah Bila, a libertarian pundit, was fired in September 2017, for being too agreeable. And Sara Haines exited *The View* in August 2018, trading political headlines for celebrity chatter as the cohost of a later, poorly watched hour of *GMA,* with Michael Strahan. Sherwood got little satisfaction from seeing his dream realized. In the summer of 2018, he was axed by Bob Iger, who felt Sherwood was no longer capable of running ABC's TV networks.

To add more balance to the table, *The View* hired Meghan McCain (in 2017) and Abby Huntsman (in 2018)—both of whom came from Fox News. It was the first time two conservative women occupied the table at the same time, although neither of them support Trump. In Season 23, which kicked off in September 2019, the rest of the panel consisted of Whoopi, Joy, and Sunny, and the ratings for the show continue to remain strong.

"With this liar-in-chief, there's material constantly with him," Joy told me. "It was the same with Clinton, except with Clinton it was just a blow job. Trump is screwing the whole country. It's not so funny, because you can see by his daily mishaps that he's incompetent. He's amoral. He has no clue what he's doing. He's greedy. He's jealous. He's insecure. And those are his good points."

The renewed appeal of *The View*—as it has always been during its most successful years—lies in its ability to educate. "I think that we're an informative show," Joy said. "I read *The New York Times* and *The Washington Post* every day. I read Facebook. People have a confidence we are telling them something that's the unvarnished truth. We have no axe to grind. Even though I'm 100 percent against Trump, if he were to do something right, which I strongly doubt, I would say it. I haven't seen it yet."

Producers still regularly call the White House to see if Trump will come on. But they know that it's an unlikely request. "I did not know how bad he would be," Joy said of Trump's presidency. "I just thought he was a big old egomaniac, who was in love with his daughter."

Other presidential hopefuls, from Bernie Sanders to Pete Buttigieg, have made repeated visits during the 2020 election cycle. "I think it's worth noting that interviews with politicians on other shows are different than our show," said Candi Carter, the show's second executive producer. "We have five women at the table who are smart and engaged."

With Meghan, *The View* has finally found a conservative who, like Elisabeth Hasselbeck, frequently opposes the rest of the table. "Look, I think Trump has helped ratings for all of news," Meghan told me. (Disclosure: Meghan is a close friend of mine. I was her editor at *Newsweek* and *The Daily Beast*, and she joined the show long after I'd started writing the book.) "But I think the show got the panel right. I think if you had someone who wasn't a hard-lined conservative and was more scared to go against the rest of the panel sitting in my chair, I don't think it would be as effective. I'm trying to tell the truth of a perspective that is wildly underrepresented in the swath of all media except for Fox News."

Meghan joined *The View* at the suggestion of her father, who had been on the show as a presidential candidate. When we spoke again for this epilogue, Meghan talked about how her father's death from glioblastoma in 2018 had shaped her time on the show. "Grief is so intense," Meghan said. "Prince Harry called it a wound that festers, and that's how I would describe it. It's been so much harder to deal with than I ever could have imagined. And I often think that I must have been out of my fucking mind to do the most historically controversial show in all of television at a time when I was going through so much emotionally. I just wish people at home would give me a break, because I've been dealing with so much."

She admitted that she has been bothered by stories in the press about conflicts backstage detailing turmoil between her and the other hosts. Although she's complained to the network, no efforts have been made to stop the leaks. "It's been a lot to deal with the drama of the show, the leaking in the press, and then my grief all at the same time," Meghan said. "There are times when I have wanted to completely give up and leave.

And then I just keep trying to remind myself that my dad really wanted me to be here and wanted me to do it. And I keep trying to remind myself of that anytime I feel like maybe this is no longer the right decision."

On an afternoon in the fall of 2019, I asked the three people in charge of *The View*—Teta, Carter, and Hilary Estey McLoughlin—if they were keeping the panel intact.

An awkward silence hung in the air, before they assured me that they had no plans to make any changes. "There's no topic these women can't speak about," Teta said. "Obviously, there's dust ups. And they are able to leave it behind."

On September 25, 2019, *The View* wished Barbara Walters a happy ninetieth birthday, but she wasn't able to join them on TV. As her health has deteriorated, Barbara has stopped receiving visitors and corresponding with friends. Some of her closest colleagues recall how, in better days, Barbara would gaze out of her apartment and talk about looking forward to the day where she could just sit idly for a day and enjoy the view of Central Park. They try to imagine her peacefully doing that.

Bryant Renfroe, who hadn't spoken to Barbara in two years, sent her a special present for her birthday. He always remembered when they were traveling for a story, Barbara would ask for two things upon arriving at her hotel room. She wanted a copy of *The New York Times* and her spiral-bound red notebook, where she kept her schedule and the phone numbers of everyone from her sources to her doctors.

Renfroe mailed Barbara ninety front pages of *The New York Times* from every birthday she ever had, starting in 1929, all bound in a book with a red cover. "So she got her *Times* and her red book," Renfroe said.

After I'd submitted my updated epilogue for the paperback edition of *Ladies Who Punch,* I thought I'd written my final words (for now) on the show. But of course, when it comes to *The View,* it's never that easy.

In early 2020, more stories leaked about conflicts with Meghan and the cohosts backstage. Then, on January 13, Abby Huntsman announced that she was stepping down from the show to work on her father, Jon's, campaign for governor of Utah. Although she'd reportedly had a fight with Meghan (with whom she remains friends), that wasn't the reason she was leaving.

Abby, who had spent just over a year on *The View,* reached her decision after multiple conversations with ABC executives about the toxicity at the root of the show. When they didn't respond to her, she told them that she'd like to move on, according to sources with knowledge of those conversations. Abby didn't think that anyone at ABC was looking out for her.

There was also confusion about Abby's role, like there had been with Nicolle Wallace, as a moderate conservative. Producers sometimes gave her the impression they wanted her to make more outrageous statements. But she felt it was more important to be true to what she really believed.

When Abby told Whoopi that she was leaving *The View,* Whoopi looked her in the eye and said, "This is the best decision you'll make in your career."

In interviews with more than ten current and former staff on the show, they confirmed the portrait of a talk show hobbled by constant dysfunction. They described a work environment where three executive producers play a game of hot potato, not dealing with resentments or festering tensions among the cohosts or staff. "There's no leadership and no management," said one high-ranking staff member. "Whenever there's a problem, nobody communicates."

Although multiple staffers have lodged complaints to ABC News executives about bad morale, these calls for help have been ignored. In the eyes of the network, there are much bigger problems on their hands.

Good Morning America has dipped by 38 percent in the ratings over the last five years in the key demographic that advertisers care about, a drop that's put the show back in second place behind *Today*. "*The View* just isn't a priority," said one person at ABC News. "Nobody thinks it's worth the time."

Why is *The View* always on fire? Part of that is a symptom of Trump's America, where Republicans and Democrats are at war on every issue (and the press celebrates clips where Whoopi cuts off Meghan from making a point). But the cohosts have all expressed frustration at the notion that the producers can't—or won't—do their part to curtail the drama.

One person close to the show compared the network's current management style to the way Bravo tries to stoke the rivalries between its *Real Housewives* stars, to make for more explosive moments on TV. That's not what Barbara Walters had in mind when she created *The View*, which aspired to be something classier on daytime TV.

There are other ways in which *The View* has diverged from Barbara's vision. The morning meetings, where the cohosts used to sketch out the Hot Topics debates, have been permanently canceled, because there would be too much arguing between the cohosts before they were on TV. Instead, the ladies are now kept in isolation and they see each other for the first time when they are live on the set.

In January 2020, after more gossip items had been published about Meghan, she took a few days off to spend with her family. Sunny decided to hold her own morning meeting, without telling the executive producers. As she gathered the two guest cohosts that day—Yvette Nicole Brown and Ana Navarro—along with Joy and Abby, Teta came into the room.

"Sunny, what are you doing?" he asked. "You can't hold a meeting without producers."

What followed was a shouting match loud enough for the entire staff to hear. "You can't tell me who to speak to," Sunny said. "I'm the face of the show! You're not on the air! Who are you to tell me what to do?"

Sunny was trying to prove that Meghan was the one who had derailed the morning meetings by pushing back on too many things. But the confrontation seemed to disprove her point.

After the fight, Sunny accused the producers of knowing about the meeting because they were secretly reading the emails from her ABC account. (A source said they weren't—at least not for this. Everyone had been talking about the secret morning meeting, which is how Teta got wind of it.)

Even though Abby willingly left *The View,* there was a false gossip story that suggested the network had planned on firing her. *The View* is supposed to be a program that elevates opinionated women, with cohosts who speak out about against injustices and abuse. But at ABC, the network can't even keep their own house in order.

So will *The View* ever end? Joy revealed to me that she's agreed to stay on through 2022, and that will likely be her last year. "I have a three-year contract," Joy said. "But that doesn't mean I can't leave if I want to, because they can't really do anything to me at this point. I don't see myself staying for more than three years. That's it! I could be wrong. If I'm as fabulous in three years as I am now, I'll think about it. But the chances of that happening . . ." She'd just celebrated her 77th birthday. "You know, time marches on. I'm not a kid."

As for Whoopi or Meghan, it's anyone's guess.

For many years, TV pundits tried to handicap who could become the next Oprah. Perhaps nobody will ever fill her shoes, because the talk show as a form is in decline, and viewer habits are more fractured. But the argument could be made that, of all the options, one talk show has come the closest to replicating Oprah's influence. *The View* has surpassed *The Oprah Winfrey Show* with more than five thousand episodes.

When asked for her greatest career accomplishment, Barbara Walters never wavered, once telling me, "What makes me feel good is when a young woman—it's almost always a woman—says, 'You influenced me and you're the reason I became a journalist.' They watched, and they said, 'If she could do it, I could do it.'"

A Note on Sources

The first one out was the first one in. One spring afternoon, I drove to *The Insider* in Los Angeles, where Debbie Matenopoulos invited me to her dressing room after a taping. She was eager to share all her memories about working on *The View*. It all happened so quickly, I thought maybe I could line up everybody else in the next few months. But I came to learn that nothing associated with *The View* is easy. The research for this book took three years and involved more than 150 interviews with producers, agents, network executives, and guests.

But none of that mattered if I couldn't hear directly from the stars of the show. Ultimately, I conducted lengthy conversations with eleven of the cohosts, with periodic follow-ups over the phone or email. Barbara Walters, who gave me her blessing, met me for an iced tea near her home shortly after I'd sold this book. She connected me to her trusted executive producer, Bill Geddie. Eventually, he and I spent many hours over several months talking near his home on the West Coast. He was always gracious in helping me tell his story. And this is the first time he's told many of these anecdotes to a reporter.

If someone passed on participating, I'd just do what Barbara would do, which is never accept no for an answer. And so I'd wait a few months and try again. Over time, I was able to schedule one-on-one interviews with Meredith Vieira, Star Jones, Rosie O'Donnell, Sherri Shepherd, and Jenny McCarthy, in either New York or Los Angeles. I visited Joy Behar and Meghan McCain at *The View*, where I'd spent so much time backstage that I sometimes felt like Michael Wolff at the White House. Nicolle Wallace welcomed me to 30 Rockefeller Center, where we chatted before she taped her afternoon program on MSNBC. Lisa Ling agreed to a phone conversation. The two cohosts who never sat down with me—even though I'd interviewed them both before—were Whoopi Goldberg and Elisabeth Hasselbeck.

This book is primarily based on new interviews. Since I've been covering *The View* for more than ten years, I relied on some of my unpublished manuscripts for quotes that couldn't be re-created due to time passing. In 2014, I wrote a cover story for *Variety* on Barbara prior to her retirement, spending multiple days with her in different settings. I also wrote a cover story on Rosie the second time she joined *The View*, and I profiled Whoopi for *Newsweek* in 2011.

It was important for me to tell the full story of the show. And I understood that not everyone could talk for attribution. This is *The View*, after all.

Acknowledgments

Barbara Walters knew what she was doing when she coined the phrase "Hot Topics." Of all the articles that I've written as a journalist, *The View* is the one subject that always draws the most readers. When it comes to online traffic, stories about Barbara's TV show often outperform those about Marvel's *The Avengers* or *Fifty Shades of Grey*. Forget Jamie Dornan. What the internet really wants to know is what's going on behind closed doors at *The View*.

I have a theory about why so many people—even those who don't regularly tune in—can't stop themselves from reading about *The View*. The show touches on a cross-section of important themes: political polarization, red states vs. blue states, feminism, the challenges women face in Hollywood and beyond, and, of course, Donald Trump. When I first pitched this book, my thesis was that *The View* defined a turning point in American society, before the election of the first female president. That hasn't happened (yet). But for the last twenty years, *The View* has elevated opinionated heroines who believe the future is female, foreshadowing our current climate.

Bill Geddie once told me that he suggested to a prominent journalist who was covering David Letterman that he should write a book about *The View*. I'm glad that the other writer didn't take Geddie up on the offer. And I'm indebted to all the producers who worked tirelessly on the show for the last two decades. Many of them invited me into their homes or agreed to lengthy phone conversations to talk about what it was like to be on such a groundbreaking program.

I'd like to thank my brilliant friend Kate Aurthur, for navigating me through my first book. I might never have been ready if it weren't for her genuine enthusiasm for this project. Kate read and edited every page from its early draft stages, providing invaluable suggestions and questions. When I'd gain her approval—with notes like "LITERAL LOL"—I knew that I was on the right track and had to keep going.

I started as an editor at the age of twenty-one at *Newsweek*, when newsmagazines were still a force in journalism. Thank you to Marcus Mabry, Mark Whitaker, and Kathy Deveny, for hiring me and turning me into the reporter I became. And to Marc Peyser, who, as culture editor, made me rewrite every story at least five times; he has unquestionably good taste. For proof: he assigned me several stories about *The View*, which led me to this book.

Meghan McCain championed this idea, declaring it a bestseller, even before she became a cohost on the show. Melissa Durliat has been a loyal friend, who always pushes me to be better—usually with a glass of rosé in her hand.

At *Variety*, I'm grateful for my boss, Claudia Eller, who never wavers in supporting great journalism. The same goes for Jay Penske. I'm lucky to work with so many talented colleagues, including Michelle Sobrino, Gerry Byrne, Owen Gleiberman, John Ross, Lauren Utecht, Mary Corbet, Brent Lang, Stuart Oldham, Elizabeth Wagmeister, Sylvia Tan, Dea Lawrence, Donna Pennestri, Daniel D'Addario, Caroline Framke, Brian Steinberg, Robert Festino, Michael Ausiello, Meredith Woerner, Rebecca Rubin, Nicholas Stango, and Dayna Wolpa.

More than twenty publishing houses passed on this project, because they weren't interested in a book about "women in media" (whatever that means!). At St. Martin's Press, I'm beholden to Emily Angell, for believing in this manuscript. The penetrating Stephen S. Power inherited this book, without having ever seen *The View*, and he devoured every chapter. I couldn't have asked for a wiser or more energetic editor. Also, thank you to Sally Richardson, Jennifer Enderlin, Thomas Dunne, Laura Clark, Tracey Guest, Kathryn Hough Boutross, and Samantha Zukergood. My agent, David Kuhn, helped inspire the structure of this book and found it a good home.

At the start of this process, Brian Stelter took me out to lunch and gave me some incredibly helpful advice. Susan Szeliga, my old friend from the *Newsweek* library, was invaluable at finding old newspaper and magazine clips. Cindi Berger at PMK/BNC is a vault of information related to *The View*. At ABC, Julie Townsend and Lauri Hogan were crucial in helping with archival research and overseeing interview requests. At Warner Bros., Chris Circosta assisted with impossible-to-find episodes of *The Rosie O'Donnell Show*.

I've wanted to be a writer all of my life. I learned how to do that through my teachers, starting in high school with Demetra Chamberlain, Kathy Brandes, Karen Kyer, Pam Rakis, and Deborah Ledford, who encouraged me at fourteen to write, write, write, even though she taught math. At Stanford, I learned from ZZ Packer, Elizabeth Tallent, and Tobias Wolff in the creative writing department.

Thank you to my boyfriend, Christophe Hollocou, for reading early pages, acting as my secret brainstorming partner, and never getting tired of me asking him to watch old clips of *The View*.

And finally, thank you to my parents, for your love and kindness, and for teaching me your strength and determination. As immigrants from Iran, they grew up with a rich tradition of storytelling. My mom would take my sister, Sheila, and me to the library every few days, so that we couldn't live without books. And my dad would tape-record my shaky voice working its way through *A Little House on the Prairie*, because he knew I'd learn how to read faster if I could hear myself doing it. I love you all more than I can say.

Index

About the Author

Matt Sayles

RAMIN SETOODEH, an award-winning journalist, is the New York bureau chief for *Variety*. He was formerly a senior writer at *Newsweek* and has also written for *The Wall Street Journal*, the *Los Angeles Times*, and *U.S. News & World Report*, among other publications. *Ladies Who Punch* is his first book. He lives in New York City.